T0139786

Discriminative Learning in Biometrics

David Zhang · Yong Xu
Wangmeng Zuo

Discriminative Learning in Biometrics

 Springer

David Zhang
Department of Computing
The Hong Kong Polytechnic University
Kowloon, Hong Kong
China

Wangmeng Zuo
Harbin Institute of Technology
Harbin, Heilongjiang
China

Yong Xu
Shenzhen Graduate School
Harbin Institute of Technology
Shenzhen, Guangdong
China

ISBN 978-981-10-9515-3   ISBN 978-981-10-2056-8   (eBook)
DOI 10.1007/978-981-10-2056-8

Printed on acid-free paper

This Springer imprint is published by Springer Nature
The registered company is Springer Nature Singapore Pte Ltd.
The registered company address is: 152 Beach Road, #22-06/08 Gateway East, Singapore 189721, Singapore

Preface

Biometrics, defined as the automated recognition of individuals based on their behavioral and physiological characteristics, can provide more stable and feasible solutions to personal verification and identification than traditional token-based and knowledge-based methods. In the past few decades, tremendous progress has been achieved in biometrics. Versatile biometric recognition techniques have been developed, including fingerprint, face, iris, palmprint, and ear recognition, and various biometric systems have been deployed in the applications of assess control, forensics, border crossing, network security, etc. Recently, with the ever-growing need for reliable authentication of human identity in the complex physical and network environments, much attention have been given to biometric research for reliable recognition of low-quality data or under unconstrained scenarios, which has imposed new challenges to the field of biometrics.

The development and popularization of sensors shed some light on improving the accuracy and stability of biometric recognition. The deployment of national ID programs, e.g., in India and Mexico, can provide large-scale datasets to facilitate biometric research. Moreover, the emergence of social networks and surveillance networks has reshaped the methodologies in constructing several modalities of large-scale biometric datasets, which offer new opportunities for extending the application scenarios of biometric systems while enhancing the robustness and usability.

Learning method that aims at extracting discriminative features and building powerful classifiers is a core topic in machine learning and pattern recognition community. With the popularity of large-scale biometric datasets, discriminative learning is also becoming increasingly important in biometric research, and has demonstrated its superior performance in developing biometric recognition methods. Linear discriminant analysis and its variants have been widely adopted in biometric feature extraction. Metric learning can provide an elaborate solution for personal verification. Discriminative classifiers, such as discriminative dictionary learning and support vector machines, are also prominent in various biometric recognition systems.

Rather than direct applications of discriminative learning in biometric recognition, new methods can also be developed by considering the characteristics of biometrics. For example, personal identification generally is a classification task with ultrahigh number of classes, while the within-class variations cannot be ignored and the number of available samples for each individual is limited. Moreover, several classifiers suggested for biometric recognition, e.g., sparse representation-based classification, have also achieved great success in image classification and other vision tasks.

This book aims to provide the readers with several representative methods of discriminative learning for biometric recognition. The ideas, algorithms, experimental evaluation, and underlying rationales are also given for the better understanding of these methods. The book is organized into six parts. In Part I, Chap. 1 first introduces some basic knowledge on biometrics, and then provides an overview of representative discriminative learning methods. In Part II, in-depth description is given for two representative discriminative learning methods, viz. metric learning and sparse representation. In Chap. 2, we investigate metric learning from kernel perspective, and suggest two metric learning models, doublet-SVM and triplet-SVM, which can be efficiently solved using the off-the-shelf SVM solvers. We also introduce two other models, PCML and NCML, by enforcing positive semi-definite constraint on the learned matrix. In Chap. 3, we first summarize the framework of sparse representation and discriminative dictionary learning, and then present a multiple representation-based method for face recognition.

In Part III, we describe the feature extraction and matching methods for palmprint recognition. In Chap. 4, we introduce two coding-based methods, namely-improved competitive code based on fuzzy C-means and binary orientation co-occurrence vector. In Chap. 5, we further investigate some issues on multi-scale coding and accurate angular representation. We first introduce a multi-scale competitive coding scheme and further improve it by using sparse coding. Then we utilize steerable filters for accurate extraction and robust matching of angular representation. In Chap. 6, we describe a multifeature palmprint authentication method using both competitive code-based 2D and surface curvature-based 3D palmprint features.

The Part IV introduces the application of representation-based classification in face recognition. To alleviate the adverse effect of insufficient training sample per person, Chap. 7 presents some effective schemes to generate virtual face images. In Chap. 8, we introduce several sparse representation-based methods for face recognition, viz. inverse sparse representation and robust sparse representation.

In Part V, Chap. 9 presents two fusion methods to combine multi-modality of biometric features for enhanced recognition. By investigating the cross-modality correlation, both within- and cross-modality matching scores are combined for the fusion of left and right palmprint. A dynamic score level fusion method is then introduced for joint palmprint and palmvein verification. Finally, Chap. 10 provides a brief recapitulation of the main contents of this book, and points out several encouraging topics on discriminative biometric recognition for future researches.

The book is based on our years of research experience in discriminative learning in biometrics. Since 1998, under the grant support from National Natural Science Foundation of China (NSFC), Hong Kong Polytechnic University, and Harbin Institute of Technology, we had begun our studies on palmprint recognition, and gradually expanded our researches to representative discriminative learning methods, including discriminant analysis, metric learning, and sparse representation-based classification, together with their applications in face recognition and multi-biometrics. We would like to express our special thanks to Mr. Zhaotian Zhang, Mr. Ke Liu, and Ms. Xiaoyun Xiong from NSFC, who consistently supported our research work for decades.

We would like to express our gratitude to our colleagues and Ph.D. students: Profs. Jian Yang, Jie Zhou, Kuanquan Wang, Zhouchen Lin, Guangming Lu, Jane You, Qinghua Hu, and Jinhui Tang, Dr. Hongzhi Zhang, Dr. Zhihui Lai, Dr. Feng Yue, Dr. Wei Li, Dr. Meng Yang, Dr. Jinhua Wang, Dr. Pengfei Zhu, Dr. Yahui Liu, and Dr. Faqiang Wang, for their contributions to the research achievements on discriminative learning in biometrics. It is our great honor to work with them in this inspiring topic recently. The authors owe a debt of gratitude to Xiaohe Wu, Hongliang Yan, and Weiqi Zhang for their careful reading and checking of draft of the manuscript. We are also hugely indebted to Ms. Celine L. Chang and Ms. Jane Li of Springer for their consistent help and encouragement.

Finally, the work in this book was mainly sponsored by the NSFC Program under Grant No.s 61332011, 61271093, and 61272292.

Kowloon, Hong Kong
April 2016

David Zhang

Contents

Part I
Background Knowledge

Chapter 1
Discriminative Learning in Biometrics

Abstract Biometrics, similar to other pattern recognition systems, are essentially based on data collection and learning techniques. In this chapter, we will first give an overview on the systems in terms of the input features and common applications. After that, we will provide a self-contained introduction to some discriminative learning tools that are commonly used in biometrics. A clear understanding of these techniques could be of essential importance in the sense that it forms the foundation for much of the subsequent parts in this book.

1.1 Biometric Recognition

Recent years have witnessed a bloom in biometric recognition systems. There are many examples in our daily life, such as ATM with a face recognition module to verify whether the user have the permission for subsequent operations; season tickets to an amusement park by including the purchaser's biometric template; confidential delivery of health care through iris recognition; online payment with automatic facial recognition system. While these applications adopt different technologies to achieve their goals, each of those uses biometric recognition in some way. Compared with traditional password and token-based methods, biometric recognition has its distinct advantages and has been widely known as the future of identification technology (Jafri and Arabnia 2009).

Biometric recognition is defined as the automated methods of verifying or recognizing the identity of an individual based on his/her physiological and behavioral characteristics. From the definition, the term 'automated methods' excludes the personal recognition methods based on human experts. That is, biometric recognition is generally performed by the automated acquisition and analysis of the biometric data. Another characteristics of biometrics is that the recognition is conducted based on the subject's physiological and behavioral characteristics. Although it is generally believed that fingerprint is physiological, but the user habit is a behavior feature that affects the acquired fingerprint image and can be utilized in the development of fingerprint recognition. On the other hand, gait is known as a

© Springer Science+Business Media Singapore 2016
D. Zhang et al., *Discriminative Learning in Biometrics*,
DOI 10.1007/978-981-10-2056-8_1

behavior feature, but some physiological measurements, such as body height and fatness, can be extracted from gait image sequence to enhance the recognition performance. In this book, we use the term 'biometric authentication', 'biometric recognition' and 'biometrics' indiscriminately.

A biometric system is essentially a pattern recognition system that operates by acquiring biometric data from an individual, extracting a feature set from the acquired data, and comparing this feature set against the template set in the database. While there are various applications based on biometric recognition systems, we can mainly divide them into two categories: verification and identification. In the common cases, the first kind of applications aim to validate the user's identity by comparing the biometric features from the candidate with that stored in dataset for a claimed identity. The identity can be a personal identification number (PIN), user name, or smart card. In the second kind of applications, one should compare the biometric from a user with all those stored and finally give a prediction on the identity. Taking a fingerprint recognition system as an example, the block diagrams of a verification system and an identification system are illustrated in Fig. 1.1.

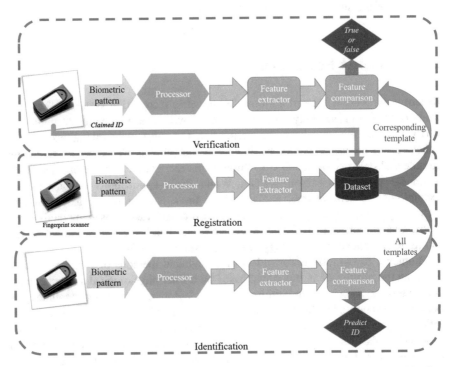

Fig. 1.1 Illustration of verification and identification. Block diagrams of registration, verification, and identification tasks are shown using the four main modules of a biometric system, i.e., acquisition, feature extraction, feature comparison, and system database. From the first and the third diagram, it is obviously that in verification task we wonder whether the ID matches his fingerprint, while in identification tasks, the prediction is made by comparing the given fingerprint and the system dataset

1.1.1 Ideal and Practical Biometric Trait

Various physiological and behavioral characteristics have been applied to biometric recognition, including fingerprint, face (Jafri and Arabnia 2009), palmprint (Zhang et al. 2012), iris, tongue (Li et al. 2008), etc. Actually, not all physiological and behavioral characteristics can be utilized for personal authentication. According to (Wayman et al. 2005), an ideal biometric trait should have the following properties:

- Universality. The biometric trait should be owned by each individual.
- Distinctiveness. Any two persons can be distinguished based on the biometric trait.
- Permanence. For a person, the biometric trait should keep invariant in his/her lifetime.
- Collectability. The biometric trait should be quantitatively acquired.

Actually, a practical biometric trait only approximately satisfies the requirements above. For examples, the finger of someone may be damaged by accident, and it is hard to distinguish identical twins from their face images. In general, biometric characteristics are not lifelong invariant but are sufficiently stable over a period of time.

Moreover, when developing a real biometric system, one should take into account several other practical issues including the following:

- Performance. This term takes three things into consideration, i.e., achievable recognition accuracy and speed; the resources required to achieve the desired recognition accuracy, as well as the operational and environmental factors that affect the accuracy.
- Acceptability. This indicates the extent to which people are willing to accept the use of a particular biometric identifier in their daily lives.
- Circumvention. To avoid being fooled, we must take into consideration how easily the system can be fooled using fraudulent methods.

1.1.2 Representative Biometric Recognition Techniques

Various biometric characteristics have been used for automatic recognition, including fingerprints, voices, iris, retina, hand, face, handwriting, keystroke, and finger shape. Some examples of biometric characteristics are shown in Fig. 1.2. In the following, we will discuss several representative biometric characteristics which have been well studied in biometric community.

Fingerprint. Fingerprint, the pattern of friction ridges on the skin of fingertip, is formed during fetal development and keeps stable over the life of an individual. Minutia descriptors of the ending and bifurcation of ridges are the major features used in fingerprint recognition. When the scan resolution is sufficiently high (e.g.,

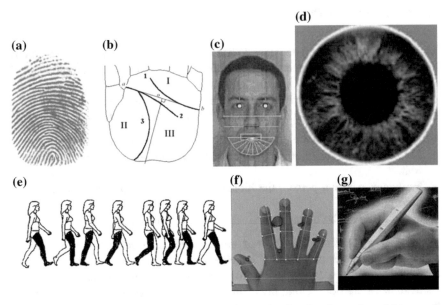

Fig. 1.2 Illustration of seven biometric traits: **a** fingerprint, **b** palmprint, **c** face, **d** iris, **e** gait, **f** hand geometry, and **g** signature

1000 ppi), extended features such as pores and ridge contours can also be extracted to improve the matching performance. Automatic fingerprint identification systems (AFIS) have been adopted as routine tools in forensics and law enforcement, and national security. Many laptop and cell phones have provide the fingerprint authentication model to enhance system security. Refer to Maltoni et al. (2009) for more detailed description on fingerprint recognition.

Face. Face recognition aims to verify or identify the identities of one or more individual in a scene based on face images or videos. Recently, driven by the development of deep convolutional neural network (CNN) and the availability of large scale training dataset, great progress has been made in this field (Schroff et al. 2015). Nowadays, the accuracy of several representative methods has surpassed human-level performance in face verification. Face recognition can be performed nonintrusively, making it applicable to both conventional biometric authentication and surveillance. Moreover, due to its multidisciplinary characteristics, the advances in face recognition can also provide useful support to related tasks, such as human–computer interaction, face animation, cognitive science, and psychological studies.

Ear. Among various biometric traits, ear is a stable structure that is not changing through the ages and satisfies the requirements of a biometric trait. Compared with face, ear is insensitive to the changes such as facial expression and makeup, glasses, and ages. Ear is a large and passive trait, making ear image acquisition more easily from a distance without person awareness. As studied in Nejati et al. (2012), ear verification can also be applied for verifying identical twins. Due to its promising characteristics, human ears have been used as a basic evidence in the law enforcement as a proof in more than hundreds of cases in United States and Netherlands since 2006, and ear biometrics has received considerable research interest. Refer to (Pflug and Busch 2012) and (Abaza et al. 2013) for comprehensive surveys on ear recognition.

Palmprint. Palmprint recognition is a relatively novel but promising biometric technology. The rich unique features contained in palmprint include principal lines and wrinkles, patterns of ridges and valleys, minutiae, and even pores. Among these features, ridges are crucial for latent palmprint recognition and have shown great potential in forensics and law enforcement (Jain and Feng 2009). On the other hand, creases, including principal lines and wrinkles, are obvious structural features which can be extracted from low resolution palmprint image and adopted for palmprint recognition (Zhang and Shu 1999). The existing low resolution palmprint recognition algorithms can be grouped into three categories: holistic-based, feature-based, and hybrid methods (Zhang et al. 2012). Among these methods, feature coding-based methods can achieve promising performance in terms of error rate and matching speed, and it is encouraging to investigate effective and compact representation of local palmprint features in the future studies. With advances in sensor techniques and computational power, novel palmprint recognition methods have recently been investigated, for example, multispectral, latent, and 3-D palmprint recognition.

Iris. Human iris refers to the annular region of the eye bounded by the pupil and the sclera (white of the eye) on either side (Burge and Bowyer 2013). The complex visual texture of iris is of the high degree of randomness and is stable since the first few years of life. Daugman suggested an IrisCode method for compact encoding of the 2-D Gabor phase information and developed the first commercial iris recognition system (Daugman 1993). A typical iris recognition system usually involves four modules: image acquisition, iris region segmentation, iris texture representation, and matching. By far, iris recognition has been studied explosively, and the system has been adopted in border control of United Arab Emirates, India Unique ID program, and Airports in London and Amsterdam (Burge and Bowyer 2013). Despite the great advance in iris recognition, several issues, such as iris quality metrics, iris dynamics, liveness detection, and unconstrained recognition of low quality images, remain unsolved.

Signature and handwriting. Handwritten signature has a long history on its applications in government, legal, and commercial transactions as a means of personal authentication. However, the studies on automatic signature recognition began in 1990s (Wirtz 1995; Lee et al. 1996). Based on the acquisition approaches, there are two types of automatic signature recognition methods, i.e., online and offline signature recognition. With the popularity of social network and online transactions, online signature verification can provide a new secure access authentication without any additional devices and has attracted the interests of many researchers. On the other hand, offline signature recognition is closely related to text dependent/independent writer identification, which plays an important role in important for forensic analysis and documents authorization.

Gait. Human gait is defined as the periodic activity with each gait cycle. Therefore, gait can be regarded as a kind of behavioristic characteristics, where a number of methods have been suggested to extract and depict the dynamics of gait, e.g., rate of transition. Moreover, physiological measurements, such as the configuration or shape of the persons, are also useful features for gait recognition. Compared with other biometric traits, gait can be acquired 300 m away, making it very suitable for surveillance scenarios. Even notable progress has been made, due to its intrinsic difficulty, more efforts should be given to further boost the performance of gait recognition to satisfy the practical requirements.

1.1.3 Multi-biometrics

For practical applications, biometric system based on single biometric trait, e.g., fingerprint, face, palmprint, and iris, usually cannot meet all the requirements. Multi-biometric system combines the information from multiple sources, including different modalities of biometric traits, different instances of a subject, and different features extracted from a sample. Thus, multi-biometrics provide an effective solution to address the inherent limitations of uni-biometric systems. In the following, we explain three typical scenarios where multi-biometrics can be utilized to improve the performance of uni-biometric system:

(1) Accuracy. When the accuracy of a uni-biometric system cannot match the performance requirement, multi-biometrics can be used to improve performance by combining the information from different modalities.
(2) Speed. When the matching speed of the top performance uni-biometric system cannot match the real-time requirement, multiple biometric traits can be utilized to build a hierarchical system. By this way, one can first employ some uni-biometric system with high speed to narrow the search range, and gradually use the high performance uni-biometric systems to guarantee the matching accuracy.
(3) Universality. Most uni-biometric traits only approximately satisfy the universality property. Therefore, it is natural to utilize multi-biometrics to improve the population coverage.

Due to their distinct advantages, multi-biometrics has been intensively studied in the last decade. Based on the levels of information, the fusion methods used in multi-biometrics are divided into four categories, i.e., sensor-level, feature-level, score-level, and decision-level fusion methods, which are briefly introduced as follows:

(1) Sensor-level fusion: If the multiple sources of acquired signals are compatible, sensor-level fusion can be used to improve the signal quality or combine the signals to form a new type of signal.

(2) Feature-level fusion: Parallel and serial feature fusion methods have been proposed to combine features from multiple sources. If the features from different sources are homogeneous, we can simply adopt weighted average for feature fusion. To save computational cost, feature selection and dimensionality reduction can be employed to reduce the feature dimension after fusion.

(3) Score-level fusion: It is believed that score-level fusion provides the best trade-off between the information content and the fusion complexity. Therefore, many score-level fusion schemes have been proposed, which can be further divided into three subcategories, i.e., transformation-based, classifier-based, and density-based approaches.

(4) Decision-level fusion: For some commercial biometric systems, one can only obtain the final decision information, making the fusion can only happen in the decision level. By far, a number of decision-level fusion methods have been suggested, to name a few, majority voting, weighted majority voting, and the Dempster-Shafer theory of evidence.

1.2 Discriminative Learning

Learning methods are generally divided into two categories: generative and discriminative methods. The key of generative learning is on modeling and learning joint probability distribution function $p(\mathbf{x}, y)$ from data. While discriminative learning directly learns the decision function $f(\mathbf{x})$ or the conditional probability distribution function $p(y|\mathbf{x})$ based on the given dataset and then form the prediction model. Discriminative learning is task-oriented and does not require any cumbersome intermediate joint probability modeling. By far, a great number of discriminative models have been studied, including k-nearest neighbor (KNN), perceptron machine, decision tree, support vector machine (SVM), boosting, and so on.

In this section, we will focus on three representative discriminative learning methods, i.e., support vector machine, metric learning, and sparse representation-based classification. For each method, some basic knowledge on models and algorithms is provided for better understanding the remaining chapters of this book.

1.2.1 Support Vector Machine

Support vector machine (SVM) and its extension have been one of the most frequently used classification techniques and have been adopted in various fields (Shawe-Taylor and Cristianini 2004; Smola and Schölkopf 2004; Samanta et al. 2003; Collobert et al. 2011; Guyon et al. 2002; Wu et al. 2015), including computer vision (Heisele et al. 2001), signal processing (Shawe-Taylor and Cristianini 2004;

Smola and Schölkopf 2004; Samanta et al. 2003), natural language processing (Collobert et al. 2011), and bioinformatics (Guyon et al. 2002).

In this section, we aim to offer a self-contained introduction on SVM by using two-class classification as an example. Denote by $\{(\mathbf{x}_i, y_i)|i = 1, \ldots, N\}$ a training dataset, $\mathbf{x}_i \in \mathbb{R}^d$ denotes the ith training sample, $y_i \in \{-1, +1\}$ denotes the corresponding label of $\mathbf{x}_i$. SVM is a max-margin classifier. When the training set is linearly separable, among all the feasible classifiers $(\mathbf{w}, b)$ that correctly classify all training samples (i.e., $y_i(\mathbf{w}^T\mathbf{x}_i + b) \geq 1, \forall i$), the classifier of SVM is the one that maximizes the margin between the classification hyperplane and training set, i.e., $1/\|\mathbf{w}\|^2$. Figure 1.3a illustrates an example of SVM for the linearly separable case. As shown in Fig. 1.3a, we define the margin as the perpendicular distance between the decision boundary and the closest samples in training set, and the closest training samples is then called as support vectors.

However, the linearly separate assumption generally does not hold. For linearly inseparable case, as depicted in Fig. 1.3b, we introduce N slack variables $\{\xi_i \geq 0, i = 1, 2, \ldots, N\}$ to penalize the misclassified samples adaptively, resulting in the following formulation (Cortes and Vapnik 1995).

$$
\begin{aligned}
\min_{\mathbf{w}, b, \boldsymbol{\xi}} \quad & \frac{1}{2}\|\mathbf{w}\|^2 + C\sum_{i=1}^{N}\xi_i \\
\text{s.t.} \quad & y_i(\langle\mathbf{w}, \mathbf{x}_i\rangle + b) \geq 1 - \xi_i, \quad i = 1, 2, \ldots, N \\
& \xi_i \geq 0, \qquad\qquad\qquad\qquad i = 1, 2, \ldots, N
\end{aligned}
\tag{1.1}
$$

According to the analysis in Bishop et al. (2006), the margin is inversely proportional to $\|\mathbf{w}\|^2$. Thus, the first part in the objective corresponds to the maximum margin principle. The second part, i.e., $\sum_{i=1}^{N}\xi_i$, describes the errors arisen from the

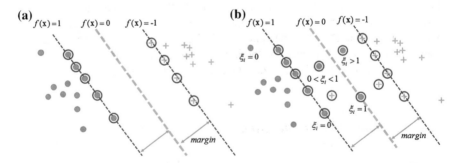

Fig. 1.3 Illustration of the SVM model. **a** the linearly separable case, and **b** linearly inseparable case. This model maximizes the margin between the positive ($y_i = +1$) and negative ($y_i = -1$) samples, and the decision boundary, i.e., $\mathbf{w}^T\mathbf{x} + b = 0$, is also shown in this figure. For the linearly separable case, the margin is defined as the perpendicular distance between the decision boundary and the closest samples in training set, and the closest training samples is known as support vectors, which are highlighted by a *circle*. For the linearly inseparable case, all the data points that do not satisfy $y_i(\mathbf{w}^T\mathbf{x}_i + b) > 1$ are support vectors

misclassified samples. And the constant C controls the trade-off between the slack variable penalty and the margin.

The model in Eq. (1.1) is a quadratic programming (QP) problem, which can be directly solved using the general-purpose QP solver. Actually, SVM is a special QP problem, and we can develop more efficient solution algorithms. For the best understanding of SVM, we present the dual problem of Eq. (1.1) as follows: (Shawe-Taylor and Cristianini 2004; Smola and Schölkopf 2004),

$$\max_{\alpha} \quad \sum_{i=1}^{N} \alpha_i - \frac{1}{2} \sum_{i=1}^{N} \sum_{j=1}^{N} \alpha_i \alpha_j y_i y_j \langle \mathbf{x}_i, \mathbf{x}_j \rangle$$
$$\text{s.t.} \quad \sum_{i=1}^{N} \alpha_i y_i = 0$$
$$\alpha_i \geq 0, \quad i = 1, 2, \ldots, N \tag{1.2}$$

where α_i is the Lagrangian multiplier.

The KKT condition can be represented as:

$$\mathbf{w} = \sum_{i=1}^{N} \alpha_i y_i \mathbf{x}_i$$
$$b = y_j - \sum_{i=1}^{N} \alpha_i y_i \langle \mathbf{x}_i, \mathbf{x}_j \rangle, \quad \text{for } j \ \alpha_j > 0 \tag{1.3}$$

And the decision function $f(\mathbf{x})$ in dual space can be represented as:

$$f(\mathbf{x}) = \sum_{i=1}^{N} \alpha_i y_i \langle \mathbf{x}_i, \mathbf{x} \rangle + b \tag{1.4}$$

Again the problem (1.2) takes the form of quadratic programming problem, and many efficient solvers for this problem have been studied, e.g., Pegasos (Shrivastava et al. 2012), SMO (Platt 1999), coordinate descent method (Hsieh et al. 2008). Implementations of theses solvers are also included in many popular open-sourced machine learning packages, such as LibSVM (Chang and Lin 2011), Liblinear (Fan et al. 2008), OpenCV, and VLFEAT (Vedaldi and Fulkerson 2010). The details of these solvers are beyond the cover of this book. For further reading, readers are encouraged to refer to the related papers and webpages.

The SVM model in Eqs. (1.1) and (1.2) is basically a linear model. In most cases, the decision function $f(\mathbf{x})$ is nonlinear, and it is required to generalize linear SVM for nonlinear classification. Cortes and Vapnik (1995) suggested an elaborate solution by mapping the data point from input space $\mathbb{R}^d$ into a high or even indefinite dimensional feature space $\mathcal{H}$ via an implicit mapping $\Phi : \mathbb{R}^d \to \mathcal{H}$. Given two samples x and y, rather than explicitly computing $\Phi(\mathbf{x})$ and $\Phi(\mathbf{y})$, one can adopt their inner product by the following kernel function

$$K(\mathbf{x}, \mathbf{y}) = \langle \Phi(\mathbf{x}), \Phi(\mathbf{y}) \rangle. \tag{1.5}$$

Fortunately, if the kernel function $K(\mathbf{x}, \mathbf{y})$ satisfies Mercer's condition, we can guarantee that there must exist a mapping $\Phi : \mathbb{R}^d \to \mathcal{H}$ implicitly. Here we introduce two commonly used kernels, i.e., polynomial kernel and Gaussian kernel. For polynomial kernel, the kernel function is defined by:

$$K(\mathbf{x}, \mathbf{y}) = (\langle \mathbf{x}, \mathbf{y} \rangle + 1)^p. \tag{1.6}$$

For Gaussian kernel, the kernel function is defined by:

$$K(\mathbf{x}, \mathbf{y}) = \exp\left(-\frac{\|\mathbf{x} - \mathbf{y}\|^2}{2\sigma^2}\right). \tag{1.7}$$

With the introduction of kernel function, the dual problem of the nonlinear can then be written as:

$$
\begin{aligned}
\min_{\alpha} \quad & \frac{1}{2}\sum_{i=1}^{N}\sum_{j=1}^{N} \alpha_i \alpha_j y_i y_j K(\mathbf{x}_i, \mathbf{x}_j) - \sum_{i=1}^{N} \alpha_i \\
\text{s.t.} \quad & \sum_{i=1}^{N} \alpha_i y_i = 0 \\
& \alpha_i \geq 0, \quad i = 1, 2, \ldots, N,
\end{aligned}
\tag{1.8}
$$

and the nonlinear decision function can be represented as:

$$f(\mathbf{x}) = \sum_{i=1}^{N} \alpha_i y_i K(\mathbf{x}_i, \mathbf{x}) + b. \tag{1.9}$$

With the kernel trick, various kernel methods, including variants of SVM, have been proposed in the last two decades. Refer to (Shawe-Taylor and Cristianini 2004) for in-depth and detailed introduction on SVM.

1.2.2 Metric Learning

How to measure the distance or similarity between data is a fundamental issue in both unsupervised and supervised learning. For example, in k-means, distance metric is used to measure the dissimilarity of data points. In k-nearest neighbors, classifiers use a metric to choose the k-nearest neighbors. Obviously, the performance of these models depends heavily on the quality of the adopted metric. Since general-purpose metrics, e.g., the Euclidean distance or the cosine similarity, often fail to capture task-specific information from given data, improved performance are expected when the metric is tuned to a particular task. Handcrafted metric is generally infeasible due to too many parameters involved. Metric learning automatically learns a metric from given data and thus can provide a natural solution to this issue.

Generally speaking, distance metric learning aims to learn an effective distance metric that maximizes the distance between dissimilar pairs while minimizing the distance between similar pairs. Unlike the standard supervised learning scenario where the class labels are known in advance, metric learning usually considers constraints imposed on either doublets or triplets of training samples. Doublet constraints are often formulated as two sets: the Must-link/cannot link constraints, and triplet constraints are often formed as one set: relative constraints.

- Must-link/cannot link constraints (a.k.a., similar/dissimilar pairs)

$$
\begin{aligned}
\mathcal{S} &= \{(\mathbf{x}_i, \mathbf{x}_j) : \mathbf{x}_i \text{ and } \mathbf{x}_j \text{ should be similar}\}, \\
\mathcal{D} &= \{(\mathbf{x}_i, \mathbf{x}_j) : \mathbf{x}_i \text{ and } \mathbf{x}_j \text{ should be dissimilar}\}.
\end{aligned}
\tag{1.10}
$$

- Relative constraints (sometimes called training triplet)

$$
\mathcal{R} = \{(\mathbf{x}_i, \mathbf{x}_j, \mathbf{x}_k) : \mathbf{x}_i \text{ should be more similar to } \mathbf{x}_j \text{ than to } \mathbf{x}_k\}.
\tag{1.11}
$$

Given the class labels, it is straightforward to conclude that samples with the same label should be similar rather than those with different labels. Thus, given a training set $\{(\mathbf{x}_i, y_i) | i = 1, \ldots, N\}$, we can construct doublet or triplet constraints in Eqs. (1.10) and (1.11) (Bellet et al. 2013; Wang et al. 2015).

Among numerous metric learning methods, Mahalanobis distance metric learning has attracted most interests due to its simplicity and nice interpretation in terms of a linear projection (Bellet et al. 2013; Yang 2007). Mahalanobis distance implicitly corresponds to computing the squared Euclidean distance after applying a linear transformation parameterized by transform matrix $\mathbf{L}$ (Davis et al. 2007). In the context of metric leaning, given two samples $\mathbf{x}_i$ and $\mathbf{x}_j$, the Mahalanobis distance between them is defined as:

$$
d_{\mathbf{M}}^2(\mathbf{x}_i, \mathbf{x}_j) = \|\mathbf{L}(\mathbf{x}_i - \mathbf{x}_j)\|^2 = (\mathbf{x}_i - \mathbf{x}_j)^{\mathrm{T}} \mathbf{M}(\mathbf{x}_i - \mathbf{x}_j).
\tag{1.12}
$$

where $\mathbf{M} = \mathbf{L}^{\mathrm{T}}\mathbf{L}$, and $\mathbf{M}$ should be positive semidefinite (PSD) (Zuo et al. 2015).

The Mahalanobis distance metric learning is to adapt the parameter matrix, either $\mathbf{L}$ or $\mathbf{M}$, to the problem of interest based on the information from the training data. Based on which one of $\mathbf{L}$ and $\mathbf{M}$ are learned, the learning methods can be divided into two groups. For methods that learn $\mathbf{L}$, including NCA (Roweis et al. 2004), LMCA (Torresani and Lee 2006), NRML (Lu et al. 2014), metric learning is mostly formulated as nonconvex problems, optimized by gradient-based solvers. In LMNN (Weinberger et al. 2009), MCML (Pérez-Suay et al. 2013), taking the PSD constraint into consideration, the problem can be formulated as convex program. In ITML (Davis et al. 2007), the problem is modeled in an information-theoretic setting.

Large Margin Nearest Neighbors (LMNN) (Weinberger and Saul 2009) suggested an effective way to learn distance metric for KNN classification. It adaptively penalizes the distance between inputs and its target neighbors to be smaller than the distance between inputs and its nearest non-similar neighbors. This leverages the full power of KNN classification. Correspondingly, the sets $\mathcal{S}$ and $\mathcal{R}$ are redefined in LMNN:

$$
\begin{aligned}
\mathcal{S} &= \{(\mathbf{x}_i, \mathbf{x}_j) : y_i = y_j \text{ and } \mathbf{x}_j \text{ belongs to the } k\text{-nearest neighbors of } \mathbf{x}_i\}, \\
\mathcal{R} &= \{(\mathbf{x}_i, \mathbf{x}_j, \mathbf{x}_k) : (\mathbf{x}_i, \mathbf{x}_j) \in \mathcal{S}, y_i \neq y_k\}.
\end{aligned}
\tag{1.13}
$$

Additionally, margin loss is imposed on violation of constraints in $\mathcal{R}$. The optimization problem of LMNN is finally an instance of semidefinite programming and can be stated as follows:

$$
\begin{aligned}
\min_{M \in \mathbb{S}_+^d} \quad & (1 - \mu) \sum_{(\mathbf{x}_i, \mathbf{x}_j) \in \mathcal{S}} d_{\mathbf{M}}^2(\mathbf{x}_i, \mathbf{x}_j) + \mu \sum_{i,j,k} \xi_{i,j,k} \\
\text{s.t.} \quad & d_{\mathbf{M}}^2(\mathbf{x}_i, \mathbf{x}_j) - d_{\mathbf{M}}^2(\mathbf{x}_i, \mathbf{x}_j) \geq 1 - \xi_{ijk} \quad \forall(\mathbf{x}_i, \mathbf{x}_j, \mathbf{x}_k) \in \mathcal{R},
\end{aligned}
\tag{1.14}
$$

where ξ_{ijk} is the slack variable. The final objective consists of two terms with the hyper parameter μ controlling the trade-off between them. The first term, based on doublet constraints, penalizes the large distance between the given data point and their target neighbors, thus pulling the target neighbors closer together. The second term, based on triplet constraints, penalizes the small distance between differently labeled samples, thus pushing differently labeled samples further apart. LMNN has been one of the most widely used Mahalanobis distance learning methods and has been extended to many application scenarios.

We further introduce another representative method, i.e., Information-Theoretic Metric Learning (ITML) (Davis et al. 2007). It introduces the logdet divergence regularization in its model, operating on the doublets constraints. It formulated the Mahalanobis metric learning problem as that of minimizing the differential relative entropy between the multivariate Gaussian distribution under constraints on the distances function. Given doublets constraints, along with an initial distance parameterized by $\mathbf{M}_0$, the optimization problem is formulated as:

$$
\begin{aligned}
\min_{\mathbf{M} \in \mathbb{S}_+^d} \quad & D_{ld}(\mathbf{M}, \mathbf{M}_0) + \gamma \sum_{i,j} \xi_{ij} \\
\text{s.t.} \quad & d_{\mathbf{M}}^2(\mathbf{x}_i, \mathbf{x}_j) \leq u + \xi_{ij} \quad \forall(\mathbf{x}_i, \mathbf{x}_j) \in \mathcal{S} \\
& d_{\mathbf{M}}^2(\mathbf{x}_i, \mathbf{x}_j) \geq v + \xi_{ij} \quad \forall(\mathbf{x}_i, \mathbf{x}_j) \in \mathcal{D},
\end{aligned}
\tag{1.15}
$$

where $D_{ld}(\cdot, \cdot)$ refers to the Bregman divergence of two matrices, defined by:

$$D_{ld}(\mathbf{M}, \mathbf{M}_0) = \mathrm{tr}(\mathbf{M}\mathbf{M}_0^{-1}) - \log\det(\mathbf{M}\mathbf{M}_0^{-1}) - d, \qquad (1.16)$$

where d denotes the dimension of input vectors. By introducing the logdet regularization on $\mathbf{M}$, this model aims to learn a distance that is close to $\mathbf{M}_0$. In practice, $\mathbf{M}_0$ is often set to $\mathbf{I}$ (the identity matrix), which corresponds to Euclidean distance. Thus, the regularization aims at keeping the learned distance close to the Euclidean distance. The inherent limitation of this model is that $\mathbf{M}_0$ needs to be picked by hand and often have non-negligible influence on performance of the learned metric $\mathbf{M}$. The ITML model can be effectively and efficiently solved by an iterative Bregman projection algorithm and converges to global minimum.

Many other trends and extensions on metric learning has been well studied, e.g., metric learning via dual approaches and kernel methods has been studied in Shen et al. (2009) and (Der and Saul 2012), the connection between SVM and metric learning with doublet-based constraints has been studied in (Pérez-Suay et al. 2013). Additionally, many open-sourced toolkits have been available for metric learning, e.g., DistLearnKit,[1] MetricLearn,[2] and so on.

1.2.3   Sparse Representation-Based Classification

In this subsection, we offer a self-contained introduction on sparse representation-based classification (SRC), which has received considerable research interests in both theoretical studies and practical applications. It has been proven to be a powerful solution in numerous domains, including signal processing, machine learning, and computer vision (Wright et al. 2010; Shi et al. 2009; Mairal et al. 2009).

Basically, SRC imposes a sparsity-based regularization on the representation-based classification. Denote by $\mathbf{y} \in \mathbb{R}^m$ a query sample, and $\mathbf{D} = [\mathbf{d}_1, \mathbf{d}_2, \ldots \mathbf{d}_p] \in \mathbb{R}^{m \times p}$ a dictionary. Representation-based classifier first represents (or approximate) the query samples as a linear combination of atoms in the dictionary $\mathbf{D}$, i.e., $\mathbf{y} = \mathbf{D}\mathbf{x}$. $\mathbf{x}$ denotes the representation coefficient vector. Secondly, it exploits the deviation between $\mathbf{y}$ and the reconstruction results of every class. Finally, $\mathbf{y}$ will be classified into the class which minimizes the deviation. However, the representation problem in the first step is often underdetermined, which suggests that infinite solutions are often available. Hence constraints must be set to the solution in order to learn a desired one (Aharon et al. 2006). The solution with the fewest number of nonzero coefficients is certainly an appealing representation. A nature way to formulate this is to introduce the sparsity constraints. Sparsity

---

[1]http://www.cs.cmu.edu/~liuy/distlearn.htm.
[2]https://all-umass.github.io/metric-learn/.

constraints often come as a L_p-norm regularizer. By presetting the limit of sparsity ε, the sparse representation can be obtained by solving the problem:

$$\min_{\mathbf{x}} \quad ||\mathbf{y} - \mathbf{D}\mathbf{x}||_2$$
$$\text{s.t.} \quad ||\mathbf{x}||_p \leq \varepsilon, \tag{1.17}$$

where $|| \cdot ||_p$ denotes L_p-norm, And the choice value of p will be further discussed.

A wide range of models and methods have been investigated based on SRC. The taxonomy of SRC methods can be studied from various viewpoints, and a symmetric investigation is provided in Zhang et al. (2015). Moreover, to improve the robustness, the L_1-norm has also been introduced to the reconstruction term. Therefore, one typical SRC model can be written as:

$$\hat{\mathbf{x}} = \arg\min_{\mathbf{x}} ||\mathbf{y} - \mathbf{D}\mathbf{x}||_1 + \lambda ||\mathbf{x}||_1. \tag{1.18}$$

Many optimization algorithms, such as L_1-regularized least squares (L1LS) (Kim et al. 2007), fast iterative shrinkage and thresholding algorithm (FISTA) (Gong et al. 2013), alignment or registration errors (Luo et al. 2012), and orthogonal matching pursuit (OMP) (Needell and Vershynin 2010), have been suggested to solve the model in Eq. (1.18).

Learning the dictionary $\mathbf{D}$ from the training data is another crucial issue for sparse representation-based classification. Based on whether the class label of training sample is exploited in the process of learning, we roughly grouped the developed dictionary learning methods into two categories (Zhang and Li 2010; Jiang et al. 2011; Jiang et al. 2013; Bryt and Elad 2008; Wang et al. 2010), i.e., supervised and unsupervised dictionary learning. Here we focus on KSVD (Aharon et al. 2006), as well as its two discriminative extensions, i.e., D-KSVD (Zhang et al. 2015) and LC-KSVD (Rubinstein et al. 2010).

Before our further discussion, we first make some notations declaration. In the following, $\mathbf{Y} = \{\mathbf{y}_i\}_{i=1}^{N}$ is the matrix composed of N known data samples, and each column corresponds to a sample. $\mathbf{X} = \{\mathbf{x}_i\}_{i=1}^{N}$ represents the coefficient matrix, and $\mathbf{x}_i$ denotes the representation coefficient vectors of $\mathbf{y}_i$. KSVD aims to learn the dictionary $\mathbf{D}$ by enforcing sparsity constraint on each coefficient vector $\mathbf{x}_i$, resulting in the following formulation:

$$\{\mathbf{D}, \mathbf{X}\} = \arg\min_{\mathbf{D}, \mathbf{X}} ||\mathbf{Y} - \mathbf{D}\mathbf{X}||_F^2$$
$$\text{s.t.} \quad \forall i, ||\mathbf{x}_i||_0 \leq T_0. \tag{1.19}$$

KSVD solves the above model by alternating minimization. Given $\mathbf{D}$, we can use the MOD algorithm to update $\mathbf{X}$. Then, $\mathbf{D}$ and $\mathbf{X}$ are simultaneously updated by using SVD.

Several discriminative extensions of KSVD, including discriminative KSVD (D-KSVD) (Zhang and Li 2010) and label-consistent KSVD (LC-KSVD), have been developed. The objective of D-KSVD is defined as:

$$\{\mathbf{D}, \mathbf{C}, \mathbf{X}\} = \underset{\mathbf{D}, \mathbf{C}, \mathbf{X}}{\arg\min} ||\mathbf{Y} - \mathbf{D}\mathbf{X}||_F^2 + \mu ||\mathbf{H} - \mathbf{C}\mathbf{X}||_F^2 + \eta ||\mathbf{C}||_F^2$$
$$\text{s.t.} \quad ||\mathbf{x}_i||_0 \leq T_0, \tag{1.20}$$

where $\mathbf{H} = \{\mathbf{h}_i\}_{i=1}^{N}$ are the class label vectors of input samples $\mathbf{Y}$, $\mathbf{h}_i = [0, 0, \ldots, 1, \ldots, 0]^t$ is a label vector corresponding to an input signal $\mathbf{y}_i$, and the nonzero position indicates the class of $\mathbf{y}_i$. $\mathbf{C}$ represents the parameter term for classifier, i.e., $\mathbf{C}\mathbf{X}$ can be interpreted as the classification results of classifier. The model in Eq. (1.20) includes three terms. The first term is the common reconstruction error in SRC. The second and third terms are related to classifier parameters, respectively, denoting a structure risk and a regularizer based on the classifier parameter $\mathbf{C}$. η and μ are the parameters to control the trade-off of the three terms. With simple algebra, D-KSVD can also be solved by KSVD.

In classification phase, given the optimal dictionary $\hat{\mathbf{D}}$ and classifier $\hat{\mathbf{C}}$, along with the matrix $\mathbf{Y}'$ composed of test samples, there are mainly two steps to infer the labels. First, the sparse representation matrix $\mathbf{X}'$ can be obtained by exploiting the efficient OMP algorithm (Needell and Vershynin 2010). Second, the learned classifier is operated on the coefficient vector for classification.

Another extension of KSVD, i.e., LC-KSVD, is to introduce a label consistency regularization (Jiang et al. 2011; Jiang et al. 2013). Label consistency is intuitively based on the consideration that the class distributions that a dictionary element 'contributes' during classification are highly peaked in one class (Jiang et al. 2013). This is achieved by minimizing a discriminative sparse-code error

$$||\mathbf{L} - \mathbf{A}\mathbf{X}||_F^2, \tag{1.21}$$

where $\mathbf{L}$ is described as the 'discriminative' sparse codes of input samples $\mathbf{Y}$ for classification, $\mathbf{A}$ denotes a linear transformation to be learned. The optimization problem of LC-KSVD can be formulated as:

$$\{\mathbf{D}, \mathbf{A}, \mathbf{C}, \mathbf{X}\} = \underset{\mathbf{D}, \mathbf{A}, \mathbf{C}, \mathbf{X}}{\arg\min} ||\mathbf{Y} - \mathbf{D}\mathbf{X}||_F^2 + \eta ||\mathbf{L} - \mathbf{A}\mathbf{X}||_F^2 + \mu ||\mathbf{H} - \mathbf{C}\mathbf{X}||_F^2$$
$$\text{s.t.} \quad ||\mathbf{x}_i||_0 \leq T_0, \tag{1.22}$$

where η and μ are scalars controlling the relative contribution of the corresponding items.

1.3 Summary

In this chapter, some basic knowledge on biometrics and discriminative learning are introduced. First, we described the properties for an ideal and practical biometric trait, and then provide a brief introduction on several representative traits used in biometrics. To address the inherent limitations of uni-biometrics, multi-biometrics have been introduced, and a short survey is provided to summarize the main fusion methods used in multi-biometrics. In the second part, we introduced three representative discriminative learning methods: support vector machine, metric learning, and sparse representation-based classification. These methods not only play an important role in biometrics, but also have been extensively adopted in many real world applications.

References

A. Abaza, A. Ross, C. Hebert, M.A.F. Harrison, M.S. Nixon, A survey on ear biometrics. ACM Comput Surv (CSUR) **45**(2), 22 (2013)

M. Aharon, A. Bruckstein, M. Elad, *K-svd: an Algorithm for Designing Overcomplete Dictionaries for Sparse Representation* (2006)

A. Bellet, A. Habrard, M. Sebban, A survey on metric learning for feature vectors and structured data. *arXiv preprint* arXiv:1306.6709 (2013)

C.M. Bishop, Pattern recognition. Mach. Learn. **128** (2006)

O. Bryt, M. Elad, Compression of facial images using the K-SVD algorithm. J. Vis. Commun. Image Represent. **19**(4), 270–282 (2008)

M.J. Burge, K. Bowyer (eds.), *Handbook of Iris Recognition* (Springer Science & Business Media, 2013)

C.C. Chang, C.J. Lin, LIBSVM: a library for support vector machines. ACM Trans. Intell. Syst. Technol. (TIST), **2**(3), 27 (2011)

R. Collobert, J. Weston, L. Bottou, M. Karlen, K. Kavukcuoglu, P. Kuksa, Natural language processing (almost) from scratch. J. Mach. Learn. Res. **12**, 2493–2537 (2011)

C. Cortes, V. Vapnik, Support-vector networks. Mach. Learn. **20**(3), 273–297 (1995)

J.G. Daugman, High confidence visual recognition of persons by a test of statistical independence. Pattern Anal. Mach. Intell., IEEE Trans. **15**(11), 1148–1161 (1993)

J.V. Davis, B. Kulis, P. Jain, S. Sra, I.S. Dhillon, in *Information-theoretic metric learning*. Proceedings of the 24th International Conference on Machine Learning (ACM, 2007), pp. 209–216

M. Der, L.K. Saul, Latent coincidence analysis: a hidden variable model for distance metric learning. Adv. Neural Inf. Process. Syst., 3230–3238 (2012)

R.E. Fan, K.W. Chang, C.J. Hsieh, X.R. Wang, C.J. Lin, LIBLINEAR: a library for large linear classification. J. Mach. Learn. Res. **9**, 1871–1874 (2008)

P. Gong, C. Zhang, Z. Lu, J.Z. Huang, J. Ye, in *A general iterative shrinkage and thresholding algorithm for non-convex regularized optimization problems*. International Conference on Machine Learning, vol. 28, no. 2 (NIH Public Access, 2013), p. 37

I. Guyon, J. Weston, S. Barnhill, V. Vapnik, Gene selection for cancer classification using support vector machines. Mach. Learn. **46**(1–3), 389–422 (2002)

B. Heisele, P. Ho, T. Poggio, in *Face recognition with support vector machines: global versus component-based approach*. 2001 Proceedings of IEEE International Conference on Computer Vision (ICCV 2001), vol. 2, Eighth (IEEE, 2001), pp. 688–694

C.J. Hsieh, K.W. Chang, C.J. Lin, S.S. Keerthi, S. Sundararajan, in *A dual coordinate descent method for large-scale linear SVM*. Proceedings of the 25th International Conference on Machine Learning (ACM, 2008), pp. 408–415

R. Jafri, H. Arabnia, Information-theoretic metric learning recognition techniques. J. Inf. Process. Syst. 5(2), 41–68 (2009)

A.K. Jain, J. Feng, Latent palmprint matching. Pattern Anal. Mach. Intell. IEEE Trans. 31(6), 1032–1047 (2009)

Z. Jiang, Z. Lin, L.S. Davis, in *Learning a discriminative dictionary for sparse coding via label consistent K-SVD*. 2011 IEEE Conference on Computer Vision and Pattern Recognition (CVPR) (IEEE, 2011), pp. 1697–1704

Z. Jiang, Z. Lin, L.S. Davis, Label consistent K-SVD: learning a discriminative dictionary for recognition. Pattern Anal. Mach. Intell., IEEE Trans. 35(11), 2651–2664 (2013)

S.J. Kim, K. Koh, M. Lustig, S. Boyd, D. Gorinevsky, An interior-point method for large-scale l 1-regularized least squares. Signal Process., IEEE J. 1(4), 606–617 (2007)

L.L. Lee, T. Berger, E. Aviczer, Reliable online human signature verification systems. Pattern Anal. Mach. Intell., IEEE Trans. 18(6), 643–647 (1996)

L. Liu, D. Zhang, A. Kumar, X. Wu, in *Tongue line extraction*. 19th International Conference on Pattern Recognition, 2008 (ICPR 2008) (IEEE), pp. 1–4

J. Lu, X. Zhou, Y.P. Tan, Y. Shang, J. Zhou, Neighborhood repulsed metric learning for kinship verification. Pattern Anal. Mach. Intell., IEEE Trans. 36(2), 331–345 (2014)

H.Z. Luo, H.X. Wu, G.T. Chen, On the convergence of augmented Lagrangian methods for nonlinear semidefinite programming. J. Global Optim. 54(3), 599–618 (2012)

J. Mairal, J. Ponce, G. Sapiro, A. Zisserman, F.R. Bach, Supervised dictionary learning. Adv. Neural Inf. Process. Syst. 1033–1040 (2009)

D. Maltoni, D. Maio, A. Jain, S. Prabhakar, *Handbook of Fingerprint Recognition* (Springer Science & Business Media, 2009)

D. Needell, R. Vershynin, Signal recovery from incomplete and inaccurate measurements via regularized orthogonal matching pursuit. Signal Process., IEEE J. 4(2), 310–316 (2010)

H. Nejati, L. Zhang, T. Sim, E. Martinez-Marroquin, G. Dong, in *Wonder ears: identification of identical twins from ear images*. International Conference on Pattern Recognition (ICPR) (IEEE, 2012 21st), pp. 1201–1204

A. Pérez-Suay, F.J. Ferri, M. Arevalillo-Herráez, J.V. Albert, in *Comparative evaluation of batch and online distance metric learning approaches based on margin maximization*. 2013 IEEE International Conference on Systems, Man, and Cybernetics (SMC) (IEEE, 2013), pp. 3511–3515

A. Pflug, C. Busch, Ear biometrics: a survey of detection, feature extraction and recognition methods. Biometrics, IET 1(2), 114–129 (2012)

J.C. Platt, 12 fast training of support vector machines using sequential minimal optimization. Adv. Kernel Methods, 185–208 (1999)

S. Roweis, G. Hinton, R. Salakhutdinov, Neighbourhood component analysis. Adv. Neural Inf. Process. Syst. (NIPS) 17, 513–520 (2004)

R. Rubinstein, A.M. Bruckstein, M. Elad, Dictionaries for sparse representation modeling. Proc. IEEE 98(6), 1045–1057 (2010)

B. Samanta, K.R. Al-Balushi, S.A. Al-Araimi, Artificial neural networks and support vector machines with genetic algorithm for bearing fault detection. Eng. Appl. Artif. Intell. 16(7), 657–665 (2003)

F. Schroff, D. Kalenichenko, J. Philbin, in *Facenet: a unified embedding for face recognition and clustering*. Proceedings of the IEEE Conference on Computer Vision and Pattern Recognition (2015), pp. 815–823

J. Shawe-Taylor, N. Cristianini, *Kernel Methods for Pattern Analysis* (Cambridge University Press, 2004)

C. Shen, J. Kim, L. Wang, A. Hengel, Positive semidefinite metric learning with boosting. Adv. Neural Inf. Process. Syst., 1651–1659 (2009)

Y. Shi, D. Dai, C. Liu, H. Yan, Sparse discriminant analysis for breast cancer biomarker identification and classification. Prog. Nat. Sci. **19**(11), 1635–1641 (2009)

A. Shrivastava, J.K. Pillai, V.M. Patel, R. Chellappa, in *Learning discriminative dictionaries with partially labeled data*. 2012 19th IEEE International Conference on Image Processing (ICIP) (IEEE, 2012), pp. 3113–3116

A.J. Smo La, B. Schölkopf, A tutorial on support vector regression. Stat. Comput. **14**(3), 199–222 (2004)

L. Torresani, K.C. Lee, Large margin component analysis. Adv. Neural Inf. Process. Syst., 1385–1392 (2006)

Vedaldi, B. Fulkerson, in *VLFeat: an open and portable library of computer vision algorithms*. Proceedings of the 18th ACM International Conference on Multimedia (ACM, 2010), pp. 1469–1472

J. Wang, J. Yang, K. Yu, F. Lv, T. Huang, Y. Gong, in *Locality-constrained linear coding for image classification*. 2010 IEEE Conference on Computer Vision and Pattern Recognition (CVPR) (IEEE, 2010), pp. 3360–3367

F. Wang, W. Zuo, L. Zhang, D. Meng, D. Zhang, A kernel classification framework for metric learning. Neural Netw. Learn. Syst., IEEE Trans. **26**(9), 1950–1962 (2015)

J. Wayman, A. Jain, D. Maltoni, D. Maio, *An Introduction to Biometric Authentication Systems* (Springer, London, 2005), pp. 1–20

K.Q. Weinberger, L.K. Saul, Distance metric learning for large margin nearest neighbor classification. J. Mach. Learn. Res. **10**, 207–244 (2009)

B. Wirtz, in *Stroke-based time warping for signature verification*. Proceedings of the Third International Conference on Document Analysis and Recognition, vol. 1 (IEEE, 1995), pp. 179–182

J. Wright, Y. Ma, J. Mairal, G. Sapiro, T.S. Huang, S. Yan, Sparse representation for computer vision and pattern recognition. Proc. IEEE **98**(6), 1031–1044 (2010)

X. Wu, W. Zuo, Y. Zhu, L. Lin, F-SVM: combination of feature transformation and SVM learning via convex relaxation. arXiv preprint arXiv:1504.05035 (2015)

L. Yang, in *An overview of distance metric learning*. Proceedings of the Computer Vision and Pattern Recognition Conference (2007)

D. Zhang, W. Shu, Two novel characteristics in palmprint verification: datum point invariance and line feature matching. Pattern Recogn. **32**(4), 691–702 (1999)

Q. Zhang, B. Li, in *Discriminative K-SVD for dictionary learning in face recognition*. 2010 IEEE Conference on Computer Vision and Pattern Recognition (CVPR) (IEEE, 2010), pp. 2691–2698

D. Zhang, W. Zuo, F. Yue, A comparative study of palmprint recognition algorithms. ACM Comput. Surv. (CSUR) **44**(1), 2 (2012)

Z. Zhang, Y. Xu, J. Yang, X. Li, D. Zhang, A survey of sparse representation: algorithms and applications. Access, IEEE **3**, 490–530 (2015)

W. Zuo, F. Wang, D. Zhang, L. Lin, Y. Huang, D. Meng, L. Zhang, Iterated Support Vector Machines for Distance Metric Learning. *arXiv preprint* arXiv:1502.00363 (2015)

Part II
Metric Learning and Sparse Representation-Based Classification

Chapter 2
Metric Learning with Biometric Applications

Abstract Learning a desired distance metric from given training samples plays a significant role in the field of machine learning. In this chapter, we first present two novel metric learning methods based on a support vector machine (SVM). We then present a kernel classification framework for metric learning that can be implemented efficiently by using the standard SVM solvers. Some novel kernel metric learning methods, such as the double-SVM and the triplet-SVM, are also introduced in this chapter.

2.1 Introduction

Distance metric learning aims to train a valid distance metric that enables samples of different classes to have larger distances and samples of the same class to have smaller distances (Bellet et al. 2013). Distance metric learning has been adopted successfully in many real-world applications, such as face verification (Guillaumin et al. 2009), object classification (Mensink et al. 2012), and visual tracking (Li et al. 2012).

In past years, numerous distance metric learning algorithms have been proposed (Balcan et al. 2008; Kedem et al. 2012; Guillaumin et al. 2009; Fu et al. 2008; Wang et al. 2011). On the basis of the availability of labels, available distance metric learning algorithms can be categorized into two groups: supervised distance metric learning and unsupervised distance metric learning (Yang and Jin 2006). Unsupervised distance metric learning can be viewed as a dimension reduction approach, including principal component analysis (PCA) and locally linear embedding (LLE), which aim to learn an underlying low-dimensional manifold without label information. Supervised distance metric learning methods utilize the information of class labels to improve the discrimination of the distance metric, and can be further divided into two groups: learn metrics with triplet or pairwise constraints. For each triplet, triplet constraint-based metric learning approaches restrict that the distance between a pair of samples from the same class should be smaller than that of those from different classes. The large margin nearest neighbor

© Springer Science+Business Media Singapore 2016
D. Zhang et al., *Discriminative Learning in Biometrics*,
DOI 10.1007/978-981-10-2056-8_2

(LMNN) (Weinberger et al. 2009), BoostMetric (Shen et al. 2009) and FrobMetric (Shen et al. 2011) are typical triplet constraint-based metric learning methods. Compared to triplet constraint-based metric learning methods, pairwise constraint-based methods are more generally used in real applications of metric learning. For example, only pairwise constraint-based methods are available for face verification, particularly for the LFW face database (Huang et al. 2007). The neighborhood-component analysis method (NCA) (Goldberger et al. 2004), the information theoretic metric learning algorithm (ITML) (Davis et al. 2007), and the logistic discriminative-based metric learning method (LDML) (Guillaumin et al. 2009) are typical pairwise constraint-based metric learning methods. The NCA method learns a distance metric from the input data by finding a linear transformed space that has the maximum performance of the average leave-one-out classification. Globerson and Roweis (2005) proposed an effective metric learning method by maximizing intraclass distances while collapsing the interclass distance to zero. Huang et al. (2012) proposed a distance metric learning method which restricts distances between the same classes to be smaller than that of those from different classes. Both pairwise constraint-based and triplet constraint-based metric learning methods work in a fully supervised metric learning manner.

The remainder of this chapter is organized as follows. Section 2.2 presents two novel distance metric learning models based on SVM. In Sect. 2.3, we present a kernel classification framework for metric learning. The framework provides a new perspective on developing metric learning methods. Based on this framework, two novel kernel metric learning methods, doublet-SVM and triplet-SVM, are also presented.

2.2 Support Vector Machines for Metric Learning

2.2.1 Positive Semidefinite Constrained Metric Learning (PCML)

Suppose $\{(\mathbf{x}_i, y_i) | i = 1, 2, \ldots, N\}$ represents a training set, where $\mathbf{x}_i \in \mathbb{R}^d$ and y_i denote the ith training sample and its class label. The Mahalanobis distance of two samples $\mathbf{x}_i$ and $\mathbf{x}_j$ is defined as

$$d_{\mathbf{M}}^2(\mathbf{x}_i, \mathbf{x}_j) = \mathrm{tr}\left(\mathbf{M}^{\mathrm{T}}(\mathbf{x}_i - \mathbf{x}_j)(\mathbf{x}_i - \mathbf{x}_j)^{\mathrm{T}}\right) = \left\langle \mathbf{M}, (\mathbf{x}_i - \mathbf{x}_j)(\mathbf{x}_i - \mathbf{x}_j)^{\mathrm{T}} \right\rangle, \quad (2.1)$$

where $\mathbf{M}$ is a positive semidefinite (PSD) matrix, $\langle \mathbf{A}, \mathbf{B} \rangle = \mathrm{tr}(\mathbf{A}^{\mathrm{T}}\mathbf{B})$ is defined as the Frobenius inner product of two matrices $\mathbf{A}$ and $\mathbf{B}$, and $\mathrm{tr}(\cdot)$ denotes the matrix trace operator. For each pair samples $\mathbf{x}_i$ and $\mathbf{x}_j$, we define $\mathbf{X}_{ij} = (\mathbf{x}_i - \mathbf{x}_j)(\mathbf{x}_i - \mathbf{x}_j)^{\mathrm{T}}$. Thus, the Mahalanobis distance can be rewritten as $d_{\mathbf{M}}^2(\mathbf{x}_i, \mathbf{x}_j) = \langle \mathbf{M}, \mathbf{X}_{ij} \rangle$.

2.2.1.1 PCML and Its Dual Problem

Suppose $\mathcal{S} = \{(\mathbf{x}_i, \mathbf{x}_j): \mathbf{x}_i$ and $\mathbf{x}_j$ have the same class labels$\}$ represents the set of similar pairs, and $\mathcal{D} = \{(\mathbf{x}_i, \mathbf{x}_j) : \mathbf{x}_i$ and $\mathbf{x}_j$ have different class labels$\}$ denotes the set of dissimilar pairs. The objective function of the PCML model is

$$
\begin{aligned}
\min_{\mathbf{M}, b, \xi} \quad & \frac{1}{2} \|\mathbf{M}\|_F^2 + C \sum_{ij} \xi_{ij} \\
\text{s.t.} \quad & h_{ij}\left(\langle \mathbf{M}, \mathbf{X}_{ij} \rangle + b\right) \geq 1 - \xi_{ij}, \quad \xi_{ij} \geq 0, \quad \forall\ i, j, \mathbf{M} \succeq 0,
\end{aligned}
\tag{2.2}
$$

where ξ_{ij} is the slack variables, b is the bias, and $\|\cdot\|_F$ denotes the Frobenius norm. h_{ij} is an indicator variable, and is defined as:

$$
h_{ij} = \begin{cases} 1, & \text{if } (\mathbf{x}_i, \mathbf{x}_j) \in \mathcal{D} \\ -1, & \text{if } (\mathbf{x}_i, \mathbf{x}_j) \in \mathcal{S}. \end{cases}
\tag{2.3}
$$

The PCML model is convex and can be solved by the standard semidefinite programming (SDP) solvers. However, the general-purpose interior-point SDP solver is very complex, which is not suitable for metric learning with large samples. In order to improve the efficiency of the Mahalanobis distance metric learning, we present an iterating SVM training algorithm based on the PSD projection in this chapter.

First, a Lagrange multiplier λ and a PSD matrix $\mathbf{Y}$ are introduced to the PCML model. The Lagrange dual problem of the PCML model in Eq. (2.3) can be formulated as

$$
\begin{aligned}
\max_{\lambda, \mathbf{Y}} \quad & -\frac{1}{2} \left\| \sum_{ij} \lambda_{ij} h_{ij} \mathbf{X}_{ij} + \mathbf{Y} \right\|_F^2 + \sum_{ij} \lambda_{ij} \\
\text{s.t.} \quad & \sum_{ij} \lambda_{ij} h_{ij} = 0, \quad 0 \leq \lambda_{ij} \leq C, \quad \mathbf{Y} \succeq 0.
\end{aligned}
\tag{2.4}
$$

The detailed derivation of the dual problem can be found in Appendix 2.1. Based on the Karush-Kuhn-Tucker (KKT) conditions, matrix $\mathbf{M}$ can be calculated by

$$
\mathbf{M} = \sum_{ij} \lambda_{ij} h_{ij} \mathbf{X}_{ij} + \mathbf{Y}.
\tag{2.5}
$$

Based on the strong duality, if the Lagrange dual problem in Eq. (2.4) can be solved, matrix $\mathbf{M}$ can also be obtained by Eq. (2.5). However, due to the PSD constraint $\mathbf{Y} \succeq 0$, the Lagrange dual problem in Eq. (2.4) is still difficult to solve.

2.2.1.2 Alternative Optimization Algorithm

In order to improve the efficiency of general SDP solvers, we present an optimization scheme by updating λ and $\mathbf{Y}$ alternatively. When $\mathbf{Y}$ is obtained, we introduce a new variable η with $\eta_{ij} = 1 - h_{ij}\langle \mathbf{X}_{ij}, \mathbf{Y} \rangle$ to obtain λ. Therefore, λ can be updated by solving the following formula:

$$\max_{\lambda} \quad -\frac{1}{2}\sum_{ij}\sum_{kl}\lambda_{ij}\lambda_{kl}h_{ij}h_{kl}\langle \mathbf{X}_{ij}, \mathbf{X}_{kl}\rangle + \sum_{ij}\eta_{ij}\lambda_{ij}$$
$$\text{s.t.} \quad \sum_{ij}\lambda_{ij}h_{ij} = 0, \quad 0 \le \lambda_{ij} \le C, \quad \forall \; i,j. \tag{2.6}$$

The above subproblem is a QP problem, and can be solved efficiently by using existing SVM solvers, such as LibSVM (Chang and Lin 2011). When λ is updated by solving Eq. (2.6), $\mathbf{Y}$ also can be updated by solving the following objective function:

$$\min_{\mathbf{Y}} \quad \|\mathbf{Y} - \mathbf{Y}_0\|_F^2 \quad \text{s.t.} \quad \mathbf{Y} \succeq 0, \tag{2.7}$$

where $\mathbf{Y}_0 = -\sum_{ij}\lambda_{ij}h_{ij}\mathbf{X}_{ij}$. Through the eigen-decomposition of $\mathbf{Y}_0$, i.e., $\mathbf{Y}_0 = \mathbf{U}\Lambda\mathbf{U}^T$, $\mathbf{Y}$ can be rewritten as $\mathbf{Y} = \mathbf{U}\Lambda_+\mathbf{U}^T$, where $\Lambda_+ = \max(\Lambda, 0)$, Λ denotes the diagonal matrix of eigenvalues. Finally, the alternative optimization scheme of PCML algorithm is summarized in Algorithm 1.

Algorithm 2.1 Algorithm of PCML

  Input: $S = \{(\mathbf{x}_i, \mathbf{x}_j)$: the class labels of $\mathbf{x}_i$ and $\mathbf{x}_j$ are the same$\}$, $\cdot D = \{(\mathbf{x}_i, \mathbf{x}_j)$: the class labels of $\mathbf{x}_i$ and $\mathbf{x}_j$ are different$\}$, and $\{h_{ij}\}$.

  Output: $\mathbf{M}$.

1. **Initialize** $\mathbf{Y}^{(0)}$, $t \leftarrow 0$.
2. **Repeat**
3. Update $\eta^{(t+1)}$ with $\eta_{ij}^{(t+1)} = 1 - h_{ij}\langle \mathbf{X}_{ij}, \mathbf{Y}^{(t)}\rangle$.
4. Update $\lambda^{(t+1)}$ by solving the subproblem (2.6) using an SVM solver.
5. Update $\mathbf{Y}_0^{(t+1)} = -\sum_{ij}\lambda_{ij}^{(t+1)}h_{ij}\mathbf{X}_{ij}$.
6. Update $\quad \mathbf{Y}^{(t+1)} = \mathbf{U}^{(t+1)}\Lambda_+^{(t+1)}\mathbf{U}^{(t+1)T}, \quad$ where $\quad \mathbf{Y}_0^{(t+1)} = \mathbf{U}^{(t+1)}\Lambda^{(t+1)}\mathbf{U}^{(t+1)T}$ and $\Lambda_+^{(t+1)} = \max(\Lambda^{(t+1)}, 0)$.
7. $t \leftarrow t + 1$.
8. **Until** convergence
9. $\mathbf{M} = \sum_{ij}\lambda_{ij}^{(t)}h_{ij}\mathbf{X}_{ij} + \mathbf{Y}^{(t)}$.
10. **Return** $\mathbf{M}$

2.2.1.3 Optimality Condition

The general alternating minimization approach would converge to the correct solution (Gunawardana and Byrne 2005; Csisz and Tusnády 1984). By updating λ and $\mathbf{Y}$ alternatively, the presented optimization PCML algorithm can find the global optimum of the problems in Eqs. (2.2) and (2.4) quickly. Figure 2.1 shows an example convergence curve of the PCML algorithm in the *PenDigits dataset*, and we can see that it converges in less than 20 iterations.

We further use the duality gap in each iteration to verify the optimality condition of the presented optimization PCML algorithm. The duality gap is defined as the difference between the primal and dual objective values, and is calculated as

$$
\text{DualGap}_{\text{PCML}}^{(n)} = \frac{1}{2} \left\| \mathbf{M}^{(n)} \right\|_F^2 + C \sum_{ij} \xi_{ij}^{(n)} - \sum_{ij} \lambda_{ij}^{(n)} + \frac{1}{2} \left\| \sum_{ij} \lambda_{ij}^{(n)} h_{ij} \mathbf{X}_{ij} + \mathbf{Y}^{(n)} \right\|_F^2,
$$

(2.8)

where $\text{DualGap}_{\text{PCML}}^{(n)}$ denotes the duality gap in the nth iteration, and $\mathbf{M}^{(n)}$, $\xi^{(n)}$, $\lambda^{(n)}$, and $\mathbf{Y}^{(n)}$ are feasible primal and dual variables. According to Eq. (2.5), we can derive that

$$
\mathbf{M}^{(n)} = \sum_{i,j} \lambda_{ij}^{(n)} h_{ij} \mathbf{X}_{ij} + \mathbf{Y}^{(n)} = \mathbf{Y}^{(n)} - \mathbf{Y}_0^{(n)}.
$$

(2.9)

As discussed in Sect. 2.2.1.2, $\mathbf{Y}_0^{(n)} = \mathbf{U}^{(n)} \Lambda^{(n)} \mathbf{U}^{(n)\text{T}}$, $\mathbf{Y}^{(n)} = \mathbf{U}^{(n)} \Lambda_+^{(n)} \mathbf{U}^{(n)\text{T}}$; therefore, $\mathbf{M}^{(n)} = \mathbf{U}^{(n)} \Lambda_-^{(n)} \mathbf{U}^{(n)\text{T}}$, where $\Lambda_-^{(n)} = \Lambda_+^{(n)} - \Lambda^{(n)}$. Thus, $\left\| \mathbf{M}^{(n)} \right\|_F^2$ can be calculated by

$$
\begin{aligned}
\left\| \mathbf{M}^{(n)} \right\|_F^2 &= \text{tr}\left(\mathbf{M}^{(n)\text{T}} \mathbf{M}^{(n)} \right) = \text{tr}\left(\mathbf{U}^{(n)} \Lambda_-^{(n)} \mathbf{U}^{(n)\text{T}} \mathbf{U}^{(n)} \Lambda_-^{(n)} \mathbf{U}^{(n)\text{T}} \right) \\
&= \text{tr}\left(\mathbf{U}^{(n)} \Lambda_-^{(n)2} \mathbf{U}^{(n)\text{T}} \right) = \text{tr}\left(\Lambda_-^{(n)2} \right).
\end{aligned}
$$

(2.10)

From Eqs. (2.8)–(2.10), we can obtain the duality gap

$$
\text{DualGap}_{\text{PCML}}^{(n)} = C \sum_{i,j} \xi_{ij}^{(n)} - \sum_{i,j} \lambda_{ij}^{(n)} + \text{tr}\left(\Lambda_-^{(n)2} \right).
$$

(2.11)

Based on the KKT conditions of the PCML dual problem in Eq. (2.4), $\xi_{ij}^{(n)}$ can be obtained by

$$
\xi_{ij}^{(n)} = \begin{cases} 0 & \text{for all } \lambda_{ij}^{(n)} < C \\ \left[1 - h_{ij}\left(\langle \mathbf{M}^{(n)}, \mathbf{X}_{ij} \rangle + b^{(n)} \right) \right]_+ & \text{for all } \lambda_{ij}^{(n)} = C, \end{cases}
$$

(2.12)

where

$$b^{(n)} = \frac{1}{h_{ij}} - \left\langle \mathbf{M}^{(n)}, \mathbf{X}_{ij} \right\rangle \quad \text{for all} \ \ 0 < \lambda_{ij}^{(n)} < C. \tag{2.13}$$

The detailed derivation of $\xi_{ij}^{(n)}$ and $b^{(n)}$ can be found in Appendix 2.1. The duality gap is always nonnegative, and approaches zero when the primal problem is convex. Thus, it can be used as the termination condition of the presented iterative algorithm. From Fig. 2.1, we can see that the duality gap would converge to zero, which indicates that the presented algorithm would reach the global optimum. In the implementation of Algorithm 2.1, the following termination condition is adopted:

$$\text{DualGap}_{\text{PCML}}^{(t)} - \text{DualGap}_{\text{PCML}}^{(t-1)} < \varepsilon \cdot \text{DualGap}_{\text{PCML}}^{(1)}, \tag{2.14}$$

where ε is a small constant and is set at 0.01 in the experiment.

2.2.1.4 Remarks

Warm start: In the presented optimization PCML algorithm, we use a simple warm-start strategy to iteratively calculate λ. The solution to the previous iteration is used as the initialization for the next iteration. By using the iteration scheme, the optimal λ can be obtained rapidly, and the efficiency of the PCML algorithm can be greatly improved.

Construction of pairwise constraints: Suppose there are N^2 pairwise constraints in the training set. This involves a high computation cost as a result of using the N^2 pairwise constraints directly for metric learning. In practice, we can reduce the computational cost by using a subset of pairwise constraints rather than the entire dataset. For each sample, we select its k-nearest neighbors to construct similar pairs and its k farthest neighbors to construct dissimilar pairs. Thus, $2kN$ pairwise

Fig. 2.1 Duality gap versus number of iterations in the PenDigits dataset for PCML (Zuo et al. 2015)

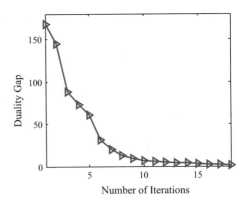

constraints are achieved in total. In practice, k is generally chosen as $1 \sim 3$. Thus, compared with N^2 pairwise constraints, the $2kN$ pairwise constraints can improve the efficiency effectively.

Computational Complexity: In the training of SVM, we use the LibSVM library, where the computational complexity of SMO-type algorithms (Platt 1999) is $O(N^2 d)$. For PSD projection, the complexity of the conventional SVD algorithm is $O(d^3)$.

2.2.2 Nonnegative-Coefficient Constrained Metric Learning (NCML)

Given a set of rank-1 PSD matrices $\mathbf{M}_t = \mathbf{m}_t \mathbf{m}_t^T$ ($t = 1, \ldots, T$), a linear combination of $\mathbf{M}_t$ is defined as $\mathbf{M} = \sum_t \alpha_t \mathbf{M}_t$, where αt denotes the scalar combination coefficient. One can easily prove the following Theorem 2.1.

Theorem 2.1 *Assume the scalar coefficient $\alpha_t \geq 0$, $\forall\, t$, matrix $\mathbf{M} = \sum_t \alpha_t \mathbf{M}_t$ is a PSD matrix, where $\mathbf{M}_t = \mathbf{m}_t \mathbf{m}_t^T$ is a rank-1 PSD matrix.*

Proof Suppose $\mathbf{u} \in \mathbb{R}^d$ is a random vector. Based on the expression of $\mathbf{M}$, we have

$$\mathbf{u}^T \mathbf{M} \mathbf{u} = \mathbf{u}^T \left(\sum_t \alpha_t \mathbf{m}_t \mathbf{m}_t^T \right) \mathbf{u} = \sum_i \alpha_i \mathbf{u}^T \mathbf{m}_t \mathbf{m}_t^T \mathbf{u} = \sum_i \alpha_i \left(\mathbf{u}^T \mathbf{m}_t \right)^2.$$

Since $\left(\mathbf{u}^T \mathbf{m}_t \right)^2 \geq 0$ and $\alpha_t \geq 0$, $\forall\, t$, we have $\mathbf{u}^T \mathbf{M} \mathbf{u} \geq 0$. Therefore, $\mathbf{M}$ is a PSD matrix.

2.2.2.1 NCML and Its Dual Problem

Inspired by Theorem 2.1, we present a nonnegative-coefficient constrained metric learning (NCML) method by reparameterizing the distance metric $\mathbf{M}$. Given the training data $\mathcal{S}$ and $\mathcal{D}$, a rank-1 PSD matrix $\mathbf{X}_{ij}$ can be constructed for each pair of $(\mathbf{x}_i, \mathbf{x}_j)$. By assuming that the learned matrix should be the linear combination of $\mathbf{X}_{ij}$ with the nonnegative-coefficient constraint, the NCML model can be formulated as

$$\min_{\mathbf{M}, b, \alpha, \xi} \quad \frac{1}{2} \|\mathbf{M}\|_F^2 + C \sum_{ij} \xi_{ij}$$

$$\text{s.t.} \quad h_{ij} \left(\langle \mathbf{M}, \mathbf{X}_{ij} \rangle + b \right) \geq 1 - \xi_{ij}, \xi_{ij} \geq 0, \quad \alpha_{ij} \geq 0, \quad \forall\, i, j, \quad \mathbf{M} = \sum_{ij} \alpha_{ij} \mathbf{X}_{ij}.$$

$$(2.15)$$

By substituting $\sum_{ij} \alpha_{ij} \mathbf{X}_{ij}$ for $\mathbf{M}$, the NCML model is transformed as follows:

$$\min_{\alpha,b,\xi} \quad \frac{1}{2} \sum_{ij} \sum_{kl} \alpha_{ij} \alpha_{kl} \langle \mathbf{X}_{ij}, \mathbf{X}_{kl} \rangle + C \sum_{ij} \xi_{ij}$$

$$\text{s.t.} \quad h_{ij} \left(\sum_{kl} \alpha_{kl} \langle \mathbf{X}_{ij}, \mathbf{X}_{kl} \rangle + b \right) \geq 1 - \xi_{ij}, \quad \xi_{ij} \geq 0, \quad \alpha_{ij} \geq 0, \quad \forall\, i,j. \tag{2.16}$$

By introducing two variables η and β, the Lagrange dual of the primal problem in Eq. (2.16) can be formulated as

$$\max_{\eta,\beta} \quad -\frac{1}{2} \sum_{ij} \sum_{kl} (\beta_{ij} h_{ij} + \eta_{ij})(\beta_{kl} h_{kl} + \eta_{kl}) \langle \mathbf{X}_{ij}, \mathbf{X}_{kl} \rangle + \sum_{ij} \beta_{ij}$$

$$\text{s.t.} \quad \sum_{kl} \eta_{kl} \langle \mathbf{X}_{ij}, \mathbf{X}_{kl} \rangle \geq 0, \quad 0 \leq \beta_{ij} \leq C, \quad \forall i,j, \quad \sum_{ij} \beta_{ij} h_{ij} = 0. \tag{2.17}$$

The detailed derivation of the dual problem can be found in Appendix 2.2. Based on KKT conditions of the dual problem, coefficient α_{ij} can be obtained by

$$\alpha_{ij} = \beta_{ij} h_{ij} + \eta_{ij}. \tag{2.18}$$

Matrix $\mathbf{M}$ can then be obtained by

$$\mathbf{M} = \sum_{ij} (\beta_{ij} h_{ij} + \eta_{ij}) \mathbf{X}_{ij}. \tag{2.19}$$

2.2.2.2 Optimization Algorithm

If the two Lagrange multipliers η and β are obtained from Eq. (2.19), the distance metric can also be obtained. In this subsection, an alternative optimization approach to calculate the two groups of variables is presented. First, assuming η is known, variable β can be obtained by solving the following formula:

$$\max_{\beta} \quad -\frac{1}{2} \sum_{ij} \sum_{kl} \beta_{ij} \beta_{kl} h_{ij} h_{kl} \langle \mathbf{X}_{ij}, \mathbf{X}_{kl} \rangle + \sum_{ij} \delta_{ij} \beta_{ij}$$

$$\text{s.t.} \quad 0 \leq \beta_{ij} \leq C, \quad \forall i,j, \quad \sum_{ij} \beta_{ij} h_{ij} = 0, \tag{2.20}$$

where $\delta_{ij} = 1 - h_{ij} \sum_{kl} \eta_{kl} \langle \mathbf{X}_{ij}, \mathbf{X}_{kl} \rangle$. β also can be solved efficiently by the standard SVM solvers, such as LibSVM (Chang and Lin 2011).

After β has been solved, η can be obtained by solving the following formula:

$$\min_{\eta} \quad \frac{1}{2}\sum_{ij}\sum_{kl}\eta_{ij}\eta_{kl}\langle \mathbf{X}_{ij}, \mathbf{X}_{kl}\rangle + \sum_{ij}\eta_{ij}\gamma_{ij}$$
$$\text{s.t.} \quad \sum_{kl}\eta_{ij}\langle \mathbf{X}_{ij}, \mathbf{X}_{kl}\rangle \geq 0, \quad \forall i,j, \tag{2.21}$$

where $\gamma_{ij} = \sum_{kl}\beta_{kl}h_{kl}\langle \mathbf{X}_{ij}, \mathbf{X}_{kl}\rangle$. Based on the KKT condition of the Lagrange dual problem, the subproblem of η can be simplified as:

$$\eta_{ij} = \mu_{ij} - h_{ij}\beta_{ij}, \quad \forall i,j, \tag{2.22}$$

where μ is the Lagrange dual multiplier. The Lagrange dual problem of Eq. (2.21) is transformed as follows:

$$\max_{\mu} \quad -\frac{1}{2}\sum_{ij}\sum_{kl}\mu_{ij}\mu_{kl}\langle \mathbf{X}_{ij}, \mathbf{X}_{kl}\rangle + \sum_{ij}\gamma_{ij}\mu_{ij}$$
$$\text{s.t.} \quad \mu_{ij} \geq 0, \quad \forall i,j. \tag{2.23}$$

The detailed derivation of above dual problem can be found in Appendix 2.3. The Lagrange dual problem of Eq. (2.23) can also be solved efficiently by standard SVM solvers, such as LibSVM.

After updating μ and β alternatively, the optimal solutions of μ and β can be obtained; the optimal solution for α in Eq. (2.16) can then be obtained as follows:

$$\alpha_{ij} = \mu_{ij}, \quad \forall i,j, \tag{2.24}$$

and the distance metric matrix $\mathbf{M} = \sum_{ij}\alpha_{ij}\mathbf{X}_{ij}$ is then obtained. The presented NCML algorithm is summarized in Algorithm 2.2.

Algorithm 2.2 Algorithm of NCML
   Input: Training set $\{(\mathbf{x}_i, \mathbf{x}_j), h_{ij}\}$.
   Output: The matrix $\mathbf{M}$.

1. **Initialize** $\eta^{(0)}$ with small random values, $t \leftarrow 0$.
2. **Repeat**
3. Update $\delta^{(t+1)}$ with $\delta_{ij}^{(t+1)} = 1 - h_{ij}\sum_{kl}\eta_{kl}^{(t)}\langle \mathbf{X}_{ij}, \mathbf{X}_{kl}\rangle$.
4. Update $\beta^{(t+1)}$ by solving the subproblem (2.20) using an SVM solver.
5. Update $\gamma^{(t+1)}$ with $\gamma_{ij}^{(t+1)} = \sum_{kl}\beta_{kl}^{(t+1)}h_{kl}\langle \mathbf{X}_{ij}, \mathbf{X}_{kl}\rangle$.
6. Update $\mu^{(t+1)}$ by solving the subproblem (2.23) using an SVM solver.
7. Update $\eta^{(t+1)}$ with $\eta_{ij}^{(t+1)} \leftarrow \mu_{ij}^{(t+1)} - h_{ij}\beta_{ij}^{(t+1)}$.

8. $t \leftarrow t + 1$.
9. **Until** convergence
10. $\mathbf{M} = \sum_{ij} \mu_{ij}^{(t)} \mathbf{X}_{ij}$
11. **Return M**

Similarly to the PCML method presented, the Lagrange dual multipliers β and μ of the NCML method can also be obtained rapidly by using the warm-start strategy. Figure 2.2 shows the duality gap versus the number of iterations in the PenDigits dataset for NCML. Figure 2.2, one can see that the presented NCML algorithm would converge after 10–15 iterations.

2.2.2.3 Optimality Condition

In this subsection, we also use the duality gap to analyze the optimality condition of NCML. From the primal and dual objectives in Eqs. (2.16) and (2.17), the duality gap of the NCML method in the nth iteration is

$$
\begin{aligned}
\mathrm{DualGap}_{\mathrm{NCML}}^{(n)} =\ & \frac{1}{2} \sum_{ij} \sum_{kl} \alpha_{ij}^{(n)} \alpha_{kl}^{(n)} \langle \mathbf{X}_{ij}, \mathbf{X}_{kl} \rangle + C \sum_{ij} \xi_{ij}^{(n)} \\
& + \frac{1}{2} \sum_{ij} \sum_{kl} \left(\beta_{ij}^{(n)} h_{ij} + \eta_{ij}^{(n)} \right) \left(\beta_{kl}^{(n)} h_{kl} + \eta_{kl}^{(n)} \right) \langle \mathbf{X}_{ij}, \mathbf{X}_{kl} \rangle - \sum_{ij} \beta_{ij}^{(n)},
\end{aligned}
$$
$$(2.25)$$

where $\alpha_{ij}^{(n)}$ and $\xi_{ij}^{(n)}$ denote the feasible solutions to the primal problem, and $\beta_{ij}^{(n)}$ and $\eta_{ij}^{(n)}$ represent the feasible solutions to the dual problem, as $\eta_{ij}^{(n)}$ and $\mu_{ij}^{(n)}$ are the optimal solutions to the primal subproblem of η in Eq. (2.21) and its dual problem in Eq. (2.23), respectively; thus, the duality gap of subproblem of η is zero

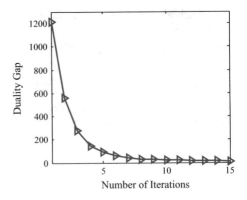

Fig. 2.2 Duality gap versus number of iterations in the PenDigits dataset for NCML (Zuo et al. 2015)

$$\frac{1}{2} \sum_{ij} \sum_{kl} \eta_{ij}^{(n)} \eta_{kl}^{(n)} \langle \mathbf{X}_{ij}, \mathbf{X}_{kl} \rangle + \sum_{ij} \eta_{ij}^{(n)} \gamma_{ij}^{(n)}$$

$$+ \frac{1}{2} \sum_{ij} \sum_{kl} \mu_{ij}^{(n)} \mu_{kl}^{(n)} \langle \mathbf{X}_{ij}, \mathbf{X}_{kl} \rangle - \sum_{ij} \gamma_{ij}^{(n)} \mu_{ij}^{(n)} = 0. \tag{2.26}$$

As shown in Eq. (2.24), $\alpha_{ij}^{(n)}$ and $\mu_{ij}^{(n)}$ should be equal. Substituting Eq. (2.26) into Eq. (2.25) produces the following:

$$\text{DualGap}_{\text{NCML}}^{(n)} = C \sum_{i,j} \xi_{ij}^{(n)} - \sum_{i,j} \beta_{ij}^{(n)} + \sum_{i,j} \mu_{ij}^{(n)} \gamma_{ij}^{(n)}. \tag{2.27}$$

Based on the KKT conditions of the dual problem in Eq. (2.15), we can obtain $\xi_{ij}^{(n)}$ as follows:

$$\xi_{ij}^{(n)} = \begin{cases} 0 & \text{for all } \beta_{ij}^{(n)} < C \\ \left[1 - h_{ij} \left(\sum_{k,l} \alpha_{kl}^{(n)} \langle \mathbf{X}_{ij}, \mathbf{X}_{kl} \rangle + b^{(n)} \right) \right]_+ & \text{for all } \beta_{ij}^{(n)} = C, \end{cases}$$
$$= \begin{cases} 0 & \text{for all } \beta_{ij}^{(n)} < C \\ \left[\delta_{ij}^{(n+1)} - h_{ij} \left(\gamma_{ij}^{(n)} + b^{(n)} \right) \right]_+ & \text{for all } \beta_{ij}^{(n)} = C \end{cases} \tag{2.28}$$

where $[z] = \max(z, 0)$ and

$$b^{(n)} = \frac{1}{h_{ij}} - \sum_{k,l} \alpha_{kl}^{(n)} \langle \mathbf{X}_{ij}, \mathbf{X}_{kl} \rangle = \frac{\delta_{ij}^{(n+1)}}{h_{ij}} - \gamma_{ij}^{(n)} \quad \text{for all } 0 < \beta_{ij}^{(n)} < C. \tag{2.29}$$

The detailed derivation of $\xi_{ij}^{(n)}$ and $b^{(n)}$ can be found in Appendix 2.2. Figure 2.2 shows the duality gap versus the number of iterations of the presented NCML method in the PenDigits dataset. From Fig. 2.2, we can see that the duality gap would converge to zero in 15 iterations, and the presented NCML method reaches the global optimum. In the implementation of the NCML algorithm, the following termination condition is chosen:

$$\text{DualGap}_{\text{NCML}}^{(t)} - \text{DualGap}_{\text{NCML}}^{(t-1)} < \varepsilon \cdot \text{DualGap}_{\text{NCML}}^{(1)}, \tag{2.30}$$

where ε is a small constant. In the experiment, we simply set $\varepsilon = 0.01$.

2.2.2.4   Remarks

Computational Complexity: In Sect. 2.2.1.4, we discussed the pairwise constraint construction scheme for the PCML method. For the NCML method, the same scheme is used to construct the pairwise constraints. In each iteration, NCML uses the SVM solver twice, while the PCML only uses it once. When the SMO-type algorithm (Bellet et al. 2012) is used for SVM training, the computational complexity of the presented NCML algorithm is $O(N^2 d)$. This indicates that the computational cost of the NCML algorithm is only with respect to d, which involves two parts: the computation of $\langle \mathbf{X}_{ij}, \mathbf{X}_{kl} \rangle$ and the construction of matrix $\mathbf{M}$. Since $\langle \mathbf{X}_{ij}, \mathbf{X}_{kl} \rangle = \left((\mathbf{x}_i - \mathbf{x}_j)^{\mathrm{T}} (\mathbf{x}_k - \mathbf{x}_l) \right)^2$, the computation cost of $\langle \mathbf{X}_{ij}, \mathbf{X}_{kl} \rangle$ is $O(d)$. After the convergence of β and μ, matrix $\mathbf{M}$ can be directly obtained; thus, the construction cost of matrix $\mathbf{M}$ is less than $O(kNd^2)$.

Nonlinear extensions: Note that $\langle \mathbf{X}_{ij}, \mathbf{X}_{kl} \rangle = \mathrm{tr} \left(\mathbf{X}_{ij}^{\mathrm{T}} \mathbf{X}_{kl} \right)$ can be treated as an inner product of two pairs of samples: $(\mathbf{x}_i, \mathbf{x}_j)$ and $(\mathbf{x}_k, \mathbf{x}_l)$. If some kernels $K\left((\mathbf{x}_i, \mathbf{x}_j), (\mathbf{x}_k, \mathbf{x}_l) \right)$ are performed on $(\mathbf{x}_i, \mathbf{x}_j)$ and $(\mathbf{x}_k, \mathbf{x}_l)$, we can extend the presented method to new linear or even nonlinear metric learning algorithms by using $K\left((\mathbf{x}_i, \mathbf{x}_j), (\mathbf{x}_k, \mathbf{x}_l) \right)$ to replace $\langle \mathbf{X}_{ij}, \mathbf{X}_{kl} \rangle$. Furthermore, the Mahalanobis distance between any two samples $\mathbf{x}_m$ and $\mathbf{x}_n$ can be rewritten as $(\mathbf{x}_m - \mathbf{x}_n)^{\mathrm{T}} \mathbf{M} (\mathbf{x}_m - \mathbf{x}_n) = \sum_{i,j} \alpha_{ij} K\left((\mathbf{x}_i, \mathbf{x}_j), (\mathbf{x}_m, \mathbf{x}_n) \right)$. Another nonlinear extension strategy is to perform a kernel $k(\mathbf{x}_i, \mathbf{x}_j)$ on $\mathbf{x}_i$ and $\mathbf{x}_j$; following this, we can substitute $\left(k(\mathbf{x}_i, \mathbf{x}_k) - k(\mathbf{x}_i, \mathbf{x}_l) - k(\mathbf{x}_j, \mathbf{x}_k) + k(\mathbf{x}_j, \mathbf{x}_l) \right)^2$ for $\langle \mathbf{X}_{ij}, \mathbf{X}_{kl} \rangle$ and rewrite the Mahalanobis distance between $\mathbf{x}_m$ and $\mathbf{x}_n$ as $(\mathbf{x}_m - \mathbf{x}_n)^{\mathrm{T}} \mathbf{M} (\mathbf{x}_m - \mathbf{x}_n) = \sum_{i,j} \alpha_{ij} \left(k(\mathbf{x}_i, \mathbf{x}_m) - k(\mathbf{x}_i, \mathbf{x}_n) - k(\mathbf{x}_j, \mathbf{x}_m) + k(\mathbf{x}_j, \mathbf{x}_n) \right)^2$. This illustrates that the NCML method has the ability to learn nonlinear metrics for histogram and structural data by using proper kernel functions and incorporating appropriate regularizations in α. Metric learning for structural data beyond vector data has received much attention in recent years (Kedem et al. 2012; Bellet et al. 2012), and NCML can provide a new perspective on this topic.

Other SVM Solvers: Although the implementation of the presented algorithm is based on LibSVM, there are some well-studied SVM training algorithms, such as core vector machines (Tsang et al. 2005, 2007), LaRank (Bordes et al. 2007), BMRM (Teo et al. 2007), and Pegasos (Shalev-Shwartz et al. 2011), which can be utilized for large-scale metric learning. Moreover, we can refer to the progress in kernel methods (Evgeniou and Pontil 2004; Belkin et al. 2006; Andrews et al. 2002), and extend the presented scheme to semi-supervised, multiple instance, and multitask metric learning approaches.

2.2.3 Experimental Results

In this subsection, we use four handwritten digit datasets to evaluate the PCML and NCML models for k-NN classification ($k = 1$). The PCML and NCML algorithms are compared to the Euclidean distance metric and the state-of-the-art metric learning models, including NCA (Goldberger et al. 2004), ITML (Davis et al. 2007), MCML (Globerson and Roweis 2005), LDML (Guillaumin et al. 2009), LMNN (Weinberger et al. 2009), PLML (Wang et al. 2012), and DML-eig (Ying and Li 2012). PCML and NCML are implemented using the LibSVM[1] toolbox. The source codes for NCA[2], ITML[3], MCML[4], LDML[5], LMNN[6], PLML[7], and DML-eig[8] are available online, and we tune their parameters to get the best results.

Table 2.1 lists the basic information of the four handwritten digit datasets. We use the defined training sets to train the metrics, and classify the defined test sets to get the classification error rates. For the Semeion dataset, we use 10-fold cross-validation to evaluate the metric learning methods, and the classification error rate and training time are obtained by averaging over 10 runs of 10-fold cross-validation.

For MNIST, Semeion and USPS datasets, we first reduce the feature dimension to 100 by using the principal component analysis (PCA) method, and then learn the distance metrics in the PCA subspace. Table 2.2 shows the classification error rates of the ten competing methods on the four handwritten digit datasets. The last row in Table 2.2 lists the average ranks of the competing methods. In the experiment, we do not list the error rate and training time of MCML in the MNIST dataset, because MCML requires too large a memory space (more than 30 GB) for this dataset and cannot run on our PC. From Table 2.2, one can see that both PCML and NCML achieve the best performances.

Figure 2.3 shows the training time of the above distance metric learning algorithms. We can see that the PCML and NCML methods are much faster than the other models.

Finally, we compare the training time of PCML and NCML on different feature dimensions. The computation complexities of PCML and NCML are $O(N^2d + d^3)$ and $O(N^2d)$, respectively. Figure 2.4 shows the training time versus the PCA dimension in the PenDigits dataset. From Fig. 2.4, one can see that when the PCA dimension is lower than 110, the training time of NCML is longer than that of

---

[1]http://www.csie.ntu.edu.tw/cjlin/libsvm/

[2]http://www.cs.berkeley.edu/~fowlkes/software/nca/

[3]http://www.cs.utexas.edu/~pjain/itml/

[4]http://homepage.tudelft.nl/19j49/Matlab_Toolbox_for_Dimensionality_Reduction.html

[5]http://lear.inrialpes.fr/people/guillaumin/code.php

[6]http://www.cse.wustl.edu/~kilian/code/code.html/

[7]http://cui.unige.ch/~wangjun/

[8]http://empslocal.ex.ac.uk/people/staff/yy267/software.html

Table 2.1 The handwritten digit datasets used in the experiments (Zuo et al. 2015)

Dataset	# of training samples	# of test samples	Dimension	PCA dimension	# of classes
MNIST	60,000	10,000	784	100	10
PenDigits	7494	3498	16	N/A	10
Semeion	1434	159	256	100	10
USPS	7291	2007	256	100	10

PCML. When the PCA dimension is higher than 110, the training time of PCML increases and becomes longer than that of NCML.

2.3 A Kernel Classification Framework for Metric Learning

Most metric learning models depend on convex or non-convex optimization techniques. However, these algorithms are inefficient for learning the distance metrics for large-scale problems. In this section, we present a kernel classification framework that can unify many state-of-the-art metric learning methods, and that can improve the efficiency greatly. The connections between the kernel framework and LMNN, ITML, and LDML will also be discussed in this section.

2.3.1 Doublets and Triplets

Unlike conventional supervised learning problems, metric learning usually uses a set of constraints imposed on the doublets or triplets of the training samples to learn the desired distance metric. It is very interesting and useful to evaluate whether metric learning can be cast as a conventional supervised learning problem. To build a connection between the two problems, we model metric learning as a kind of supervised learning problem operating on a set of doublets or triplets in the following.

Suppose $D = \{(\mathbf{x}_i, y_i)|i = 1, 2, \ldots, n\}$ denotes a training dataset, $\mathbf{x}_i \in \mathbb{R}^d$ is the vector of ith training sample, and y_i is the class label of $\mathbf{x}_i$. For any two samples, we define a doublet $(\mathbf{x}_i, \mathbf{x}_j)$, and assign a class label h to this doublet as follows: $h = -1$ if $y_i = y_j$ and $h = 1$ if $y_i \neq y_j$. For each training sample $\mathbf{x}_i$, we find its m_1 most similar samples from D, denoted by $\{\mathbf{x}_{i,1}^s, \ldots, \mathbf{x}_{i,m_1}^s\}$, and its m_2 nearest dissimilar neighbors, denoted by $\{\mathbf{x}_{i,1}^d, \ldots, \mathbf{x}_{i,m_2}^d\}$; we then construct $(m_1 + m_2)$ doublets $\{(\mathbf{x}_i, \mathbf{x}_{i,1}^s), \ldots, (\mathbf{x}_i, \mathbf{x}_{i,m_1}^s), (\mathbf{x}_i, \mathbf{x}_{i,1}^d), \ldots, (\mathbf{x}_i, \mathbf{x}_{i,m_2}^d)\}$. We define a doublet set $\{\mathbf{z}_1, \cdots, \mathbf{z}_{N_d}\}$ as denoting all such doublets constructed from the training dataset, where $\mathbf{z}_l = (\mathbf{x}_{l,1}, \mathbf{x}_{l,2})$, and $l = 1, 2, \ldots, N_d$. h_l represents the class label of each

Table 2.2 Comparison of the classification error rate on the handwritten digit datasets (%) (Zuo et al. 2015)

c	Euclidean	NCA	ITML	MCML	LDML	LMNN	DML-eig	PLML	PCML	NCML
MNIST	2.87	5.46	2.89	N/A	6.05	2.28	5.06	2.54	3.85	2.80
PenDigits	2.26	2.23	2.29	2.26	6.20	2.52	3.75	2.46	2.06	2.06
Semeion	8.54	8.60	5.71	11.23	11.98	6.09	5.72	7.66	4.83	5.53
USPS	5.08	5.68	6.33	5.08	8.77	5.38	11.36	6.73	5.33	5.43
Average rank	4.00	6.25	5.25	4.67	9.50	4.50	7.50	5.75	2.75	2.75

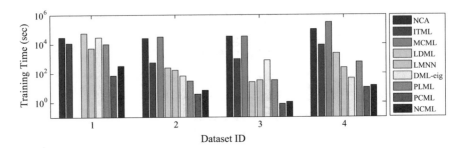

Fig. 2.3 Training time (s) of NCA, ITML, MCML, LDML, LMNN, DML-eig, PLML, PCML and NCML. From 1–4, the Dataset ID represents MNIST, PenDigits, Semeion, and USPS (Zuo et al. 2015)

Fig. 2.4 Training time (s) versus PCA dimension in the PenDigits dataset (Zuo et al. 2015)

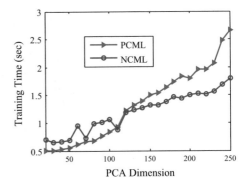

doublet z_l. Note that doublet-based constraints are used in ITML (Davis et al. 2007) and LDML (Guillaumin et al. 2009), but the details of the construction of the doublets are not introduced.

For any three samples $\mathbf{x}_i$, $\mathbf{x}_j$, and $\mathbf{x}_k$ from D, we define a triplet $(\mathbf{x}_i, \mathbf{x}_j, \mathbf{x}_k)$, and their class labels satisfy $y_i = y_j \neq y_k$. We adopt the following strategy to construct a triplet set. For each training sample $\mathbf{x}_i$, we find its m_1 nearest neighbors $\{\mathbf{x}_{i,1}^s, \ldots, \mathbf{x}_{i,m_1}^s\}$ that have the same class label as $\mathbf{x}_i$, and m_2 nearest neighbors $\{\mathbf{x}_{i,1}^d, \ldots, \mathbf{x}_{i,m_2}^d\}$ that have different class labels from $\mathbf{x}_i$. Thus, for each sample $\mathbf{x}_i$, we can construct $m_1 m_2$ triplets $\{(\mathbf{x}_i, \mathbf{x}_{i,j}^s, \mathbf{x}_{i,k}^d) | j = 1, \ldots, m_1; \ k = 1, \ldots, m_2\}$. Combining all the triplets, we form a triplet set $\{\mathbf{t}_1, \ldots, \mathbf{t}_{N_t}\}$, where $\mathbf{t}_l = (\mathbf{x}_{l,1}, \mathbf{x}_{l,2}, \mathbf{x}_{l,3})$, $l = 1, 2, \ldots, N_t$. Note that, for the convenience of expression, we have removed the superscript "s" and "d" from $\mathbf{x}_{l,2}$ and $\mathbf{x}_{l,3}$, respectively. A similar way to construct the triplets was used in LMNN (Weinberger et al. 2009), based on the k-nearest neighbors of each sample.

2.3.2   A Family of Degree-2 Polynomial Kernels

In this subsection, we introduce a family of degree-2 polynomial kernel functions that can operate on pairwise constraints of the doublets or triplets. With the degree-2 polynomial kernels, distance metric learning can be readily formulated as a kernel classification problem.

For two samples $\mathbf{x}_i$ and $\mathbf{x}_j$, we define the following kernel function:

$$K_p(\mathbf{x}_i, \mathbf{x}_j) = \mathrm{tr}(\mathbf{x}_i \mathbf{x}_i^\mathrm{T} \mathbf{x}_j \mathbf{x}_j^\mathrm{T}), \tag{2.31}$$

where $\mathrm{tr}(\cdot)$ is the trace operator of a matrix. $K_p(\mathbf{x}_i, \mathbf{x}_j) = (\mathbf{x}_i^\mathrm{T} \mathbf{x}_j)^2$ is a degree-2 polynomial kernel, and $K_p(\mathbf{x}_i, \mathbf{x}_j)$ satisfies Mercer's condition (Shawe-Taylor and Cristianini 2004).

The kernel function can also be extended to a pair of doublets or triplets. For two doublets $\mathbf{z}_i = (\mathbf{x}_{i,1}, \mathbf{x}_{i,2})$ and $\mathbf{z}_j = (\mathbf{x}_{j,1}, \mathbf{x}_{j,2})$, the corresponding degree-2 polynomial kernel function is defined as

$$\begin{aligned} K_p(\mathbf{z}_i, \mathbf{z}_j) &= \mathrm{tr}\left((\mathbf{x}_{i,1} - \mathbf{x}_{i,2})(\mathbf{x}_{i,1} - \mathbf{x}_{i,2})^\mathrm{T}(\mathbf{x}_{j,1} - \mathbf{x}_{j,2})(\mathbf{x}_{j,1} - \mathbf{x}_{j,2})^\mathrm{T} \right) \\ &= \left[(\mathbf{x}_{i,1} - \mathbf{x}_{i,2})^\mathrm{T}(\mathbf{x}_{j,1} - \mathbf{x}_{j,2}) \right]^2. \end{aligned} \tag{2.32}$$

The kernel function in Eq. (2.32) defines an inner product of two doublets. Based on the degree-2 polynomial kernel function, we can learn a decision function to obtain the class label of the doublet, and can also identity whether the two samples in the doublet are of the same class or not.

Similarly to doublets, for two triplets $\mathbf{t}_i = (\mathbf{x}_{i,1}, \mathbf{x}_{i,2}, \mathbf{x}_{i,3})$ and $\mathbf{t}_j = (\mathbf{x}_{j,1}, \mathbf{x}_{j,2}, \mathbf{x}_{j,3})$, we define the corresponding degree-2 polynomial kernel function as

$$K_p(\mathbf{t}_i, \mathbf{t}_j) = \mathrm{tr}\left(\mathbf{T}_i \mathbf{T}_j \right), \tag{2.33}$$

where

$$\begin{aligned} \mathbf{T}_i &= \left(\mathbf{x}_{i,1} - \mathbf{x}_{i,3}\right)\left(\mathbf{x}_{i,1} - \mathbf{x}_{i,3}\right)^\mathrm{T} - \left(\mathbf{x}_{i,1} - \mathbf{x}_{i,2}\right)\left(\mathbf{x}_{i,1} - \mathbf{x}_{i,2}\right)^\mathrm{T}, \\ \mathbf{T}_j &= \left(\mathbf{x}_{j,1} - \mathbf{x}_{j,3}\right)\left(\mathbf{x}_{j,1} - \mathbf{x}_{j,3}\right)^\mathrm{T} - \left(\mathbf{x}_{j,1} - \mathbf{x}_{j,2}\right)\left(\mathbf{x}_{j,1} - \mathbf{x}_{j,2}\right)^\mathrm{T}. \end{aligned}$$

The triplet kernel function in Eq. (2.33) defines an inner product of two triplets. With this triplet kernel function, a decision function to identify the class label of triplets can be learned, and the class label of the query sample can then be identified. In Sect. 2.3.3, we will discuss the connection between metric learning and kernel decision function learning.

2.3.3 Metric Learning Via Kernel Methods

With the degree-2 polynomial kernels presented in Sect. 2.3.2, the doublet-based and triplet-based distance metric learning can easily be extended to the kernel space. More specifically, any kernel classification method can be utilized to learn a kernel classifier. For doublet-based and triplet-based distance metric learning, the corresponding class label can be obtained by the following two forms:

$$g_d(\mathbf{z}) = \text{sgn}\left(\sum_l h_l \alpha_l K_p(\mathbf{z}_l, \mathbf{z}) + b \right), \tag{2.34}$$

$$g_t(\mathbf{t}) = \text{sgn}\left(\sum_l \alpha_l K_p(\mathbf{t}_l, \mathbf{t}) \right), \tag{2.35}$$

where $\mathbf{z}_l$ and $\mathbf{t}_l$, $l = 1, 2, \ldots, N$, denote the doublet and triplet constructed from the training dataset. $\mathbf{z} = (\mathbf{x}_{(1)}, \mathbf{x}_{(2)})$ is the test doublet, t represents the test triplet, α_l is the weight, and b is the bias. For the doublet-based method, kernel decision function $g_d(\mathbf{z})$ can be used to determine whether two samples $\mathbf{x}_{(1)}$ and $\mathbf{x}_{(2)}$ are from the same class.

For the doublet, we have

$$\sum_l h_l \alpha_l \text{tr}\left((\mathbf{x}_{l,1} - \mathbf{x}_{l,2})(\mathbf{x}_{l,1} - \mathbf{x}_{l,2})^{\text{T}}(\mathbf{x}_{(i)} - \mathbf{x}_{(j)})(\mathbf{x}_{(i)} - \mathbf{x}_{(j)})^{\text{T}} \right) + b$$
$$= (\mathbf{x}_{(i)} - \mathbf{x}_{(j)})^{\text{T}}\mathbf{M}(\mathbf{x}_{(i)} - \mathbf{x}_{(j)}) + b, \tag{2.36}$$

where

$$\mathbf{M} = \sum_l h_l \alpha_l (\mathbf{x}_{l,1} - \mathbf{x}_{l,2})(\mathbf{x}_{l,1} - \mathbf{x}_{l,2})^{\text{T}}, \tag{2.37}$$

where matrix $\mathbf{M}$ is the Mahalanobis distance metric.

For the triplet, matrix $\mathbf{M}$ can be derived as follows:

Theorem 2.2 *For the triplet-based decision function defined in* Eq. (2.35), *matrix* $\mathbf{M}$ *of the Mahalanobis distance metric is*

$$\mathbf{M} = \sum_l \alpha_l \mathbf{T}_l = \sum_l \alpha_l \left[(\mathbf{x}_{l,1} - \mathbf{x}_{l,3})(\mathbf{x}_{l,1} - \mathbf{x}_{l,3})^{\text{T}} - (\mathbf{x}_{l,1} - \mathbf{x}_{l,2})(\mathbf{x}_{l,1} - \mathbf{x}_{l,2})^{\text{T}} \right], \tag{2.38}$$

and $\sum_l \alpha_l K_p(\mathbf{t}_l, \mathbf{t})$ *then represents the relative difference of the Mahalanobis distance between* $\mathbf{x}_{(i)}$ *and* $\mathbf{x}_{(k)}$ *and the Mahalanobis distance between* x(i) *and* x(j).

Proof Let $\mathbf{T}_l = (\mathbf{x}_{l,1} - \mathbf{x}_{l,3})(\mathbf{x}_{l,1} - \mathbf{x}_{l,3})^{\mathrm{T}} - (\mathbf{x}_{l,1} - \mathbf{x}_{l,2})(\mathbf{x}_{l,1} - \mathbf{x}_{l,2})^{\mathrm{T}}$. Based on the definition of $K_p(\mathbf{t}_l, \mathbf{t})$, we have

$$
\begin{aligned}
\sum_l \alpha_l K_p(\mathbf{t}_l, \mathbf{t}) &= \sum_l \alpha_l \mathrm{tr}(\mathbf{T}_l \mathbf{T}) \\
&= \sum_l \alpha_l \mathrm{tr}\left(\mathbf{T}_l\left((\mathbf{x}_{(i)} - \mathbf{x}_{(k)})(\mathbf{x}_{(i)} - \mathbf{x}_{(k)})^{\mathrm{T}} - (\mathbf{x}_{(i)} - \mathbf{x}_{(j)})(\mathbf{x}_{(i)} - \mathbf{x}_{(j)})^{\mathrm{T}}\right)^{\mathrm{T}}\right) \\
&= \sum_l \alpha_l \mathrm{tr}\left(\mathbf{T}_l\left((\mathbf{x}_{(i)} - \mathbf{x}_{(k)})(\mathbf{x}_{(i)} - \mathbf{x}_{(k)})^{\mathrm{T}}\right)^{\mathrm{T}}\right) - \sum_l \alpha_l \mathrm{tr}\left(\mathbf{T}_l\left((\mathbf{x}_{(i)} - \mathbf{x}_{(j)})(\mathbf{x}_{(i)} - \mathbf{x}_{(j)})^{\mathrm{T}}\right)^{\mathrm{T}}\right) \\
&= (\mathbf{x}_{(i)} - \mathbf{x}_{(k)})^{\mathrm{T}} \sum_l \alpha_l \mathbf{T}_l (\mathbf{x}_{(i)} - \mathbf{x}_{(k)}) - (\mathbf{x}_{(i)} - \mathbf{x}_{(j)})^{\mathrm{T}} \sum_l \alpha_l \mathbf{T}_l (\mathbf{x}_{(i)} - \mathbf{x}_{(j)}) \\
&= (\mathbf{x}_{(i)} - \mathbf{x}_{(k)})^{\mathrm{T}} \mathbf{M} (\mathbf{x}_{(i)} - \mathbf{x}_{(k)}) - (\mathbf{x}_{(i)} - \mathbf{x}_{(j)})^{\mathrm{T}} \mathbf{M} (\mathbf{x}_{(i)} - \mathbf{x}_{(j)})
\end{aligned}
$$

$$(2.39)$$

By setting $\mathbf{M} = \sum_l \alpha_l \mathbf{T}_l$ as matrix $\mathbf{M}$ in the Mahalanobis distance metric, we can see that $\sum_l \alpha_l K_p(\mathbf{t}_l, \mathbf{t})$ is the difference of the Mahalanobis distance between $\mathbf{x}_{(i)}$ and $\mathbf{x}_{(k)}$ and the Mahalanobis distance between $\mathbf{x}_{(i)}$ and $\mathbf{x}_{(j)}$.

Clearly, Eqs. (2.34)–(2.39) provide us with a new perspective for understanding the distance metric matrix $\mathbf{M}$ under a kernel classification framework. Meanwhile, using this kernel framework to learn a distance metric may be much easier and more efficient than the previous metric learning methods. In the following, we introduce two kernel classification methods for metric learning: regularized kernel SVM and kernel logistic regression. It should be pointed out that, based on modifying the construction of the doublet or triplet set, this kernel framework can be extended to other, new metric learning algorithms by using different kernel classifier models, or by adopting different optimization algorithms.

2.3.3.1 Kernel SVM-Like Model

For the doublet- or triplet-based distance metric learning, a SVM-like model is defined as

$$
\min_{\mathbf{M}, b, \xi} r(\mathbf{M}) + \rho(\xi)
$$

$$
\text{s.t.} \quad f_l^{(d)}\left((\mathbf{x}_{l,1} - \mathbf{x}_{l,2})^{\mathrm{T}} \mathbf{M}(\mathbf{x}_{l,1} - \mathbf{x}_{l,2}), b, \xi_l\right) \geq 0 \text{ (doublet set)}
$$

$$
f_l^{(t)}\left((\mathbf{x}_{l,1} - \mathbf{x}_{l,3})^{\mathrm{T}} \mathbf{M}(\mathbf{x}_{l,1} - \mathbf{x}_{l,3}) - (\mathbf{x}_{l,1} - \mathbf{x}_{l,2})^{\mathrm{T}} \mathbf{M}(\mathbf{x}_{l,1} - \mathbf{x}_{l,2}), \xi_l\right) \geq 0 \text{ (triplet set)}
$$

$$
\xi_l \geq 0,
$$

$$(2.40)$$

where $r(\mathbf{M})$ is the regularization term, $\rho(\xi)$ denotes the margin loss term, constraint $f_l^{(d)}$ is a linear function of $(\mathbf{x}_{l,1} - \mathbf{x}_{l,2})^{\mathrm{T}} \mathbf{M}(\mathbf{x}_{l,1} - \mathbf{x}_{l,2})$, b, and ξ_l, and constraint $f_l^{(t)}$ is a linear function of $(\mathbf{x}_{l,1} - \mathbf{x}_{l,3})^{\mathrm{T}}\mathbf{M}(\mathbf{x}_{l,1} - \mathbf{x}_{l,3}) - (\mathbf{x}_{l,1} - \mathbf{x}_{l,2})^{\mathrm{T}}\mathbf{M}(\mathbf{x}_{l,1} - \mathbf{x}_{l,2})$ and ξ_l. In the implementation, we can simply choose a convex regularizer $r(\mathbf{M})$ and a convex margin loss $\rho(\xi)$ to guarantee that Eq. (2.40) is convex. By plugging Eq. (2.37) or (2.38) into Eq. (2.40), matrix $\mathbf{M}$ can be calculated simply by the SVM and kernel methods.

If we adopt the l_2-norm to regularize $\mathbf{M}$ and the hinge loss penalty on ξ_l, the model in Eq. (2.40) would become the standard SVM. SVM and its variants have been well studied (Schölkopf et al. 2001; Müller et al. 2001; Vapnik 2013), and various SVM-based algorithms have been proposed for large-scale problems (Tsang et al. 2005; Collobert et al. 2002). Thus, the SVM-like modeling in Eq. (2.40) enables us to learn good metrics from large-scale training data efficiently.

2.3.3.2 Kernel Logistic Regression

For the kernel logistic regression model (KLR) (Keerthi et al. 2005), we let class label $h_l = 1$ if the samples of doublet z_l belong to the same class and let $h_1 = 0$ if two samples belong to different classes. For a query doublet z_l, the probability of $h_1 = 1$ is defined as

$$P(p_l = 1|\mathbf{z}_l) = \frac{1}{1 + \exp\left((\mathbf{x}_{l,1} - \mathbf{x}_{l,2})^{\mathrm{T}}\mathbf{M}(\mathbf{x}_{l,1} - \mathbf{x}_{l,2}) + b\right)}. \qquad (2.41)$$

Matrix $\mathbf{M}$ and bias b can be obtained by solving the following log-likelihood function:

$$(\mathbf{M}, b) = \arg\max_{\mathbf{M}, b}\left\{ 1(\mathbf{M}, b) = \sum_l h_l \ln P(p_l = 1|\mathbf{z}_l) + (1 - h_l) \ln P(p_l = 0|\mathbf{z}_l) \right\}. \qquad (2.42)$$

KLR is a powerful probabilistic approach to classification. By modeling metric learning as a KLR problem, we can easily use the existing KLR algorithms to learn the desired distance metric. Moreover, the various improved KLR, such as sparse KLR (Koh et al. 2007), can also be used to develop new metric learning methods.

2.3.4 Connections with LMNN, ITML, and LDML

The kernel classification framework can be viewed as a unified model of many state-of-the-art metric learning methods. In this subsection, we show the connections of the presented framework and some typical distance metric learning methods, such as LMNN, ITML and LDML.

2.3.4.1   LMNN

LMNN (Weinberger et al. 2009) learns a distance metric that penalizes both large distances between samples with the same label and small distances between samples with different labels. LMNN is operated using a set of triplets $\{(\mathbf{x}_i, \mathbf{x}_j, \mathbf{x}_k)\}$, where $\mathbf{x}_i$ and $\mathbf{x}_j$ have the same class labels, and $\mathbf{x}_i$ and $\mathbf{x}_k$ have different class labels. The objective function of LMNN is defined as follows:

$$\min_{\mathbf{M}, \xi_{ijk}} \sum_{i,j} (\mathbf{x}_i - \mathbf{x}_j)^{\mathrm{T}} \mathbf{M} (\mathbf{x}_i - \mathbf{x}_j) + C \sum_{i,j,k} \xi_{ijk}$$
$$\text{s.t.} (\mathbf{x}_i - \mathbf{x}_k)^{\mathrm{T}} \mathbf{M} (\mathbf{x}_i - \mathbf{x}_k) - (\mathbf{x}_i - \mathbf{x}_j)^{\mathrm{T}} \mathbf{M} (\mathbf{x}_i - \mathbf{x}_j) \geq 1 - \xi_{ijk} \qquad (2.43)$$
$$\xi_{ijl} \geq 0, \quad \mathbf{M} \succcurlyeq 0.$$

For LMNN, matrix $\mathbf{M}$ is required to be positive and semidefinite; thus, we introduce the following indicator function:

$$\iota_{\succcurlyeq}(\mathbf{M}) = \begin{cases} 0, & \text{if } \mathbf{M} \succcurlyeq 0 \\ +\infty, & \text{otherwise} \end{cases}, \qquad (2.44)$$

and choose the following regularizer and margin loss:

$$r_{\mathrm{LMNN}}(\mathbf{M}) = \sum_{i,j} (\mathbf{x}_i - \mathbf{x}_j)^{\mathrm{T}} \mathbf{M} (\mathbf{x}_i - \mathbf{x}_j) + \iota_{\succcurlyeq}(\mathbf{M}), \qquad (2.45)$$

$$\rho_{\mathrm{LMNN}}(\xi) = C \sum_{ijk} \xi_{ijk}. \qquad (2.46)$$

We can then define the following SVM-like model for the same triplet set:

$$\min_{\mathbf{M}, \xi} r_{\mathrm{LMNN}}(\mathbf{M}) + \rho_{\mathrm{LMNN}}(\xi)$$
$$\text{s.t.} \quad (\mathbf{x}_i - \mathbf{x}_k)^{\mathrm{T}} \mathbf{M} (\mathbf{x}_i - \mathbf{x}_k) - (\mathbf{x}_i - \mathbf{x}_j)^{\mathrm{T}} \mathbf{M} (\mathbf{x}_i - \mathbf{x}_j) \geq 1 - \xi_{ijk}, \quad \xi_{ijk} \geq 0. \qquad (2.47)$$

From Eqs. (2.41) and (2.47), one can observe that the SVM-like model is equivalent to the LMNN model.

2.3.4.2   ITML

ITML (Davis et al. 2007) operates on a set of doublets $\{(\mathbf{x}_i, \mathbf{x}_j)\}$, and its objective model is as follows:

$$\min_{\mathbf{M},\xi} D_{ld}(\mathbf{M},\mathbf{M}_0) + \gamma \cdot D_{ld}(\mathrm{diag}(\xi),\mathrm{diag}(\xi_0))$$

$$\begin{aligned}
\text{s.t.} (\mathbf{x}_i - \mathbf{x}_j)^T \mathbf{M}(\mathbf{x}_i - \mathbf{x}_j) &\le \xi_{u(i,j)} \quad (i,j) \in \mathcal{S} \\
(\mathbf{x}_i - \mathbf{x}_j)^T \mathbf{M}(\mathbf{x}_i - \mathbf{x}_j) &\ge \xi_{l(i,j)} \quad (i,j) \in \mathcal{D} \\
\mathbf{M} &\succeq 0,
\end{aligned} \qquad (2.48)$$

where $\mathbf{M}_0$ is the given prior of the metric matrix, ξ_0 is the given prior to ξ, $\mathcal{S}$ denotes the doublet set in which two samples $\mathbf{x}_i$ and $\mathbf{x}_j$ have same class label, $\mathcal{D}$ represents the doublet set in which two samples $\mathbf{x}_i$ and $\mathbf{x}_j$ have different class labels, and $D_{ld}(\cdot,\cdot)$ is the LogDet divergence of two matrices defined as

$$D_{ld}(\mathbf{M},\mathbf{M}_0) = \mathrm{tr}(\mathbf{M}\mathbf{M}_0^{-1}) - \log\det(\mathbf{M}\mathbf{M}_0^{-1}) - n. \qquad (2.49)$$

By introducing the following regularizer and margin loss,

$$r_{\mathrm{ITML}}(\mathbf{M}) = D_{ld}(\mathbf{M},\mathbf{M}_0) + \iota_{\succeq}(\mathbf{M}), \qquad (2.50)$$

$$\rho_{\mathrm{ITML}}(\xi) = \gamma \cdot D_{ld}(\mathrm{diag}(\xi),\mathrm{diag}(\xi_0)), \qquad (2.51)$$

we can then define the following SVM-like model for the same doublet set:

$$\min_{\mathbf{M},b,\xi} r_{\mathrm{ITML}}(\mathbf{M}) + \rho_{\mathrm{ITML}}(\xi)$$

$$\begin{aligned}
\text{s.t.} \quad (\mathbf{x}_i - \mathbf{x}_j)^T \mathbf{M}(\mathbf{x}_i - \mathbf{x}_j) &\le \xi_{u(i,j)} \quad (i,j) \in \mathcal{S} \\
(\mathbf{x}_i - \mathbf{x}_j)^T \mathbf{M}(\mathbf{x}_i - \mathbf{x}_j) &\ge \xi_{l(i,j)} \quad (i,j) \in \mathcal{D} \\
\xi_{ij} &\ge 0,
\end{aligned} \qquad (2.52)$$

where $\mathbf{z}_{ij} = (\mathbf{x}_i,\mathbf{x}_j)$. From Eqs. (2.52) and (2.48), it is obvious that the SVM-like model is equivalent to the ITML model.

2.3.4.3   LDML

LDML (Guillaumin et al. 2009) is a logistic discriminant-based metric learning approach, which learns the metric from a set of doublets. Suppose $z_l = (\mathbf{x}_l^{(i)}, \mathbf{x}_l^{(j)})$ and hl are a doublet and its class label, respectively. $y_{l(i)}$ and $y_{l(j)}$ are class labels of two samples $\mathbf{x}_l^{(i)}$, $\mathbf{x}_l^{(j)}$, respectively. For LDML, the probability of $y_l^{(i)} = y_l^{(j)}$ is defined as follows:

$$p_l = P(y_{l(i)} = y_{l(j)} | \mathbf{x}_{l(i)}, \mathbf{x}_{l(j)}, \mathbf{M}, b) = \sigma(b - d_{\mathbf{M}}(\mathbf{x}_{l(i)}, \mathbf{x}_{l(j)})), \qquad (2.53)$$

where $\sigma(z)$ is the sigmoid function, b is the bias, and $d_{\mathbf{M}}(\mathbf{x}_{l(i)}, \mathbf{x}_{l(j)}) = (\mathbf{x}_{l(i)} - \mathbf{x}_{l(j)})^T \mathbf{M}(\mathbf{x}_{l(i)} - \mathbf{x}_{l(j)})$. With probability p_l defined in

Eq. (2.53), LDML learns metric matrix $\mathbf{M}$ and bias b by solving the following log-likelihood:

$$\max_{\mathbf{M},b} \left\{ l(\mathbf{M}, b) = \sum_l h_l \ln p_l + (1 - h_l) \ln(1 - p_l) \right\}. \tag{2.54}$$

Unlike LMNN, metric matrix $\mathbf{M}$ is not required to be positive definite in LDML.

With the same doublet set, suppose α is the solution obtained by the kernel logistic model in Eq. (2.42), and metric matrix $\mathbf{M}$ is the solution to LDML in Eq. (2.54). It is obvious that

$$\mathbf{M} = -\sum_l \alpha_l (\mathbf{x}_{l(i)} - \mathbf{x}_{l_1(j)})(\mathbf{x}_{l(i)} - \mathbf{x}_{l(j)})^{\mathrm{T}}. \tag{2.55}$$

Thus, LDML is equivalent to the kernel logistic regression under the presented kernel classification framework.

2.3.5   Metric Learning Via SVM

In Sect. 2.3.4, we proved that the kernel classification framework is a generalized model for existing metric learning models. In this section, we will present two metric learning models, namely, the doublet-SVM and the triplet-SVM, developed according to the kernel framework.

2.3.5.1   Doublet-SVM

In the doublet-SVM, we adopt the l_2-norm regularizer $r_{\mathrm{SVM}}(\mathbf{M}) = \frac{1}{2}\|\mathbf{M}\|_F^2$, and the margin loss term $\rho_{\mathrm{SVM}}(\xi) = C \sum_l \xi_l$. The model for the doublet-SVM is defined as follows:

$$\begin{aligned} &\min_{\mathbf{M},b,\xi} \frac{1}{2}\|\mathbf{M}\|_F^2 + C \sum_l \xi_l \\ &\text{s.t.}\quad h_l\left((\mathbf{x}_{l,1} - \mathbf{x}_{l,2})^{\mathrm{T}}\mathbf{M}(\mathbf{x}_{l,1} - \mathbf{x}_{l,2}) + b\right) \geq 1 - \xi_l, \quad \xi_l \geq 0, \quad \forall l, \end{aligned} \tag{2.56}$$

where $\|\cdot\|_F$ denotes the Frobenius norm. The Lagrange dual problem of the above doublet-SVM model is:

$$\max_{\alpha} \; -\frac{1}{2}\sum_{i,j}\alpha_i\alpha_j h_i h_j K_p\left(\mathbf{z}_i,\mathbf{z}_j\right) + \sum_i \alpha_i$$

$$\text{s.t.} \quad 0 \le \alpha_l \le C, \quad \sum_l \alpha_l h_l = 0, \quad \forall l. \tag{2.57}$$

The above Lagrange dual problem can also be easily solved by standard SVM solvers, such as LIBSVM (Chang and Lin 2011). Please refer to Appendix 2.4 for the detailed deduction of the dual problem of the doublet-SVM.

2.3.5.2 Triplet-SVM

In the triplet-SVM, we also adopt the regularization term $r_{\text{SVM}}(\mathbf{M}) = \frac{1}{2}\|\mathbf{M}\|_F^2$, and the margin loss term $\rho_{\text{SVM}}(\xi) = C\sum_l \xi_l$. Since the triplets do not have label information, we choose the linear inequality constraints that are adopted in LMNN, and the triplet-SVM model is defined as

$$\min_{\mathbf{M},\xi} \; \frac{1}{2}\|\mathbf{M}\|_F^2 + C\sum_l \xi_l$$

$$\text{s.t.} \quad (\mathbf{x}_{l,1} - \mathbf{x}_{l,3})^{\text{T}}\mathbf{M}(\mathbf{x}_{l,1} - \mathbf{x}_{l,3}) - (\mathbf{x}_{l,1} - \mathbf{x}_{l,2})^{\text{T}}\mathbf{M}(\mathbf{x}_{l,1} - \mathbf{x}_{l,2}) \ge 1 - \xi_l \tag{2.58}$$

$$\xi_l \ge 0, \quad \forall l.$$

In fact, the triplet-SVM can be regarded as a one-class SVM model, and the formulation of the triplet-SVM is similar to the one-class SVM in (Schölkopf et al. 2001). The dual problem of the triplet-SVM is

$$\max_{\alpha} \; -\frac{1}{2}\sum_{i,j}\alpha_i\alpha_j K_p\left(\mathbf{t}_i,\mathbf{t}_j\right) + \sum_i \alpha_i$$

$$\text{s.t.} \quad 0 \le \alpha_l \le C, \quad \forall l, \tag{2.59}$$

which can also be solved efficiently by the standard SVM solvers (Chang and Lin 2011). Please refer to Appendix 2.5 for the detailed deduction of the dual problem of the triplet-SVM.

2.3.6 Experimental Results

In this subsection, the doublet-SVM, the triplet-SVM and some state-of-the-art metric learning algorithms for k-NN classification are compared on 10 UCI datasets. Five representative and state-of-the-art metric learning models are selected, namely LMNN (Weinberger et al. 2009), ITML (Davis et al. 2007), LDML

Table 2.3 The UCI datasets used in the experiment

Dataset	# of training samples	# of test samples	Feature dimension	# of classes
Parkinsons	176	19	22	2
Sonar	188	20	60	2
Statlog segmentation	2079	231	19	7
Breast tissue	96	10	9	6
ILPD	525	58	10	2
Statlog satellite	4435	2000	36	6
Blood transfusion	674	74	4	2
SPECTF Heart	80	187	44	2
Cardiotocography	1914	212	21	10
Letter	16,000	4000	16	26

© 2015 IEEE. Reprinted with permission, from Wang et al. (2013)

(Guillaumin et al. 2009), neighborhood component analysis (NCA) (Goldberger et al. 2004) and maximally collapsing metric learning (MCML) (Globerson and Roweis 2005). We implemented the doublet-SVM and the triplet-SVM based on the popular SVM toolbox LINSVM[9]. The source codes for LMNN[10], ITML[11], LDML[12], NCA[13], and MCML[14] are also available online, and we tuned their parameters to get the best results.

Table 2.3 shows the basic information for the 10 UCI datasets (Frank and Asuncion 2010). For the Statlog Satellite, SPECTF Heart, and Letter datasets, we use the defined training and test sets to perform the experiment. For the other seven datasets, 10-fold cross-validation were chosen to evaluate the competing metric learning methods, and the reported error rate and training time were obtained by averaging over 10 runs.

Both the doublet-SVM and the triplet-SVM have three hyperparameters, namely, m_1, m_2, and C. Using the Statlog Segmentation dataset as an example, we analyzed the connections between the classification error rate and the hyperparameters. We first analyzed the influence of m_2 on the classification performance of the two SVM methods. Figure 2.5 shows the classification error rate versus m_2 for the doublet-SVM and the triplet-SVM when $m_1 = 1$ and $C = 1$. From Fig. 2.5, we can see that both SVM methods obtained the lowest classification error rates when

---

[9]http://www.csie.ntu.edu.tw/~cjlin/libsvm/

[10]http://www.cse.wustl.edu/~kilian/code/code.html

[11]http://www.cs.utexas.edu/~pjain/itml/

[12]http://lear.inrialpes.fr/people/guillaumin/code.php

[13]http://www.cs.berkeley.edu/~fowlkes/software/nca/

[14]http://homepage.tudelft.nl/19j49/Matlab_Toolbox_for_Dimensionality_Reduction.html

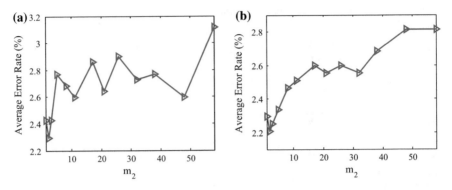

Fig. 2.5 Classification error rate (%) versus m_2 for **a** doublet-SVM and **b** triplet-SVM with $m_1 = 1$ and $C = 1$. © 2015 IEEE. Reprinted with permission, from Wang et al. (2013)

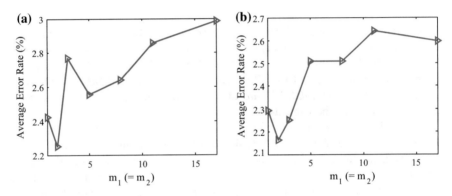

Fig. 2.6 Classification error rate (%) versus m_1 (=m_2) for **a** doublet-SVM and **b** triplet-SVM with $C = 1$. © 2015 IEEE. Reprinted with permission, from Wang et al. (2013)

$m_2 = 2$. Moreover, the error rates for both SVM methods tended to be a little higher when $m_2 > 3$. Thus, we set m_2 to $1 \sim 3$ in our experiments.

By setting $m_1 = m_2$, we investigated the influence of m_1 on the classification error rate of two SVM methods. Figure 2.6 shows the classification error rate versus $m_1(=m_2)$ for the two SVM methods, respectively. From Fig. 2.6, it is obvious that both SVM methods achieved the lowest classification error when $m_1 = m_2 = 2$. Thus, m_1 is set to $1 \sim 3$ in our experiments.

By setting $m_1 = m_2 = 2$, we further studied the relation between C and the classification error rate of the two SVM methods. Figure 2.7 shows the classification error rate versus C for the two SVM methods above. From Fig. 2.7, we can see that the error rate is insensitive to C in a wide range, but it jumps when C is no less than 10^4 for the doublet-SVM and no less than 101 for the triplet-SVM. Thus, we set $C < 10^4$ for the doublet-SVM and $C < 10^1$ for the triplet-SVM in our experiments.

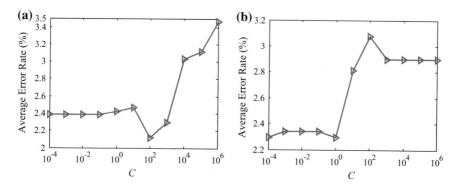

Fig. 2.7 Classification error rate (%) versus C for **a** doublet-SVM and **b** triplet-SVM with $m_1 = m_2 = 2$. © 2015 IEEE. Reprinted with permission, from Wang et al. (2013)

Table 2.4 shows the classification error rates of seven metric learning models on 10 UCI datasets. From Table 2.4, it obvious that the doublet-SVM method achieves the lowest error rates on the Letter, ILPD, and SPECTF Heart datasets. On the Statlog Segmentation dataset, the triplet-SVM achieves the best performance.

We further adopted the average ranks of these models to compare the recognition performances of different distance metric learning models. For each dataset, the rank is calculated based on classification error rates of the compared metric learning methods; thus, rank 1 denotes the best method and rank 2 is the second best method, and so on. The average rank is defined as the mean rank of one method over the 10 datasets, which can provide a fair comparison of the algorithms (Demšar 2006). The rank of different metric learning methods is shown in the last row in Table 2.4.

From Table 2.4, we can see that the doublet-SVM achieves the best average rank and the triplet-SVM achieves the fifth best average rank. This proves that, by incorporating the degree-2 polynomial kernel into the standard (one-class) kernel SVM classifier, the kernel classification based metric learning framework can lead to highly competitive classification accuracy with state-of-the-art metric learning methods. It is interesting to see that, although the doublet-SVM achieves better performance than the triplet-SVM for most datasets, the triplet-SVM performs better than the doublet-SVM for large datasets, such as Statlog Segmentation, Statlog Satellite and Cardiotocography, and achieves a very close error rate to that of the doublet-SVM for the large dataset Letter. The experiments indicate that the doublet-SVM is more suitable for small-scale datasets, while the triplet-SVM is more suitable for large-scale datasets in which each class has many training samples.

All the experiments were executed using the same hardware and software conditions. We should point out that, in the training stage, the doublet-SVM, ITML, LDML, MCML, and NCA were worked on the doublet set, while the triplet-SVM and LMNN were implemented on the triplet set. Thus, there are five doublet-based

Table 2.4 The classification error rates (%) and average ranks of the competing methods on the UCI datasets

Method	Doublet-SVM	Triplet-SVM	NCA	LMNN	ITML	MCML	LDML
Parkin sons	5.68	7.89	4.21	5.26	6.32	12.94	7.15
Sonar	13.07	14.29	14.43	11.57	14.86	24.29	22.86
Statlog segmenttion	2.42	2.29	2.68	2.64	2.51	2.77	2.86
Breast tissue	38.37	33.37	30.75	34.37	36.75	30.75	48.00
ILPD	32.09	35.16	34.79	34.12	34.12	34.79	35.84
Statlog satellite	10.80	10.75	10.95	10.05	11.75	15.65	15.90
Blood transfusion	29.47	34.37	28.38	28.78	27.86	31.89	31.40
SPECTF Heart	27.27	33.69	38.50	34.76	35.29	29.95	33.16
Cardiotocography	20.71	19.34	21.84	19.21	18.96	20.76	22.26
Letter	2.47	2.77	2.47	3.45	2.77	4.20	11.05
Average rank	2.7	3.8	3.5	2.9	3.5	5.0	6.1

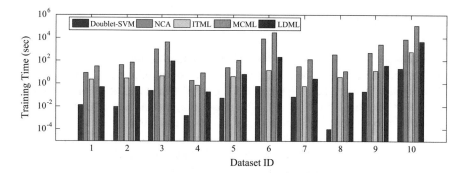

Fig. 2.8 Training time (s) for the doublet-SVM, NCA, ITML, MCML and LDML. From 1–10, the Dataset ID represents Parkinsons, Sonar, Statlog Segmentation, Breast Tissue, ILPD, Statlog satellite, Blood Transfusion, SPECTF Heart, Cardiotocography, and Letter. © 2015 IEEE. Reprinted with permission, from Wang et al. (2013)

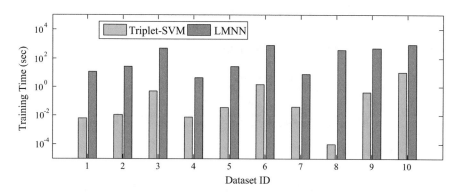

Fig. 2.9 Training time (s) for the triplet-SVM and LMNN. From 1–10, the Dataset ID represents Parkinsons, Sonar, Statlog Segmentation, Breast Tissue, ILPD, Statlog satellite, Blood Transfusion, SPECTF Heart, Cardiotocography, and Letter. © 2015 IEEE. Reprinted with permission, from Wang et al. (2013)

metric learning methods, and two triplet-based methods are compared in the experiments. Figure 2.8 shows the training time of five doublet-based distance metric learning methods. From Fig. 2.8, it is obvious that the doublet-SVM method is much faster than are the other four doublet-based methods. On average, it is 2000 times faster than the second fastest algorithm, ITML. Figure 2.9 shows the training time of two triplet-based distance metric learning methods, the triplet-SVM and LMNN. From Fig. 2.9, we can see that the triplet-SVM is about 100 times faster than LMNN on the ten datasets.

2.4   Summary

In this chapter, we first presented two distance metric learning models based on the support vector machine. The two models can be solved efficiently by the standard SVM solvers. In Sect. 2.3, we presented a general kernel classification framework for metric learning. By coupling a degree-2 polynomial kernel and a positive semidefinite constraint with some kernel methods, the framework can unify many representative and state-of-the-art metric learning methods, such as LMNN, ITML and LDML. On the basis of the kernel classification framework, two novel metric learning methods, namely the doublet-SVM and the triplet-SVM, were presented in detail. Experimental results show that the presented methods obtained better performance than state-of-the-art metric learning methods.

Appendix 1: The Dual of PCML

The original problem of PCML is formulated as

$$
\min_{\mathbf{M},b,\xi} \quad \frac{1}{2}\|\mathbf{M}\|_F^2 + C\sum_{i,j}\xi_{ij} \tag{2.60}
$$
$$
\text{s.t.} \quad h_{ij}\big(\langle\mathbf{M},\mathbf{X}_{ij}\rangle + b\big) \geq 1 - \xi_{ij}, \xi_{ij} \geq 0, \ \forall i,j, \mathbf{M} \succcurlyeq 0.
$$

Its Lagrangian is

$$
L(\lambda,\kappa,\mathbf{Y},\mathbf{M},b,\xi) = \frac{1}{2}\|\mathbf{M}\|_F^2 + C\sum_{i,j}\xi_{ij} - \sum_{i,j}\lambda_{ij}\big[h_{ij}\big(\langle\mathbf{M},\mathbf{X}_{ij}\rangle + b\big) - 1 + \xi_{ij}\big]
$$
$$
- \sum_{i,j}\kappa_{ij}\xi_{ij} - \langle\mathbf{Y},\mathbf{M}\rangle, \tag{2.61}
$$

where λ, κ, and $\mathbf{Y}$ are the Lagrange multipliers that satisfy $\lambda_{ij} \geq 0$, $\kappa_{ij} \geq 0$, $\forall i,j$, and $\mathbf{Y} \succcurlyeq 0$. Based on the KKT conditions, the original problem can be converted into the dual problem. KKT conditions are defined as follows:

$$
\frac{\partial L(\lambda,\kappa,\mathbf{Y},\mathbf{M},b,\xi)}{\partial \mathbf{M}} = 0 \Rightarrow \mathbf{M} - \sum_{i,j}\lambda_{ij}h_{ij}\mathbf{X}_{ij} - \mathbf{Y} = 0, \tag{2.62}
$$

$$
\frac{\partial L(\lambda,\kappa,\mathbf{Y},\mathbf{M},b,\xi)}{\partial b} = 0 \Rightarrow \sum_{i,j}\lambda_{ij}h_{ij} = 0, \tag{2.63}
$$

$$\frac{\partial L(\lambda, \kappa, \mathbf{Y}, \mathbf{M}, b, \xi)}{\partial \xi_{ij}} = C - \lambda_{ij} - \kappa_{ij} = 0 \Rightarrow 0 \le \lambda_{ij} \le C, \ \forall i,j, \tag{2.64}$$

$$h_{ij}\big(\langle \mathbf{M}, \mathbf{X}_{ij}\rangle + b\big) - 1 + \xi_{ij} \ge 0, \quad \xi_{ij} \ge 0, \tag{2.65}$$

$$\lambda_{ij} \ge 0, \quad \kappa_{ij} \ge 0, \quad \mathbf{Y} \succcurlyeq 0, \tag{2.66}$$

$$\lambda_{ij}\big[h_{ij}\big(\langle \mathbf{M}, \mathbf{X}_{ij}\rangle + b\big) - 1 + \xi_{ij}\big] = 0, \ \kappa_{ij}\xi_{ij} = 0. \tag{2.67}$$

Equation (2.62) implies the relationship between λ, $\mathbf{Y}$ and $\mathbf{M}$ as follows:

$$\mathbf{M} = \sum_{i,j} \lambda_{ij} h_{ij} \mathbf{X}_{ij} + \mathbf{Y}. \tag{2.68}$$

Substituting Eqs. (2.62)–(2.69) back into the Lagrangian, we get the following Lagrange dual problem of PCML:

$$\begin{aligned} \max_{\lambda, \mathbf{Y}} \quad & -\frac{1}{2}\left\| \sum_{i,j} \lambda_{ij} h_{ij} \mathbf{X}_{ij} + \mathbf{Y} \right\|_F^2 + \sum_{i,j} \lambda_{ij} \\ \text{s.t.} \quad & \sum_{i,j} \lambda_{ij} h_{ij} = 0, 0 \le \lambda_{ij} \le C, \mathbf{Y} \succcurlyeq 0. \end{aligned} \tag{2.69}$$

From Eqs. (2.68) and (2.69), we can see that matrix $\mathbf{M}$ is explicitly determined by the training procedure, and b is not. Nevertheless, b can be easily obtained by using the KKT complementarity condition in Eqs. (2.64) and (2.67), which shows that $\xi_{ij} = 0$ if $\lambda_{ij} < C$, and $h_{ij}\big(\langle \mathbf{M}, \mathbf{X}_{ij}\rangle + b\big) - 1 + \xi_{ij} = 0$ if $\lambda_{ij} > 0$. Thus, we can simply take any training point for which $0 < \lambda_{ij} < C$ to calculate b by

$$b = \frac{1}{h_{ij}} - \langle \mathbf{M}, \mathbf{X}_{ij}\rangle, \quad \text{for all } 0 < \lambda_{ij} < Cs. \tag{2.70}$$

Note that it is reasonable to take the average of all such training points. After we obtained b, we can calculate ξ_{ij} by

$$\xi_{ij} = \begin{cases} 0 & \text{for all } \lambda_{ij} < C \\ \big[1 - h_{ij}\big(\langle \mathbf{M}, \mathbf{X}_{ij}\rangle + b\big)\big]_+ & \text{for all } \lambda_{ij} = C, \end{cases} \tag{2.71}$$

where term $[z]_+ = \max(z, 0)$ denotes the standard hinge loss.

Appendix 2: The Dual of NCML

The primal problem of NCML is as follows:

$$
\min_{\alpha, b, \xi} \quad \frac{1}{2} \sum_{i,j} \sum_{k,l} \alpha_{ij} \alpha_{kl} \langle \mathbf{X}_{ij}, \mathbf{X}_{kl} \rangle + C \sum_{i,j} \xi_{ij}
$$

$$
\text{s.t.} \quad h_{ij} \left(\sum_{k,l} \alpha_{kl} \langle \mathbf{X}_{ij}, \mathbf{X}_{kl} \rangle + b \right) \geq 1 - \xi_{ij}, \quad \xi_{ij} \geq 0, \quad \alpha_{ij} \geq 0, \quad \forall i,j.
$$

(2.72)

Its Lagrangian can be defined as

$$
L(\beta, \sigma, v, \alpha, b, \xi) = \frac{1}{2} \sum_{i,j} \sum_{k,l} \alpha_{ij} \alpha_{kl} \langle \mathbf{X}_{ij}, \mathbf{X}_{kl} \rangle + C \sum_{i,j} \xi_{ij} - \sum_{i,j} \sigma_{ij} \alpha_{ij}
$$

$$
- \sum_{i,j} \beta_{ij} \left[h_{ij} \left(\sum_{kl} \alpha_{kl} \langle \mathbf{X}_{ij}, \mathbf{X}_{kl} \rangle + b \right) - 1 + \xi_{ij} \right] - \sum_{i,j} v_{ij} \xi_{ij},
$$

(2.73)

where β, σ, and v are the Lagrange multipliers that satisfy $\beta_{ij} \geq 0$, $\sigma_{ij} \geq 0$ and $v_{ij} \geq 0$, $\forall i, j$. Converting the original problem to its dual problem needs the following KKT conditions:

$$
\frac{\partial L(\beta, \sigma, v, \alpha, b, \xi)}{\partial \alpha_{ij}} = 0 \Rightarrow \sum_{k,l} \alpha_{kl} \langle \mathbf{X}_{ij}, \mathbf{X}_{kl} \rangle - \sum_{k,l} \beta_{kl} h_{kl} \langle \mathbf{X}_{ij}, \mathbf{X}_{kl} \rangle - \sigma_{ij} = 0,
$$

(2.74)

$$
\frac{\partial L(\beta, \sigma, v, \alpha, b, \xi)}{\partial b} = 0 \Rightarrow \sum_{i,j} \beta_{ij} h_{ij} = 0,
$$

(2.75)

$$
\frac{\partial L(\beta, \sigma, v, \alpha, b, \xi)}{\partial \xi_{ij}} = 0 \Rightarrow C - \beta_{ij} - v_{ij} = 0 \Rightarrow 0 \leq \beta_{ij} \leq C,
$$

(2.76)

$$
h_{ij} \left(\sum_{k,l} \alpha_{kl} \langle \mathbf{X}_{ij}, \mathbf{X}_{kl} \rangle + b \right) - 1 + \xi_{ij} \geq 0, \quad \xi_{ij} \geq 0, \quad \alpha_{ij} \geq 0, \quad \forall i,j,
$$

(2.77)

$$
\beta_{ij} \geq 0, \quad \sigma_{ij} \geq 0, \quad v_{ij} \geq 0, \quad \forall i,j,
$$

(2.78)

$$
\beta_{ij} \left[h_{ij} \left(\sum_{kl} \alpha_{kl} \langle \mathbf{X}_{ij}, \mathbf{X}_{kl} \rangle + b \right) - 1 + \xi_{ij} \right] = 0, \quad v_{ij} \xi_{ij} = 0, \quad \sigma_{ij} \alpha_{ij} = 0, \quad \forall i,j.
$$

(2.79)

Here, we introduce a coefficient vector η, which satisfies $\sigma_{ij} = \sum_{k,l} \eta_{kl} \langle \mathbf{X}_{ij}, \mathbf{X}_{kl} \rangle$,

where $\langle \mathbf{X}_{ij}, \mathbf{X}_{kl} \rangle$ denotes a positive definite kernel. Thus, we can guarantee that every η has a unique corresponding $\boldsymbol{\sigma}$, and vice versa. According to Eq. (2.74), the relationship between α, β, and η is

$$\alpha_{ij} = \beta_{ij} h_{ij} + \eta_{ij}, \quad \forall i, j. \tag{2.80}$$

Substituting Eqs. (2.74)–(2.76) back into the Lagrangian, the Lagrange dual problem of NCML can be rewritten as follows:

$$\max_{\eta, \beta} \quad -\frac{1}{2} \sum_{i,j} \sum_{k,l} (\beta_{ij} h_{ij} + \eta_{ij})(\beta_{kl} h_{kl} + \eta_{kl}) \langle \mathbf{X}_{ij}, \mathbf{X}_{kl} \rangle + \sum_{i,j} \beta_{ij}$$
$$\text{s.t.} \quad \sum_{k,l} \eta_{kl} \langle \mathbf{X}_{ij}, \mathbf{X}_{kl} \rangle \geq 0, \quad 0 \leq \beta_{ij} \leq C, \quad \forall i, j, \quad \sum_{i,j} \beta_{ij} h_{ij} = 0. \tag{2.81}$$

Analogous to PCML, we can use the KKT complementarity condition in Eq. (2.75) to compute b and ξ_{ij} in NCML. Eqs. (2.76) and (2.79) show that $\xi_{ij} = 0$ if $\beta_{ij} < C$, and $h_{ij} \left(\sum_{kl} \alpha_{kl} \langle \mathbf{X}_{ij}, \mathbf{X}_{kl} \rangle + b \right) - 1 + \xi_{ij} = 0$ if $\beta_{ij} > 0$. With any training point for which $0 < \beta_{ij} < C$, b can be obtained by

$$b = \frac{1}{h_{ij}} - \sum_{kl} \alpha_{kl} \langle \mathbf{X}_{ij}, \mathbf{X}_{kl} \rangle. \tag{2.82}$$

Therefore, β_{ij} can also be obtained by

$$\xi_{ij} = \begin{cases} 0 & \text{for all } \beta_{ij} < C \\ \left[1 - h_{ij} \left(\sum_{k,l} \alpha_{kl} \langle \mathbf{X}_{ij}, \mathbf{X}_{kl} \rangle + b \right) \right]_{+} & \text{for all } \beta_{ij} = C, \end{cases} \tag{2.83}$$

where term $[z]_{+} = \max(z, 0)$ denotes the standard hinge loss.

Appendix 3: The Dual of the Subproblem of η in NCML

The subproblem of η is defined as follows:

$$\min_{\eta} \quad \frac{1}{2} \sum_{i,j} \sum_{k,l} \eta_{ij} \eta_{kl} \langle \mathbf{X}_{ij}, \mathbf{X}_{kl} \rangle + \sum_{i,j} \eta_{ij} \gamma_{ij}$$
$$\text{s.t.} \quad \sum_{k,l} \eta_{kl} \langle \mathbf{X}_{ij}, \mathbf{X}_{kl} \rangle \geq 0, \quad \forall i, j, \tag{2.84}$$

where $\gamma_{ij} = \sum_{k,l} \beta_{kl} h_{kl} \langle \mathbf{X}_{ij}, \mathbf{X}_{kl} \rangle$. Its Lagrangian is

$$L(\mu, \eta) = \frac{1}{2} \sum_{i,j} \sum_{k,l} \eta_{ij} \eta_{kl} \langle \mathbf{X}_{ij}, \mathbf{X}_{kl} \rangle + \sum_{i,j} \eta_{ij} \gamma_{ij} - \sum_{i,j} \mu_{ij} \sum_{k,l} \eta_{kl} \langle \mathbf{X}_{ij}, \mathbf{X}_{kl} \rangle, \quad (2.85)$$

where μ is the Lagrange multiplier that satisfies $\mu_{ij} \geq 0$, $\forall i, j$. Converting the original problem to its dual problem needs the following KKT condition:

$$\frac{\partial L(\mu, \eta)}{\partial \eta_{ij}} = 0 \Rightarrow \sum_{k,l} \eta_{kl} \langle \mathbf{X}_{ij}, \mathbf{X}_{kl} \rangle + \gamma_{ij} - \sum_{k,l} \mu_{kl} \langle \mathbf{X}_{ij}, \mathbf{X}_{kl} \rangle = 0. \quad (2.86)$$

According to Eq. (2.86), the relationship between μ, η and β is

$$\eta_{ij} = \mu_{ij} - h_{ij} \beta_{ij}, \quad \forall i, j. \quad (2.87)$$

Substituting Eqs. (2.86) and (2.87) back into the Lagrangian, we get the following Lagrange dual problem of the subproblem of η

$$\begin{aligned}
\max_{\mu} \quad & -\frac{1}{2} \sum_{i,j} \sum_{k,l} \mu_{ij} \mu_{kl} \langle \mathbf{X}_{ij}, \mathbf{X}_{kl} \rangle + \sum_{i,j} \gamma_{ij} \mu_{ij} \\
& -\frac{1}{2} \sum_{i,j} \sum_{k,l} \beta_{ij} \beta_{kl} h_{ij} h_{kl} \langle \mathbf{X}_{ij}, \mathbf{X}_{kl} \rangle \\
\text{s.t.} \quad & \mu_{ij} \geq 0, \forall i, j.
\end{aligned} \quad (2.88)$$

Since β is fixed in this subproblem, $\sum_{i,j} \sum_{k,l} \beta_{ij} \beta_{kl} h_{ij} h_{kl} \langle \mathbf{X}_{ij}, \mathbf{X}_{kl} \rangle$ remains constant in Eq. (2.88). Thus, we can omit this term and derive the simplified Lagrange dual problem as follows:

$$\begin{aligned}
\max_{\mu} \quad & -\frac{1}{2} \sum_{i,j} \sum_{k,l} \mu_{ij} \mu_{kl} \langle \mathbf{X}_{ij}, \mathbf{X}_{kl} \rangle + \sum_{i,j} \gamma_{ij} \mu_{ij} \\
\text{s.t.} \quad & \mu_{ij} \geq 0, \quad \forall i, j.
\end{aligned} \quad (2.89)$$

Appendix 4: The Dual of the Doublet-SVM

According to the original problem of the doublet-SVM defined in Eq. (2.56), its Lagrange function can be defined as follows

$$L(\mathbf{M}, b, \xi, \alpha, \beta) = \frac{1}{2}\|\mathbf{M}\|_F^2 + C\sum_l \xi_l$$
$$- \sum_l \alpha_l\left[h_l\left((\mathbf{x}_{l,1} - \mathbf{x}_{l,2})^T\mathbf{M}(\mathbf{x}_{l,1} - \mathbf{x}_{l,2}) + b\right) - 1 + \xi_l\right] - \sum_l \beta_l\xi_l,$$

$$(2.90)$$

where α and β are the Lagrange multipliers that satisfy $\alpha_l \geq 0$ and $\beta_l \geq 0, \forall l$. To convert the original problem to its dual needs the following KKT conditions:

$$\frac{\partial L(\mathbf{M}, b, \xi, \alpha, \beta)}{\partial \mathbf{M}} = 0 \Rightarrow \mathbf{M} - \sum_l \alpha_l h_l(\mathbf{x}_{l,1} - \mathbf{x}_{l,2})(\mathbf{x}_{l,1} - \mathbf{x}_{l,2})^T = 0, \quad (2.91)$$

$$\frac{\partial L(\mathbf{M}, b, \xi, \alpha, \beta)}{\partial b} = 0 \Rightarrow \sum_l \alpha_l h_l = 0, \quad (2.92)$$

$$\frac{\partial L(\mathbf{M}, b, \xi, \alpha, \beta)}{\partial \xi_l} = 0 \Rightarrow C - \alpha_l - \beta_l = 0 \Rightarrow 0 < \alpha_l < C, \quad \forall l. \quad (2.93)$$

According to Eq. (2.91), the relationship between $\mathbf{M}$ and α is

$$\mathbf{M} = \sum_l \alpha_l h_l(\mathbf{x}_{l,1} - \mathbf{x}_{l,2})(\mathbf{x}_{l,1} - \mathbf{x}_{l,2})^T. \quad (2.94)$$

Substituting Eqs. (2.91)–(2.93) back into the Lagrangian function, we have

$$L(\alpha) = -\frac{1}{2}\sum_{i,j} \alpha_i\alpha_j h_i h_j K_p(\mathbf{z}_i, \mathbf{z}_j) + \sum_i \alpha_i. \quad (2.95)$$

Thus, the dual problem of the doublet-SVM can be formulated as follows:

$$\max_\alpha -\frac{1}{2}\sum_{i,j} \alpha_i\alpha_j h_i h_j K_p(\mathbf{z}_i, \mathbf{z}_j) + \sum_i \alpha_i$$
$$\text{s.t.} \quad 0 \leq \alpha_l \leq C, \quad \sum_l \alpha_l h_l = 0, \quad \forall l. \quad (2.96)$$

Appendix 5: The Dual of the Triplet-SVM

According to the original problem of the triplet-SVM in Eq. (2.58), its Lagrange function can be defined as follows:

$$L(\mathbf{M}, \xi, \alpha, \beta) = \frac{1}{2}\|\mathbf{M}\|_F^2 + C\sum_l \xi_l - \sum_l \alpha_l[(\mathbf{x}_{l,1} - \mathbf{x}_{l,3})^{\mathrm{T}}\mathbf{M}(\mathbf{x}_{l,1} - \mathbf{x}_{l,3})$$
$$- (\mathbf{x}_{l,1} - \mathbf{x}_{l,2})^{\mathrm{T}}\mathbf{M}(\mathbf{x}_{l,1} - \mathbf{x}_{l,2})] + \sum_l \alpha_l - \sum_l \alpha_l\xi_l - \sum_l \beta_l\xi_l,$$

$$(2.97)$$

where α and β are the Lagrange multipliers. To convert the original problem to its dual, we let the derivative of the Lagrangian function requires the following KKT conditions:

$$\frac{\partial L(\mathbf{M}, b, \xi, \alpha, \beta)}{\partial \mathbf{M}} = 0 \Rightarrow$$
$$\mathbf{M} - \sum_l \alpha_l \left[(\mathbf{x}_{l,1} - \mathbf{x}_{l,3})(\mathbf{x}_{l,1} - \mathbf{x}_{l,3})^{\mathrm{T}} - (\mathbf{x}_{l,1} - \mathbf{x}_{l,2})(\mathbf{x}_{l,1} - \mathbf{x}_{l,2})^{\mathrm{T}} \right] = 0, \qquad (2.98)$$

$$\frac{\partial L(\mathbf{M}, b, \xi, \alpha, \beta)}{\partial \xi_l} = 0 \Rightarrow C - \alpha_l - \beta_l = 0, \ \forall l. \qquad (2.99)$$

According to Eq. (2.98), the relationship between $\mathbf{M}$ and α is:

$$\mathbf{M} = \sum_l \alpha_l \left[(\mathbf{x}_{l,1} - \mathbf{x}_{l,3})(\mathbf{x}_{l,1} - \mathbf{x}_{l,3})^{\mathrm{T}} - (\mathbf{x}_{l,1} - \mathbf{x}_{l,2})(\mathbf{x}_{l,1} - \mathbf{x}_{l,2})^{\mathrm{T}} \right]. \qquad (2.100)$$

Substituting Eqs. (2.98) and (2.99) back into the Lagrangian, we get

$$L(\alpha) = -\frac{1}{2}\sum_{i,j} \alpha_i\alpha_j K_p(\mathbf{t}_i, \mathbf{t}_j) + \sum_i \alpha_i. \qquad (2.101)$$

Thus, the dual problem of the triplet-SVM can be rewritten as follows:

$$\max_\alpha \ -\frac{1}{2}\sum_{i,j} \alpha_i\alpha_j K_p(\mathbf{t}_i, \mathbf{t}_j) + \sum_i \alpha_i$$
$$\text{s.t.} \ \ 0 \le \alpha_l \le C, \ \ \forall l. \qquad (2.102)$$

References

S. Andrews, I. Tsochantaridis, T. Hofmann, Support vector machines for multiple-instance learning, in *Proceedings of Advances in Neural Information Processing Systems* (2002), pp. 561–568

M.-F. Balcan, A. Blum, N. Srebro, A theory of learning with similarity functions. Mach. Learn. **72** (1–2), 89–112 (2008)

M. Belkin, P. Niyogi, V. Sindhwani, Manifold regularization: a geometric framework for learning from labeled and unlabeled examples. J. Mach. Learn. Res. **7**, 2399–2434 (2006)

A. Bellet, A. Habrard, M. Sebban, Good edit similarity learning by loss minimization. Mach. Learn. **89**(1–2), 5–35 (2012)

A. Bellet, A. Habrard, M. Sebban, A survey on metric learning for feature vectors and structured data. arXiv preprint arXiv:1306.6709 (2002)

A. Bordes, L. Bottou, P. Gallinari, J. Weston, Solving multiclass support vector machines with LaRank, in *Proceedings of the 24th International Conference on Machine Learning* (ACM, 2007), pp. 89–96

C.-C. Chang, C.-J. Lin, LIBSVM: A library for support vector machines. ACM Trans. Intell. Syst. Technol. **2**(3), 27 (2011)

R. Collobert, S. Bengio, Y. Bengio, A parallel mixture of SVMs for very large scale problems. Neural Comput. **14**(5), 1105–1114 (2002)

I. Csisz, G. TUSN DY, Information geometry and alternating minimization procedures. Stat. Decis. **1**, 205–237 (1984)

J.V. Davis, B. Kulis, P. Jain, S. Sra, I.S. Dhillon, Information-theoretic metric learning, in *Proceedings of the 24th International Conference on Machine Learning* (ACM, 2007), pp. 209–216

J. Demšar, Statistical comparisons of classifiers over multiple data sets. J. Mach. Learn. Res. **7**, 1–30 (2006)

T. Evgeniou, M. Pontil, Regularized multi-task learning, in *Proceedings of the Tenth ACM SIGKDD International Conference on Knowledge Discovery and Data Mining* (ACM, 2004), pp. 109–117

A. Frank, A. Asuncion, UCI machine learning repository (2010). Available: http://archive.ics.uci.edu/ml

Y. Fu, S. Yan, T.S. Huang, Correlation metric for generalized feature extraction. IEEE Trans. Pattern Anal. Mach. Intell. **30**(12), 2229–2235 (2008)

A. Globerson, S.T. Roweis, Metric learning by collapsing classes, in *Proceedings of Advances in Neural Information Processing Systems* (2005), pp. 451–458

J. Goldberger, G.E. Hinton, S.T. Roweis, R. Salakhutdinov, Neighbourhood components analysis, in *Proceedings of Advances in Neural Information Processing Systems* (2004), pp. 513–520

M. Guillaumin, J. Verbeek, C. Schmid, Is that you? Metric learning approaches for face identification, in *Proceedings of IEEE International Conference on Computer Vision* (IEEE, 2009), pp. 498–505

A. Gunawardana, W. Byrne, Convergence theorems for generalized alternating minimization procedures. J. Mach. Learn. Res. **6**, 2049–2073 (2005)

C. Huang, S. Zhu, K. Yu, Large scale strongly supervised ensemble metric learning, with applications to face verification and retrieval. arXiv preprin arXiv:1212.6094 (2012)

G.B. Huang, M. Ramesh, T. Berg, E. Learned-Miller, Labeled faces in the wild: a database for studying face recognition in unconstrained environments. Technical Report 07-49 (University of Massachusetts, Amherst, 2007)

D. Kedem, S. Tyree, F. Sha, G.R. Lanckriet, K.Q. Weinberger, Non-linear metric learning, in *Proceedings of Advances in Neural Information Processing Systems* (2012), pp. 2573–2581

S.S. Keerthi, K. Duan, S.K. Shevade, A.N. Poo, A fast dual algorithm for kernel logistic regression. Mach. Learn. **61**(1–3), 151–165 (2005)

K. Koh, S.-J. Kim, S.P. Boyd, An interior-point method for large-scale l1-regularized logistic regression. J. Mach. Learn. Res. **8**(8), 1519–1555 (2007)

X. Li, C. Shen, Q. Shi, A. Dick, A. Van den Hengel, Non-sparse linear representations for visual tracking with online reservoir metric learning, in *Proceedings of IEEE Conference on Computer Vision and Pattern Recognition* (IEEE, 2012), pp. 1760–1767

K.-R. M Ller, S. MIKA, G. R TSCH, K. TSUDA, B. SCH LKOPF, An introduction to kernel-based learning algorithms. IEEE Trans. Neural Netw. **12**(2), 181–201 (2001)

T. Mensink, J. Verbeek, F. Perronnin, G. Csurka, Metric learning for large scale image classification: generalizing to new classes at near-zero cost, in *Proceedings of Computer Vision–ECCV* (Springer, Berlin, 2012), pp. 488–501

J. Platt, Fast training of support vector machines using sequential minimal optimization. Adv. Kernel Methods Support Vector Learn. **3**, 185–208 (1999)

B. Schlkopf, J.C. Platt, J. Shawe-Taylor, A.J. Smola, R.C. Williamson, Estimating the support of a high-dimensional distribution. Neural Comput. **13**(7), 1443–1471 (2001)

S. Shalev-Shwartz, Y. Singer, N. Srebro, A. Cotter, Pegasos: primal estimated sub-gradient solver for SVM. Math. Program. **127**(1), 3–30 (2011)

J. Shawe-Taylor, N. Cristianini, *Kernel Methods for Pattern Analysis* (Cambridge University Press, Cambridge, 2010)

C. Shen, J. Kim, L. Wang, A scalable dual approach to semidefinite metric learning, in *Proceedings of IEEE Conference on Computer Vision and Pattern Recognition* (IEEE, 2011), pp. 2601–2608

C. Shen, J. Kim, L. Wang, A. Hengel, Positive semidefinite metric learning with boosting, in *Proceedings of Advances in Neural Information Processing Systems* (2009), pp. 1651–1659

C.H. Teo, A. Smola, S. Vishwanathan, Q.V. Le, A scalable modular convex solver for regularized risk minimization, in *Proceedings of the 13th ACM SIGKDD International Conference on Knowledge Discovery and Data Mining* (ACM, 2007), pp. 727–736

I.W. Tsang, A. Kocsor, J.T. Kwok, Simpler core vector machines with enclosing balls, in *Proceedings of the 24th International Conference on Machine Learning* (ACM, 2007), pp. 911–918

I.W. Tsang, J.T. Kwok, P.-M. Cheung, Core vector machines: fast SVM training on very large data sets. J. Mach. Learn. Res. 363–392 (2005)

V. Vapnik, *The Nature of Statistical Learning Theory* (Springer Science & Business Media, Berlin, 2013)

F. Wang, W. Zuo, L. Zhang, D. Meng, D. Zhang, A kernel classification framework for metric learning (2013)

J. Wang, H.T. Do, A. Woznica, A. Kalousis, Metric learning with multiple kernels, in *Proceedings of Advances in Neural Information Processing Systems* (2011), pp. 1170–1178

J. Wang, A. Kalousis, A. Woznica, Parametric local metric learning for nearest neighbor classification, in *Proceedings of Advances in Neural Information Processing Systems* (2012), pp. 1601–1609

K.Q. Weinberger, J. Blitzer, L.K. Saul, Distance metric learning for large margin nearest neighbor classification. J. Mach. Learn. Res. **10**, 207–244 (2009)

L. Yang, R. Jin, *Distance Metric Learning: A comprehensive Survey,* vol. 2 (Michigan State University, 2006)

Y. Ying, P. Li, Distance metric learning with eigenvalue optimization. J. Mach. Learn. Res. **13**(1), 1–26 (2012)

W. Zuo, F. Wang, D. Zhang, L. Lin, Y. Huang, D. Meng, L. Zhang, Iterated support vector machines for distance metric learning. arXiv preprint arXiv:1502.00363 (2015)

Chapter 3
Sparse Representation-Based Classification for Biometric Recognition

Abstract Linear representation methods have been well studied in mathematics. As one of the typical linear representation methods, the sparse representation method has received much attention in recent years and is widely applied in many fields, such as image denoising, debluring, restoration, super-resolution, segmentation, classification, and visual tracking. In this chapter, we first summarize some frameworks of sparse representation, and then we give a brief introduction to the representation by dictionary learning algorithm. Based on the sparse representation, we present a novel multiple representations for image classification.

3.1 Introduction

Image representation is an important branch of computer vision. Proper descriptions or representations of images are the basis of achieving good image classification results (Chen et al. 2010). Once images are well represented, an object in the form of the image can be easily distinguished from the others.

Denote by vector $y \in R^m$ a query sample or image. The image representation-based method uses a dictionary $D = [d_1, d_2, \ldots d_p] \in R^{m \times p}$ to represent sample y, i.e., $y = D\alpha$. α can be viewed as the representation coefficient. In fields of image classification, especially face recognition, the representation-based algorithms can be simply divided into two groups: the first one uses all training samples as the dictionary, and the second one learns a dictionary from the training samples (Yang et al. 2014).

In terms of the minimization norm used in sparsity constraints, the sparse representation-based methods can be roughly categorized into five groups: sparse representation with l_0-norm minimization, sparse representation with l_p-norm ($0 < p < 1$) minimization, sparse representation with l_1-norm minimization, sparse representation with $l_{2,1}$-norm minimization, and sparse representation with l_2-norm minimization (Zhang et al. 2015b). In this chapter, we regard the sparse representation classification (SRC) algorithm with l_0, l_1 or l_p ($p < 1$) minimization as the conventional SRC algorithm, and treat the SRC algorithm with l_2-norm

© Springer Science+Business Media Singapore 2016
D. Zhang et al., *Discriminative Learning in Biometrics*,
DOI 10.1007/978-981-10-2056-8_3

minimization as the generalized SRC algorithm. A generalized SRC algorithm usually has a closed-form solution but conventional SRC algorithms do not have. Moreover, a generalized SRC algorithm is usually computationally efficient than the conventional SRC algorithm. However, the conventional SRC algorithm usually has a 'sparser' solution than the generalized SRC algorithm. Typical conventional sparse representation algorithms include l1 regularized least squares (L1LS) (S.P. 2008), fast iterative shrinkage and thresholding algorithm (FISTA) (Gong et al. 2013), augmented Lagrangian (Luo et al. 2012), orthogonal matching pursuit (OMP) (Needel and Vershynin 2007) etc. Typical generalized sparse representation algorithms include linear regression classification (LRC) (Naseem et al. 2012), collaborative representation (CRC) (Zhang et al. 2011), two-phase sparse representation (Xu et al. 2011) etc.

Sparse representation by dictionary learning can be roughly divided into three groups: supervised dictionary learning, semi-supervised dictionary learning, and unsupervised dictionary learning algorithms. Supervised dictionary learning embeds the class label into the process of sparse representation and dictionary learning so that this leads to the learned dictionary with discriminative information for effective classification. There are many supervised dictionary learning methods that have been proposed in recent years (Mairal et al. 2009; Wang et al. 2012). The discriminative K-SVD algorithm (D-KSVD) is one of the typical supervised dictionary learning methods (Zhang and Li 2010). D-KSVD algorithm incorporates the discriminative dictionary and classifier parameters and employs the K-SVD algorithm to obtain all the parameters for image classification. Jiang et al. (2011) proposed a label consistent KSVD (LC-KSVD) algorithm for image classification, which can be regarded as an extension of D-KSVD. LC-KSVD exploits the supervised information to learn the dictionary and integrates the process of constructing the dictionary and optimal linear classifier into a mixed reconstructive and discriminative objective function, and then jointly obtains the learned dictionary and an effective classifier. These supervised dictionary learning algorithms have achieved excellent performance for classification task. However, in many pattern classification problems, accessibility to a large set of labeled data may not be possible due to the fact that labeling data is expensive and time-consuming. Thus, insufficient labeled training data are adverse to supervised dictionary learning algorithms.

The semi-supervised dictionary learnings exploit unlabeled data, along with labeled data, to learn a better dictionary for image classification tasks. Shrivastava et al. (2012) proposed a semi-supervised dictionary learning algorithm by using labeled training samples to learn specific-class dictionaries, and then used them to predict the label information of the unlabeled training samples. However, the algorithm did not take into account the underlying geometrical structure of both labeled and unlabeled data, and generally could not preserve the locality structure and thus the learned dictionary may not be optimal for classification tasks. Especially, in the case where the data lies in the nonlinear manifold embedded in a very high-dimensional space (Roweis and Saul 2000; Tenenbaum et al. 2000), the classification performance of the above algorithm will be degraded. In order to address this problem, Zhang et al. (2013) presented an online semi-supervised dictionary learning algorithm for classification tasks by integrating the reconstruction error of labeled and unlabeled data, the discriminative sparse-code error, and the classification error into an objective function. Wang et al. (2013) proposed a semi-supervised dictionary learning algorithm to automatically optimize the dictionary size. The main shortcoming of semi-supervised dictionary learning algorithms is that they are usually sensitive to the number of labeled training samples.

Unsupervised dictionary learning just considers that the examples can be sparsely represented by the learned dictionary and leaves out the label information of the examples (Mairal et al. 2010). One of the typical unsupervised dictionary learning algorithms is the K-SVD algorithm (Aharon et al. 2006). Yu et al. (2009) proposed an unsupervised local coordinate coding algorithm (LCC) by taking advantage of the local geometric structure of training samples. In addition, some other unsupervised dictionary learning methods also have been proposed, such as the Bayesian dictionary learning algorithm (Zhou et al. 2012), tree-structured dictionary learning (Jenatton et al. 2010) etc.

This chapter is organized as follows: we first introduce some sparse representation methods with different norm constraints in Sect. 3.2. Section 3.3 summarizes some representation methods based on dictionary learning. In Sect. 3.4, a novel multiple representations classification method is presented for image classification. Section 3.5 concludes the chapter.

3.2 Frameworks of Sparse Representation with Different Norm Minimizations

3.2.1 Sparse Representation with l_0-Norm Minimization

Let $x_1, x_2, \cdots, x_n \in R^d$ be all the n known samples and matrix $X \in R^{d \times n}$ (d < n), which is constructed by known samples, is the measurement matrix or the basis dictionary and should also be an over-completed dictionary. Each column of X is one sample and the probe sample is $y \in R^d$, which is a column vector. Thus, if all the known samples are used to approximately represent the probe sample, it should be expressed as:

$$y = x_1\alpha_1 + x_2\alpha_2 + \cdots + x_n\alpha_n, \tag{3.1}$$

where $\alpha_i, (i = 1, 2, \ldots, n)$ is the coefficient of x_i and Eq. (3.1) can be simply rewritten as:

$$y = X\alpha, \tag{3.2}$$

where the matrix $X = [x_1, x_2, \cdots, x_n]$ and $\alpha = [\alpha_1, \alpha_2, \cdots, \alpha_n]^{\mathrm{T}}$.

However, Eq. (3.2) is an underdetermined linear system of equations and the main problem is how to solve it. From the viewpoint of linear algebra, if there is not any prior knowledge or any constraint imposed on the representation solution α, problem Eq. (3.2) is an ill-posed problem and will never have a unique solution. That is, it is impossible to utilize Eq. (3.2) to uniquely represent the probe sample y using the measurement matrix X. To alleviate this difficulty, it is feasible to impose an appropriate regularizer constraint or regularizer function on representation solution α. The sparse representation method demands that the obtained representation solution should be sparse. Hereafter, the meaning of 'sparse' or 'sparsity' refers to the condition that when the linear combination of measurement matrix is exploited to represent the probe sample, many of the coefficients should be zero or very close to zero and few of the entries in the representation solution are differentially large.

The sparsest representation solution can be acquired by solving the linear representation system Eq. (3.2) with the l_0-norm minimization constraint (Donoho and Elad 2003). Thus, problem (3.2) can be converted to the following optimization problem:

$$\hat{\alpha} = \arg \min \|\alpha\|_0 \text{ s.t. } y = X\alpha, \tag{3.3}$$

where $\| \cdot \|_0$ refers to the number of nonzero elements in the vector and is also viewed as the measure of sparsity. Moreover, if just $k(k < n)$ atoms from the measurement matrix X are utilized to represent the probe sample, problem (3.3) will be equivalent to the following optimization problem:

$$y = X\alpha \text{ s.t. } \|\alpha\|_0 \leq k. \tag{3.4}$$

Problem (3.4) is called the k-sparse approximation problem. Because real data always contains noise, representation noise is unavoidable in most cases. Thus, the original model (3.2) can be revised to a modified model with respect to small possible noise by denoting

$$y = X\alpha + s, \tag{3.5}$$

where $s \in R^d$ refers to representation noise and is bounded as $\|s\|_2 \leq \varepsilon$. With the presence of noise, the sparse solutions of problems (3.3) and (3.4) can be approximately obtained by resolving the following optimization problems:

$$\hat{\alpha} = \arg \min \|\alpha\|_0 \text{ s.t. } \|y - X\alpha\|_2^2 \leq \varepsilon, \tag{3.6}$$

or

$$\hat{\alpha} = \arg \min \|y - X\alpha\|_2^2 \text{ s.t. } \|\alpha\|_0 \leq k. \tag{3.7}$$

Furthermore, according to the Lagrange multiplier theorem, a proper constant λ exists such that problems (3.6) and (3.7) are equivalent to the following unconstrained minimization problem with a proper value of λ:

$$\hat{\alpha} = L(\alpha, \lambda) = \arg\min \|y - X\alpha\|_2^2 + \lambda\|\alpha\|_0, \tag{3.8}$$

where λ refers to the Lagrange multiplier associated with $\|\alpha\|_0$.

3.2.2 Sparse Representation with l_1-Norm Minimization

Although the sparse representation method with l_0-norm minimization can obtain the fundamental sparse solution of α over the matrix X, the problem is still a non-deterministic polynomial-time hard (NP-hard) problem and the solution is difficult to approximate (Amaldi and Kann 1998). Recent literature (Candes and Tao 2006; Candes et al. 2006) has demonstrated that when the representation solution obtained by using the l_1 norm minimization constraint is also content with the condition of sparsity, and the solution using l_1 norm minimization with sufficient sparsity can be equivalent to the solution obtained by l_0 norm minimization with full probability. Moreover, the l_1 norm optimization problem has an analytical solution and can be solved in polynomial time. Similar to sparse representation with l_0 norm minimization, the sparse representation with l_1-norm minimization is to solve the following problem:

$$\hat{\alpha} = \arg\min_{\alpha} \|\alpha\|_1 \text{ s.t. } y = X\alpha, \tag{3.9}$$

$$\hat{\alpha} = \arg\min_{\alpha} \|\alpha\|_1 \text{ s.t. } \|y - X\alpha\|_2 \leq \varepsilon, \tag{3.10}$$

$$\hat{\alpha} = \arg\min \|y - X\alpha\|_2^2 \text{ s.t. } \|\alpha\|_1 \leq \tau, \tag{3.11}$$

$$\hat{\alpha} = L(\alpha, \lambda) = \arg\min \frac{1}{2}\|y - X\alpha\|_2^2 + \lambda\|\alpha\|_1, \tag{3.12}$$

where λ is a small positive constant.

3.2.3 Sparse Representation with l_p-Norm $(0 < p < 1)$ Minimization

In addition to the l_0 norm minimization and l_1 norm minimization, some researchers are trying to solve the sparse representation problem with l_p-norm $(0 < p < 1)$ minimization, especially $p = 0.1, \frac{1}{2}, \frac{1}{3}$ or 0.9 (Guo et al. 2013; Lyu et al. 2013;

Xu et al. 2012). The sparse representation problem with l_p-norm $(0 < p < 1)$ minimization is to solve the following problem:

$$\hat{\alpha} = \arg\min_\alpha \, ||\alpha||_p^p \text{ s.t. } ||y - X\alpha||_2^2 \le \varepsilon, \tag{3.13}$$

or

$$\hat{\alpha} = \arg\min \, ||y - X\alpha||_2^2 + \lambda||\alpha||_p^p.$$

In spite of the fact that sparse representation methods with l_p-norm $(0 < p < 1)$ minimization are not the mainstream methods to obtain the sparse representation solution, it tremendously influences the improvement of the sparse representation theory.

3.2.4   Sparse Representation with l_2-Norm and $l_{2,1}$-Norm Minimization

The representation solution obtained by l_2 norm minimization is not rigorously sparse. It can only obtain a 'limit-sparse' representation solution, i.e., the solution has the property that it is discriminative and distinguishable but is not really sparse enough (Zhang et al. 2015a). The objective function of the sparse representation method with l_2 norm minimization is to solve the following problem:

$$\hat{\alpha} = \arg\min_\alpha \, ||\alpha||_2 \text{ s.t. } y = X\alpha, \tag{3.14}$$

or

$$\hat{\alpha} = \arg\min \, ||y - X\alpha||_2^2 + \lambda||\alpha||_2, \tag{3.15}$$

On the other hand, the $l_{2,1}$ norm is also called the rotation invariant l_1 norm, which is proposed to overcome the difficulty of robustness to outliers (Ding et al. 2006). The objective function of the sparse representation problem with $l_{2,1}$-norm minimization is to solve the following function:

$$\arg\min ||Y - XA||_{2,1} + \mu||A||_{2,1}. \tag{3.16}$$

where Y refers to the matrix composed of all the test samples, A is the corresponding coefficient matrix of X, and μ is a small positive constant.

3.3 Representation by Dictionary Learning

Unlike the sparse representation methods introduced in previous which use all training samples as the dictionary for image representation and classification, the dictionary learning-based representation methods usually first learn a dictionary from the given samples, and then use the learned dictionary to represent the query sample.

Given a training sample set $Y = [y_1, \cdots, y_N] \in \Re^{n \times N}$, let $D = [d_1, \cdots, d_K] \in \Re^{n \times K}$ be the learned dictionary matrix, where each k represents an atom in dictionary D, N is the number of all training samples. $X = [x_1, \cdots, x_N] \in \Re^{K \times N}$ is the coefficient matrix. We also assume that the training sample set contains all training samples from C categories.

3.3.1 Supervised Dictionary Learning Algorithms

Supervised dictionary learning algorithms usually exploit a regularization term on the labels of training samples and/or atoms to improve the discriminative ability of the learned dictionary. For example, Jiang et al. (2011) proposed the LC-KSVD algorithm by exploiting the classification error and discriminative sparse-code error to improve the discriminative ability of the learned dictionary. The LC-KSVD algorithm has the following objective function:

$$\min_{D, W, A, X} \|Y - DX\|_2^2 + \alpha \|Q - AX\|_2^2 + \beta \|H - WX\|_2^2, \forall i, \|x_i\|_0 \leq \psi, \quad (3.17)$$

where $Q = [q_1, \cdots, q_N] \in \Re^{K \times N}$ are discriminative sparse codes of training sample set Y. ψ is the sparsity factor. x_i denotes the i-th column of X. $q_i = \left[q_i^1, \cdots, q_i^K\right]^T = [0, \cdots, 1, 1, \cdots, 0]^T \in \Re^K$ is the discriminative sparse code corresponding to training sample y_i. The nonzero values of q_i occur at those indices where training sample y_i and atom d_k share the same label. For example, for $D = [d_1, \cdots, d_7]$ and $Y = [y_1, \cdots, y_7]$, if y_1, y_2, d_i and d_2 are from the first category, y_3, y_4, d_3 and d_4 are from the second category, y_5, y_6, y_7, d_5, d_6, and d_7 are from the third category, then Q should be defined as:

$$Q = \begin{bmatrix} 1 & 1 & 0 & 0 & 0 & 0 & 0 \\ 1 & 1 & 0 & 0 & 0 & 0 & 0 \\ 0 & 0 & 1 & 1 & 0 & 0 & 0 \\ 0 & 0 & 1 & 1 & 0 & 0 & 0 \\ 0 & 0 & 0 & 0 & 1 & 1 & 1 \\ 0 & 0 & 0 & 0 & 1 & 1 & 1 \end{bmatrix}$$

$W \in \Re^{C \times K}$ denotes the classifier parameters. ψ is the sparsity factor. $H = [h_1, \cdots, h_N] \in \Re^{C \times N}$. Each column vector of H has only one nonzero entry and all the other entries are zero. The position of the nonzero entry of a column vector of H indicates the category of training sample y_i. In other words, if the j-th entry of column vector h_i is 1, then we know that the i-th training sample is from the j-th category. Thus, we say that h_i denotes the label of the i-th training sample.

3.3.2 Semi-supervised Dictionary Learning Algorithms

Semi-supervised dictionary learning algorithms exploit both labeled and unlabeled training samples to learn a dictionary. Wang et al. (2013) proposed a semi-supervised robust dictionary learning algorithm by using the $l_{2,0+}$-norm to minimize the regularization term. The objective function is as follows:

$$\min_{D,\widetilde{X}} \left\| \left(\widetilde{Y} - D\widetilde{X} \right)^T \right\|_{2,q}^q + \lambda \sum_{j=0}^{C} \left\| X_j \right\|_{2,p}^p, \tag{3.18}$$

where $\widetilde{Y} = [Y_0, Y_1, \cdots, Y_C]$, and Y_k denotes the training sample set of the k-th category. In other words, Y_k is the matrix consisting of all training samples of the k-th category. Moreover, Y_0 is the unlabeled training samples and $Y_1, \cdots, Y_C$ denotes the labeled training samples. $\widetilde{X} = [X_0, X_1, \cdots, X_C]$ is the coding coefficient matrix, and X_k $(k = 1, \ldots, C)$ is the coding coefficient matrix of the training samples of the k-th category. X_0 is the coding coefficient matrix of the unlabeled training samples. p and q are the parameters.

3.3.3 Unsupervised Dictionary Learning Algorithms

Unsupervised dictionary learnings do not use the label information in the dictionary learning process. The K-SVD algorithm is a well-known and widely used unsupervised dictionary learning algorithm. The algorithm is based on the following objective function:

$$\min_{D,X} \|Y - DX\|_2^2 \quad \forall i, \|x_i\|_0 \leq \psi. \tag{3.19}$$

ψ is the sparsity factor. The K-SVD algorithm is totally subjected to the constraint that the dictionary is sparse and able to reconstruct training samples with the minimum error.

3.4   Multiple Representations for Image Classification

In this section, we will present a novel multiple representations method for image classification. Conventional and generalized sparse representation algorithms are applied with the original images and the novel representations of the images as the image classification algorithms.

3.4.1   To Obtain Novel Representations of Images

The novel representation of an original image is obtained as follows: Let I stands for an original image. Let I_{ij} denotes the intensity of the pixel at the i-th row and j-th column of I. Suppose that m is the maximum intensity of all pixels. For a conventional gray image we have $m = 255$. The novel representation of image I is denoted by J and defined as:

$$J_{ij} = I_{ij} \cdot (m - I_{ij}), \tag{3.20}$$

where J_{ij} stands for the intensity of the pixel at the i-th row and j-th column of J. From the definition, we have the following propositions:

Proposition 3.1 *If I_{ij} is m or zero, then J_{ij} will be zero.*

Proposition 3.2 *If I_{ij} is an even number, then J_{ij} will have its maximum value when I_{ij} equals to $\frac{m}{2}$.*

It is very easy to prove the above propositions. We can also know that the closer to $\frac{m}{2}$ the I_{ij}, the larger the J_{ij}. As a result, we can conclude that only if a pixel in the original face image is in the range of mid-level intensity, it will be enhanced in the novel representation of the original image; otherwise, it will have a relative small value in the novel representation. Hereafter, we also refer to novel representations of original images as virtual images.

3.4.2   The Algorithm to Fuse Original and Virtual Images

The fusion method of multiple representations is as follows: After virtual images are obtained, a classification algorithm can be applied to both the original and virtual images, respectively. We use the following flexible score fusion scheme to integrate the classification results. Let $d_o^j (j = 1, \ldots, C)$ denotes the distance or dissimilarity (also referred to as score) between the test sample and original face images of the j-th subject. C is the number of all subjects. Let $d_v^j (j = 1, \ldots, C)$ denotes the distance (i.e., score) between the test sample and virtual face images of the j-th subject. Let $P_o^1, \ldots, P_o^C$ stands for the sorted results of $d_o^1, \ldots, d_o^C$ and suppose that $P_o^1 \leq \ldots \leq P_o^C$. Let $P_v^1, \ldots, P_v^C$ stands for the sorted results of $d_v^1, \ldots, d_v^C$ and suppose that $P_v^1 \leq \ldots \leq P_v^C$. We define $w_{10} = P_o^2 - P_o^1$ and $w_{20} = P_v^2 - P_v^1$. We, respectively, use $w_1 = \frac{w_{10}}{w_{10}+w_{20}}$ and $w_2 = \frac{w_{20}}{w_{10}+w_{20}}$ as weights of d_o^j and d_v^j. The formula to fuse d_o^j and d_v^j is

$$q_j = w_1 d_o^j + w_2 d_v^j, j = 1, \ldots, C. \tag{3.21}$$

Furthermore, we define

$$r = \arg\min_j q_j. \tag{3.22}$$

Finally, the test sample is assigned to the r-th subject. The main steps of the multiple representations algorithm are presented as follows:

Step 1. Separate all original images into two sets, i.e., the set of training samples and set of test samples.

Step 2. Obtain virtual images of all original images using (3.20). Then, all images are converted into unit column vectors with norm of 1.

Step 3. A classification algorithm is applied to both the original and virtual face images to obtain d_o^j and d_v^j ($j = 1, \ldots, C$).

Step 4. Obtain weights $w_1 = \frac{w_{10}}{w_{10}+w_{20}}$ and $w_2 = \frac{w_{20}}{w_{10}+w_{20}}$. Integrate d_o^j and d_v^j ($j = 1, \ldots, C$) using (3.21).

Step 5. Use (3.22) to classify the test sample.

3.4.3 The Analysis of the Algorithm

Previous study also suggests that we may exploit only a subset of all image pixels for image classification (Smielik and Kuhnert 2013). This somewhat implies that different pixels play different roles in image classification. Furthermore, it also seems that to set different weights to different pixels is reasonable. It should be pointed out that the multiple representations algorithm indeed also has the idea that different pixels are of different importance in representing the object. We present it in detail below.

From the algorithm description presented in Sects. 3.4.1 and 3.4.2, we know that the virtual image is very different from the original image. In particular, we know that if the pixel intensity of a region in the original image is very large or small, then the pixel intensity of the same region in the virtual image will be very small. On the other hand, if the pixel intensity of a region in the original image is very close to one-second of the maximum intensity, then the pixel intensity of the same region in the virtual image will be quite close to the maximum intensity. In other words, more emphasis will be taken on the pixels with moderate intensities. For a deformable original image such as the face image, the pixel with mid-level intensity may be more stable, so the presented algorithm is reasonable. Moreover, in order to fully exploit complementary information contained in the original and virtual images, we simultaneously use them to perform image classification. The experiments presented in Sect. 3.4.4 show that the sparse representation algorithm is very suitable to integrate the original and virtual images to perform image classification.

3.4.4 Insight into the Multiple Representations Algorithm

In this section, we give an intuitive explanation to the rationale of the multiple representations algorithm. The ORL face dataset was first used to conduct an experiment to intuitively show the difference between the original image and its novel representation presented in this chapter. Figure 3.1 shows the original pixel intensities of the first sample of the first subject in the ORL face dataset. Figure 3.2 shows the pixel intensities of the novel representation of the same sample. From these two figures, we see that the pixels with moderate intensities in the first sample are converted into pixels with very high intensities in the novel representation.

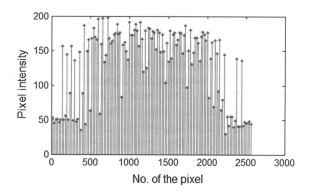

Fig. 3.1 Original pixel intensities of the first sample of the first subject in the ORL face dataset. Reprinted from Xu et al. (2015), with permission from Elsevier

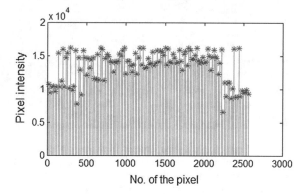

Fig. 3.2 Pixel intensities of the novel representation of the first sample in the ORL face dataset. Reprinted from Xu et al. (2015), with permission from Elsevier

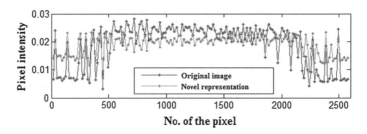

Fig. 3.3 Normalized original image of the first sample in the ORL face dataset and its normalized novel representation. Reprinted from Xu et al. (2015), with permission from Elsevier

Figure 3.3 shows normalized original image of this sample in the ORL face dataset and its normalized novel representation. Here 'normalized' means that the image vector is converted into unit vectors with the norm of 1. Figure 3.3 intuitively illustrates again that the correlation between the original image and its novel representation is not very high.

Figure 3.4 shows eight original face images and the corresponding virtual images of a subject in the Georgia Tech face database. We also see that the virtual image is directly associated with the corresponding original face image, but they also have clear difference in image appearance. As the original face image and virtual image provide multiple representations with the same face, the simultaneous use of them allows the face to be better described and recognized.

The novel representation of an original face image also appears to be a natural virtual face image. Compared with other algorithms to generate virtual face images, the presented multiple representations algorithm is very simple and computationally quite efficient. Moreover, there is no any constraint or parameter. However, most of the other algorithms to generate virtual face images are implemented with special constraints or parameters. For instance, the illumination compensation algorithm is established on the basis of a strict assumption and special parameters are needed (Hsieh and Tung 2010).

Fig. 3.4 Eight original face images (*first row*) and the corresponding novel representations (*second row*) of a subject in the Georgia Tech face database. For each column, the *upper* image is an original face image and the *lower* image is the corresponding novel representation. Reprinted from Xu et al. (2015), with permission from Elsevier

3.4.5 Experiments and Results

In this section, several representation-based methods are compared. In the experiments, besides collaborative representation, L1LS, FISTA, and PALM are directly applied to the original images to perform classification, these algorithms are also applied to the novel representation of the original image for classification. In other words, collaborative representation, L1LS, FISTA, and PALM are, respectively, used as the classification algorithm in Step 3 of the multiple representations method. In particular, the procedure is as follows: First, the novel representation of each original image is obtained. Then a conventional or generalized SRC algorithm is applied to the novel representation and original image, respectively. Finally, the scores obtained using the SRC algorithms including L1LS, FISTA, and PALM and collaborative representation are fused by the algorithm presented in Sect. 3.4.2. When collaborative representation is used in the multiple representations method, we refer to it as 'multiple representations with collaborative representation' in the corresponding tables (see Table 3.1 and Table 3.2). When collaborative representation, L1LS, FISTA, and PALM are directly applied to only the original images, we refer to it as naive collaborative representation, naive L1LS, naive FISTA, and naive PALM, respectively. We also experimentally compare the multiple representations with Gabor feature to show the advantage of the new representation. The corresponding comparison experiment is implemented by just first replacing the new representation of the presented method by the Gabor feature, and by then running the other procedures of the presented method. The same four classification algorithms, i.e., collaborative representation, L1LS, FISTA, and PALM are also used as classifiers. One can exploit the Gabor wavelet with a certain scale and orientation to perform feature extraction. In the experiments, we select an optimal Gabor filter whose wavelength is 5, and orientation is $\pi/2$ to present Gabor feature.

Table 3.1 Rate of classification errors (%) on the COIL100 dataset. Reprinted from Xu et al. (2015), with permission from Elsevier

Number of training samples per class	1	2	3	4
Multiple representations with collaborative representation	51.92	52.56	52.61	52.38
Collaborative representation + Gabor	55.83	56.19	55.80	55.79
Naive collaborative representation	55.37	55.74	55.48	55.24
Multiple representations with L1LS	54.66	53.96	53.86	53.57
L1LS + Gabor	57.96	57.24	56.51	56.37
Naive L1LS	58.00	57.00	56.42	56.25
Multiple representations with FISTA	52.00	53.56	54.91	55.65
FISTA + Gabor	55.04	59.79	63.06	64.32
Naive FISTA	53.49	54.26	55.35	55.88
Multiple representations with PALM	54.86	54.34	54.17	53.84
PALM + Gabor	58.13	57.39	56.67	56.93
Naive PALM	58.04	57.13	56.51	56.60

Table 3.2 Rate of classification errors (%) on the ORL dataset. Reprinted from Xu et al. (2015), with permission from Elsevier

Number of training samples per class	1	2	3	4	5
Multiple representations with collaborative representation	23.06	12.50	11.43	8.75	8.50
Collaborative representation + Gabor	33.61	19.38	17.86	12.92	15.00
Naive collaborative representation	31.94	16.56	13.93	10.83	11.50
Multiple representations with L1LS	25.28	15.31	14.64	11.67	12.50
L1LS + Gabor	32.78	20.00	19.29	13.75	18.50
Naive L1LS	33.33	19.69	18.93	14.58	13.50
Multiple representations with FISTA	25.28	18.75	16.07	10.42	10.50
FISTA + Gabor	34.17	24.06	29.29	28.75	30.00
Naive FISTA	31.67	18.44	16.79	12.08	13.50
Multiple representations with PALM	26.11	15.63	14.29	12.50	12.00
PALM + Gabor	33.33	19.69	18.57	14.58	19.50
Naive PALM	33.33	19.69	18.57	13.75	13.00

3.4.5.1   Experiment on the COIL100 Dataset

In this subsection, the COIL100 dataset is selected to compare the above methods. The COIL100 dataset contains 7200 images taken from 100 classes and each class has 72 images. Images were taken from several angels. The size of each image is 128×128. They are all converted into gray images in advance. Figure 3.5 shows some images of a class in the COIL100 dataset.

The first 1, 2, 3, and 4 images of each class were selected as training samples, and the remaining samples were treated as test samples, respectively. Table 3.1 shows classification results of different methods on the COIL100 database. We see

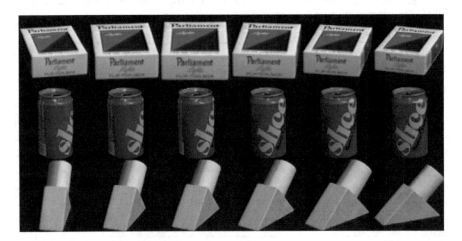

Fig. 3.5 Image examples of a class in the COIL100 dataset

that when collaborative representation, L1LS, FISTA, and PALM are integrated with the multiple representations method; the classification performance was greatly improved. This means that the multiple representations method is very useful for representing the images, and the novel representation feature is excellent in image classification.

3.4.5.2 Experiments on the ORL Dataset

In this subsection, the above methods were compared on the ORL face dataset. There are 400 face images in the ORL face dataset; it contains 40 subjects and each subject has 10 face images. Images of some subjects were taken at different time and have varying lighting, facial expressions (open/closed eyes, smiling/not smiling), and facial details (glasses/no glasses). All images were taken against a dark homogeneous background with the subjects in an upright, frontal position (with tolerance for some side movement). Each image was resized to a 56 by 46 image matrix by using the down-sampling algorithm. Figure 3.6 shows some pictures of two subjects in the ORL dataset.

The first 1, 2, 3, 4, and 5 face images of each subject were chose as training samples, and the remaining samples were treated as test samples, respectively. Table 3.2 shows classification results of above representation-based methods on the ORL dataset. From Table 3.2, we can find that, when the multiple representations method is integrated with collaborative representation, L1LS, FISTA, PALM, lower rates of classification errors can always be obtained. For example, when naive collaborative representation obtains rates of classification errors of 31.94, 16.56, and 13.93 % for 1, 2, and 3 training samples per class, the integration of the multiple representations method with collaborative representation, respectively, obtains rates of classification errors of 23.06, 12.50, and 11.43 % under the same conditions. This demonstrates that the use of the novel multiple representations of original images enable the classification accuracy to be greatly improved. We also easily find the presented novel multiple representations obtains lower rate of classification errors than the Gabor feature when four classification algorithms are used as classifies.

Fig. 3.6 Image examples of two subjects in the ORL dataset

3.5 Summary

This chapter gives a brief summarization to the sparse representation and dictionary learning. Based on the sparse representation, we present a novel multiple representations for image classification. In the experiments, some sparse representation methods are compared. The experiments show that the novel representations of images are complementary to the original images in representing the object and the combination of these two kinds of representations can lead to a very satisfactory accuracy for image classification and face recognition.

References

M. Aharon, M. Elad, A. Bruckstein, K-SVD: an algorithm for designing of overcomplete dictionaries for sparse representation Technion—Israel Inst. of Technology, 2005. IEEE Trans. Signal Process. **54**(11), 4311–4322 (2006)

E. Amaldi, V. Kann, On the approximability of minimizing nonzero variables or unsatisfied relations in linear systems. Theoret. Comput. Sci. **209**(1), 237–260 (1998)

E.J. Candes, J.K. Romberg, T. Tao, Stable signal recovery from incomplete and inaccurate measurements. Commun. Pure Appl. Math. **59**(8), 1207–1223 (2006)

E.J. Candes, T. Tao, Near-optimal signal recovery from random projections: universal encoding strategies? IEEE Trans. Inf. Theory **52**(12), 5406–5425 (2006)

J. Chen, S. Shan, C. He, G. Zhao, I.N.E.N.M. Pietik, X. CHEN, W. GAO, WLD: a robust local image descriptor. IEEE Trans. Pattern Anal. Mach. Intell. **32**(9), 1705–1720 (2010)

C. Ding, D. Zhou, X. He, H. Zha, in *R 1-PCA: rotational invariant L 1-norm principal component analysis for robust subspace factorization*. Proceedings of the 23rd International Conference on Machine Learning (ACM, 2006), pp. 281–288

D.L. Donoho, M. Elad, Optimally sparse representation in general (nonorthogonal) dictionaries via $\ell 1$ minimization. Proc. Natl. Acad. Sci. **100**(5), 2197–2202 (2003)

P. Gong, C. Zhang, Z. Lu, J.Z. Huang, J. Ye, in *A general iterative shrinkage and thresholding algorithm for non-convex regularized optimization problems*. Proceedings of International Conference on Machine Learning (NIH Public Access, 2013), p. 37

S. Guo, Z. Wang, Q. Ruan, Enhancing sparsity via ℓp $(0 < p < 1)$ minimization for robust face recognition. Neurocomputing **99**, 592–602 (2013)

P.-C. Hsieh, P.-C. Tung, Shadow compensation based on facial symmetry and image average for robust face recognition. Neurocomputing **73**(13), 2708–2717 (2010)

R. Jenatton, J. Mairal, F.R. Bach, G.R. Obozinski, in *Proximal methods for sparse hierarchical dictionary learning*. Proceedings of the 27th International Conference on Machine Learning (ICML-10) (2010). pp. 487–494

Z. Jiang, Z. Lin, L.S. Davis, in *Learning a discriminative dictionary for sparse coding via label consistent K-SVD*. Proceedings of IEEE Conference on Computer Vision and Pattern Recognition (IEEE, 2011), pp. 1697–1704

H. Luo, H. Wu, G. Chen, On the convergence of augmented Lagrangian methods for nonlinear semidefinite programming. J. Global Optim. **54**(3), 599–618 (2012)

Q. Lyu, Z. Lin, Y. She, C. Zhang, A comparison of typical ℓp minimization algorithms. Neurocomputing **119**, 413–424 (2013)

J. Mairal, F. Bach, J. Ponce, G. Sapiro, Online learning for matrix factorization and sparse coding. J. Mach. Learn. Res. **11**, 19–60 (2010)

J. Mairal, J. Ponce, G. Sapiro, A. Zisserman, F.R. Bach, in *Supervised dictionary learning*. Proceedings of Advances in Neural Information Processing Systems (2009). pp. 1033–1040

I. Naseem, R. Togneri, M. Bennamoun, Robust regression for face recognition. Pattern Recogn. **45**(1), 104–118 (2012)

D. Needel, R. Vershynin, *Signal Recovery from Inaccurate and Incomplete Measurements via Regularized Orthogonal Matching Pursuit* (2007). preprint

S.T. Roweis, L.K. Saul, Nonlinear dimensionality reduction by locally linear embedding. Science **290**(5500), 2323–2326 (2000)

B. S.P. (2008). http://web.stanford.edu/~boyd/l1_ls/

A. Shrivastava, J.K. Pillai, V.M. Patel, R. Chellappa, in *Learning discriminative dictionaries with partially labeled data*. Proceedings of IEEE International Conference on Image Processing (IEEE, 2012), pp. 3113–3116

I. Smielik, K.-D. Kuhnert, in *Statistical dependence of pixel intensities for pattern recognition*. Proceedings of IEEE International Conference on Industrial Technology (IEEE, 2013), pp. 1179–1183

J.B. Tenenbaum, V. de Silva, J.C. Langford, A global geometric framework for nonlinear dimensionality reduction. Science **290**(5500), 2319–2323 (2000)

H. Wang, F. Nie, W. Cai, H. Huang, in *Semi-supervised robust dictionary learning via efficient l-norms minimization*. Proceedings of IEEE International Conference on Computer Vision (IEEE, 2013), pp. 1145–1152

H. Wang, C. Yuan, W. Hu, C. Sun, Supervised class-specific dictionary learning for sparse modeling in action recognition. Pattern Recogn. **45**(11), 3902–3911 (2012)

Y. Xu, D. Zhang, J. Yang, J.-Y. Yang, A two-phase test sample sparse representation method for use with face recognition. IEEE Trans. Circuits Syst. Video Technol. **21**(9), 1255–1262 (2011)

Y. Xu, B. Zhang, Z. Zhong, Multiple representations and sparse representation for image classification. Pattern Recogn. **68**, 9–14 (2015)

Z. Xu, X. Chang, F. Xu, H. Zhang, regularization: a thresholding representation theory and a fast solver. IEEE Trans. Neural Networks Learn. Syst. **23**(7), 1013–1027 (2012)

M. Yang, L. Zhang, X. Feng, D. Zhang, Sparse representation based fisher discrimination dictionary learning for image classification. Int. J. Comput. Vision **109**(3), 209–232 (2014)

K. Yu, T. Zhang, Y. Gong, in *Nonlinear learning using local coordinate coding*. Proceedings of Advances in Neural Information Processing Systems (2009). pp. 2223–2231

G. Zhang, Z. Jiang, L.S. Davis, in *Online semi-supervised discriminative dictionary learning for sparse representation*. Computer Vision–ACCV 2012 (Springer, 2013)

L. Zhang, M. Yang, X. Feng, in *Sparse representation or collaborative representation: which helps face recognition?* Proceedings of IEEE International Conference on Computer Vision (IEEE, 2011), pp. 471–478

Q. Zhang, B. Li, in *Discriminative K-SVD for dictionary learning in face recognition*. Proceedings of IEEE Conference on Computer Vision and Pattern Recognition (IEEE, 2010), pp. 2691–2698

Z. Zhang, L. Wang, Q. Zhu, Z. Liu, Y. Chen, Noise modeling and representation based classification methods for face recognition. Neurocomputing **148**, 420–429 (2015a)

Z. Zhang, Y. Xu, J. Yang, X. Li, D. Zhang, A survey of sparse representation: algorithms and applications. IEEE Access **3**, 490–530 (2015b)

M. Zhou, H. Chen, J. Paisley, L. Ren, L. Li, Z. Xing, D. Dunson, G. Sapiro, L. Carin, Nonparametric Bayesian dictionary learning for analysis of noisy and incomplete images. IEEE Trans. Image Process. **21**(1), 130–144 (2012)

Part III
Discriminative Feature Extraction and Matching for Palmprint Authentication

Chapter 4
Discriminative Features for Palmprint Authentication

Abstract As an emerging biometric technology, palmprint authentication has attracted considerable attention in recent years. In this field, coding-based methods, which extract the coding features of palmprint images, are among the most promising palmprint authentication methods. In this chapter, we first give a brief review of palmprint authentication methods in Sect. 4.1. Section 4.2 describes the conventional coding-based palmprint identification methods. In Sects. 4.3 and 4.4, two improved coding-based palmprint authentication methods are presented.

4.1 Introduction

Compared with other biometric characteristics, such as face, iris, and ear, palmprint identification has the advantages of a low-price capture device, fast speed, good stability, and high accuracy. Thus, palmprint identification is very competitive among biometrics-based authentication solutions.

In recent years, various palmprint identification methods have been proposed. The existing palmprint identification methods can be divided into five groups: a line-based method (Huang et al. 2008), coding-based methods (Zhang et al. 2003; Yue et al. 2008; Yue et al. 2009), a subspace-based method (Hu et al. 2007), a representation-based method (Xu et al. 2013), and a scale-invariant feature transform (SIFT)-based method (Lowe 2004).

In most palms, there are three salient and clear lines: the heart line, head line, and life line, which are the longest and widest lines in the palmprint image and have stable line shapes and positions. On the base of these prior characteristics, line-based methods extract the palmprint principal lines and then use them to perform palmprint verification and identification (Huang et al. 2008). Palmprint principal lines can be extracted by using the Gabor filter, Sobel operation, or morphological operation. Huang et al. (2008) proposed an effective principal lines extraction algorithm, which is called the modified finite Radon transform (MFRAT) and is able to provide stable performance for palmprint verification.

© Springer Science+Business Media Singapore 2016
D. Zhang et al., *Discriminative Learning in Biometrics*,
DOI 10.1007/978-981-10-2056-8_4

Coding-based methods first perform a filtering operation on the palmprint image, and then use some rules to code the filtered result and obtain the characteristic code of each pixel of the palmprint image. Finally, the coding-based palmprint identification methods use this code to represent the palmprint image for matching and identification. The used filtering, coding rule, and matching algorithm have a great influence on the performance of palmprint identification. The PalmCode (Zhang et al. 2003), FusionCode (Kong et al. 2006), DoGCode (Wu et al. 2006), CompCode (Kong and Zhang 2004), and Ordinal Code (Sun et al. 2005) are typical coding-based methods in the field of palmprint identification.

Subspace-based methods try to find an orthogonal subspace that preserves the maximum variance of the original data and identifies the unknown palmprint in the subspace. The Eigenpalm and Fisherpalm (Cheung et al. 2006; Ribaric and Fratric 2005), which use the principal component analysis (PCA) and linear discriminant analysis (LDA) algorithms to find the subspace, are two well-known subspace-based methods for palmprint identification. The two-dimensional principal component analysis (2-DPCA) (Sang et al. 2009), two-dimensional linear discriminant analysis (2-DLDA) (Du et al. 2011), and two-dimensional locality preserving projection (2-DLPP) (Hu et al. 2007) have also been used for palmprint recognition.

Representation-based methods, such as the sparse representation classification (SRC) method, collaborative representation classification (CRC) method, linear regression classification (LRC) method, two-phase test sample sparse representation (TPTSSR) method, use all training samples or training samples of each class to represent the unknown sample, and identify the query sample as the class with the minimum residual of representation (Naseem et al. 2010; Xu et al. 2015; Zhang et al. 2011; Xu et al. 2011; Xu et al. 2013).

SIFT-based methods transform image data into scale-invariant coordinates for contactless palmprint identification (Lowe 2004; Morales et al. 2011). SIFT-based methods usually use a difference-of-Gaussian filtering to obtain potential interest points in the whole image for palmprint identification. The SIFT features are invariant to image scaling and rotation and partially invariant to the change of projection and illumination. Thus, SIFT-based methods can provide good performance for contactless palmprint identification with various scaling, rotations, and illuminations.

Because the coding-based methods, which encode the responses of a bank of filters into bitwise features, have been very successful in palmprint identification and are easy to implement, in this chapter we will mainly focus on the coding-based palmprint identification methods. In addition, some improved coding-based methods are also presented in this chapter.

4.2   Conventional Coding-Based Palmprint Identification Method

As introduced in Sect. 4.1, the filter, coding rule, and distance measure algorithm have a great influence on the performance of the palmprint identification. Therefore, in this section, we will introduce some popular coding-based methods for the above three aspects.

4.2.1   Filters

There are three types of filters: Gabor filter, Gaussian filter, and second derivative of Gaussian filter, that have good performance on line detection and are widely used in the field of palmprint identification.

4.2.1.1   Gabor Filter

Because the Gabor filter has good properties on extracting features from arbitrary directions and scales, the Gabor filter is widely used for texture extraction. Zhang et al. (2003) first proposed a coding-based method that uses a Gabor filter to extract the palmprint features for palmprint recognition. In the field of palmprint identification, the Gabor function is usually defined as follows (Lee 1996):

$$\psi(x, y, x_0, y_0, \omega, \theta, \kappa) = \frac{\omega}{\sqrt{2\pi}\kappa} e^{-\frac{\omega^2}{8\kappa^2}(4x'^2 + y'^2)} \left(e^{i\omega x'} - e^{-\frac{\kappa^2}{2}} \right), \tag{4.1}$$

where $x' = (x - x_0)\cos\theta + (y - y_0)\sin\theta$, $y' = -(x - x_0)\sin\theta + (y - y_0)\cos\theta$, (x_0, y_0) is the center of the Gabor function, ω is the radial frequency in radians per unit length, and θ is the orientation of the Gabor functions in radians. In the Gabor function $\kappa = \sqrt{2\ln 2}\left(\frac{2^\delta + 1}{2^\delta - 1}\right)$, where δ is the half-amplitude bandwidth of the frequency response. When σ and δ are fixed, ω can be obtained from $\omega = \kappa/\sigma$. The Gabor function of Eq. (4.1) is reformulated based on neurophysiology and wavelet theory. The only difference from the general Gabor filter is that the choices of parameters are limited by neurophysiological findings and the direct current of the functions is removed. Because palm lines are negative type, Kong and Zhang (2004) only use the negative real part of the Gabor filter for palmprint identification,

$$\psi(x, y, x_0, y_0, \omega, \theta, \kappa) = \frac{-\omega}{\sqrt{2\pi}\kappa} e^{-\frac{\omega^2}{8\kappa^2}(4x'^2 + y'^2)} \left(\cos(\omega x') - e^{-\frac{\kappa^2}{2}} \right). \tag{4.2}$$

Figure 4.1a shows the shape of the Gabor filter.

Fig. 4.1 Shapes of different
filters (Yue et al. 2008).
a Gabor filter. **b** Gaussian
filter. **c** Second derivative of
Gaussian filter

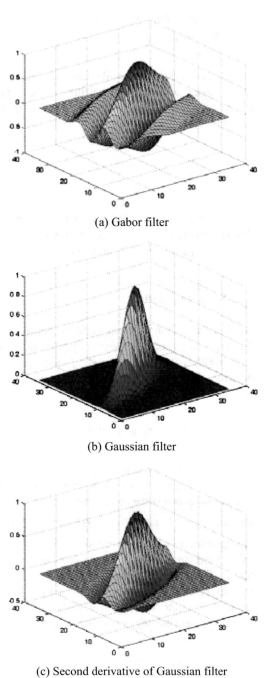

(a) Gabor filter

(b) Gaussian filter

(c) Second derivative of Gaussian filter

4.2.1.2   Gaussian Filter

In the field of image processing and pattern recognition, the Gaussian filter is usually adopted for image smoothing and removal of noise. The 2-D elliptical Gaussian filter has good performance in preserving the image edges, and can be used for the enhancement of palm lines. The 2-D elliptical Gaussian filter is formulated as follows:

$$f(x, y, x_0, y_0, \delta_x, \delta_y, \theta) = \exp\left(-\left(\frac{x'}{\delta_x}\right)^2 - \left(\frac{y'}{\delta_y}\right)^2\right), \qquad (4.3)$$

where x', y', x, y, and θ are the same as defined in Eq. (4.1), and δ_x and δ_y are the horizontal and vertical scales of the Gaussian filter, respectively. Figure 4.1b shows the shape of the real part of a typical Gaussian filter.

4.2.1.3   Second Derivative of Gaussian Filter

The second derivative of Gaussian filter is defined as

$$f(x, y, x_0, y_0, \delta, \theta) = \frac{(x'^2 - \delta^2)(y'^2 - \delta^2)}{2\pi\delta^{10}} \exp\left(-\frac{x'^2 + y'^2}{\delta^2}\right), \qquad (4.4)$$

where x', y', x, y, and θ also are the same as defined in Eq. (4.1). The shape of the second derivative of Gaussian filter is shown in Fig. 4.1c. From Fig. 4.1, we can see that the Gabor filter and second derivative of Gaussian filter have similar shapes.

4.2.2   Coding Schemes

In 1993, Daugman (1993) first proposed a coding algorithm for iris recognition. Then, several researchers extended the coding method to palmprint identification and proposed some popular coding-based palmprint identification algorithms, such as PalmCode (Zhang et al. 2003) and FusionCode (Kong et al. 2006; Kong and Zhang 2004; Zhang et al. 2003). Recently, some novel coding schemes, such as competitive code (Kong and Zhang 2004) and ordinal code, were proposed for palmprint identification. Because the competitive code method and ordinal code method were reported to have better performance than others, we compare only these two coding schemes in this section.

4.2.2.1   Competitive Coding

The competitive coding scheme chooses the dominant orientations of palmprint lines as recognition features for palmprint identification. Suppose $I(x, y)$ is the preprocessed palm image, $F(x, y, \theta)$ is the filter with orientation θ, the competitive rule is defined as

$$j = \arg \min_{\theta} \{I(x, y) \otimes F(x, y, \theta)\}, \tag{4.5}$$

where j is the winning index, and $\otimes$ denotes the convolution operator. According to the neurophysiological findings, simple cells are sensitive to specific orientations with approximate bandwidths of $\pi/6$. Thus, the original competitive coding scheme used six filters with different orientations $\theta_p = p\pi/6$, $p = \{0, 1, \ldots, 5\}$ for the competition. Figure 4.2 shows the procedure of feature extraction and representation of the competitive coding scheme.

Suppose that six orientations are used, the competitive coding scheme adopts a bitwise representation style to represent the winning index or dominant orientations of each pixel. As shown in Fig. 4.3, the winning index can be represented by three bits. In this way, the angular distance of two competitive codes of two palms can be efficiently computed with Boolean operators (Kong and Zhang 2004).

4.2.2.2   Ordinal Coding

Similar to the competitive coding scheme, the ordinal coding scheme also encodes each pixel as three bits for palmprint identification. But for each bit representation,

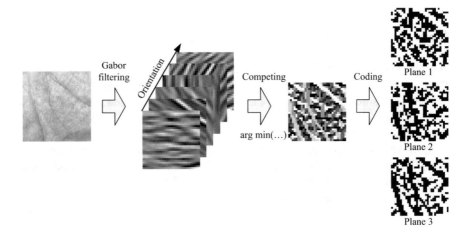

Fig. 4.2 Feature extraction of the competitive coding scheme. Reprinted from Yue et al. (2009), with permission from Elsevier

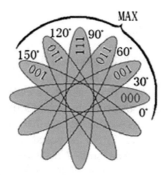

Fig. 4.3 Bitwise representation of the competitive code scheme (Yue et al. 2008)

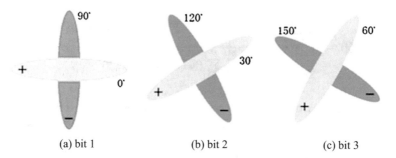

(a) bit 1   (b) bit 2   (c) bit 3

Fig. 4.4 Illustration of the ordinal coding scheme (Yue et al. 2008). **a** bit 1. **b** bit 2. **c** bit 3

the ordinal coding scheme only considers the relative magnitude of two orthogonal line-like palmprint image regions. The ordinal coding rule is defined as follows:

$$
\begin{aligned}
OF(\theta) &= \iint I(x,y)F(x,y,\theta)\mathrm{d}x\mathrm{d}y - \iint I(x,y)F\left(x,y,\theta+\frac{\pi}{2}\right)\mathrm{d}x\mathrm{d}y. \\
&= \iint I(x,y)\left(F(x,y,\theta) - F\left(x,y,\theta+\frac{\pi}{2}\right)\right)\mathrm{d}x\mathrm{d}y.
\end{aligned}
\tag{4.6}
$$

Figure 4.4 shows the ordinal coding scheme. For a preprocessed palmprint image, three ordinal filters, $OF(0)$, $OF(\pi/6)$, and $OF(\pi/3)$ are performed, and three-bit codes are obtained to represent the feature of each pixel.

Note that the code size of both coding schemes is the same: for an image, the code length of each pixel is three bits. However, compared with the competitive coding scheme, the ordinal code scheme only uses three convolution operations to encode the palm image, which makes it save half of the time for feature extraction. Furthermore, three bits can encode $2^3 = 8$ different patterns, while the competitive code scheme only has six patterns.

4.2.3 Distance Measure

Several distance measures have been proposed for coding-based palmprint identification methods. For example, Kong and Zhang (2004) used the minimum angle required to rotate in the clockwise or counterclockwise sense to be the same as the other orientation as the distance measure. Jia et al. (2008) calculated the distance by the orientation equivalence, which examines the two orientations to check if they are the same or not. (Guo et al. 2010) proposed a unified distance measure to compare different orientations. The unified distance of two orientations can be viewed as a weighted sum of the angular distance and orientation equivalence.

Kong and Zhang (2004) used the following formula to calculate the angular distance:

$$D(P,Q) = \frac{\sum\limits_{y=1}^{M} \sum\limits_{x=1}^{N} \sum\limits_{i=0}^{2} (P_i^b(x,y) \otimes Q_i^b(x,y)) \cap (P_M(x,y) \cap Q_M(x,y))}{3 * \sum\limits_{y=1}^{M} \sum\limits_{x=1}^{N} P_M(x,y) \cap Q_M(x,y)}, \tag{4.7}$$

where P and Q are two competitive codes of two palms, $P_i^b (Q_i^b)$ is the i-th bit plane of P (Q), $\otimes$ is the bitwise exclusive OR operator, and $\cap$ is the bitwise AND operator. P_M and Q_M are the corresponding masks of P and Q, respectively. The masks are used to record the palmprint pixels (Zhang et al. 2003). Because the orientation is in the range $[0, \pi)$, it is obvious that the maximum angular distance is $\pi/2$ and the minimum angular distance is 0.

The robust line orientation code (RLOC) method also represents one orientation feature by three bits. The orientation equivalence can then be computed by

$$D_{D\_o} = (P_0^b \otimes Q_0^b)|(P_1^b \otimes Q_1^b)|(P_2^b \otimes Q_2^b), \tag{4.8}$$

where | is the bitwise OR operator.

4.3 Fuzzy C-Means-Based Palmprint Authentication

4.3.1 Orientations Selection Problem in Competitive Code

The original competitive coding scheme simply uses six Gabor filters with different orientations of $\theta_p = p\pi/6$, $p = \{0, 1, \ldots, 5\}$, and thus ignores the orientation distribution characteristics of palm lines. Because the orientations of palmprint lines are not uniformly distributed, the significance of different orientations for palmprint representations would vary greatly. We verified this hypothesis on a gallery of PolyU palmprints from the palmprints database that were captured under similar conditions. The gallery contains more than 4000 palmprint images from 200 palms of 100 persons. First, we performed 180 Gabor filters with orientations of 0, 1, ..., 179 degrees on the palmprint image, and then using the competitive rule computed the winning index of orientation. Figure 4.5a shows the statistical distribution of winning indices. The horizontal axis denotes the winning index of orientation, and the vertical axis represents the corresponding percentage of the winning index. Figure 4.5b is another representation of Fig. 4.5a using the polar coordinate system. In Fig. 4.5b, the range of angles is [0,180), which starts from the horizontal axis and grows clockwise, and different values of the radius represent the percentage of the winning index.

Figure 4.5b shows two evident characteristics. The first is that the top and bottom parts are approximately symmetric. This means for the left and right palms of a person, orientations of palmprint lines are roughly symmetric. The second is that the orientations of palmprint lines are not uniformly distributed. There are several distinct peaks observed from the orientation distribution of palm lines. For example, there are four peaks around 40, 70, 110, and 140 degrees, which approximately correspond to the life line and head line on the left and right palms, respectively. Figure 4.5 shows that two nonevident peaks are around 30° and 160°.

In the determination of the orientation of each Gabor filter, two factors should be taken into account. First, the significance of the orientations of palm lines is not the same, and the orientations with larger percentage are relatively more significant for palmprint representation and recognition. Thus, the orientations selection problem can be viewed as a quantization problem of 1-D data. The selected orientations should be dominant with the minimum quantization error. Second, because the angular distances of every two neighbor orientations are assumed to be equal in

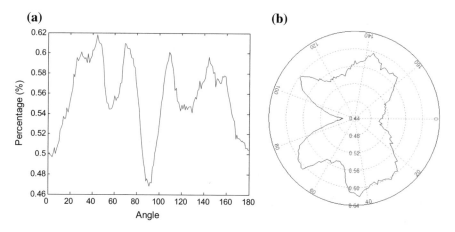

Fig. 4.5 The statistical distribution of orientations of palmprint lines. The angle starts from the horizontal axis and increases clockwise. **a** Shown in the Cartesian coordinate system, **b** shown in the polar coordinate system. Reprinted from Yue et al. (2009), with permission from Elsevier

competitive code, the selected orientations should have the smallest similarity and the largest separation from each other.

4.3.2 Fuzzy C-Means-Based Orientations Selection

In this section, we present a modified fuzzy C-means (FCM) algorithm to overcome the problem discussed in Sect. 4.3.1. First, the difference between two orientations should be measured using the sine distance rather than the Euclidean distance. Thus, we modify the objective function and the updating rule according to the sine distance. Second, to promote the separation of cluster centers, a regularization term is further integrated into the objective function. With these improvements, the modified FCM algorithm is expected to be more suitable for the orientation selection problem described in Sect. 4.3.1.

FCM allows a data point to belong to multiple clusters and all of the cluster centers can be influenced by a data point through the membership matrix. It has a distinct advantage over hard C-means when the data are not well separated (Bezdek 2013). By virtue of these features, FCM has been successfully applied to color quantization (Özdemir and Akarun 2001), image segmentation (Cheng et al. 1998), and gene expression data analysis (Dembélé and Kastner 2003). For our orientation selection problem, the data will be clustered as the orientation distribution data, as shown in Fig. 4.5. Obviously, the data are not well separated and embedded clusters might overlap each other. Therefore, FCM would be a good choice for this problem. The input to the FCM algorithm is the 180 orientations and their corresponding percentages, and the goal is to find c cluster centers as the selected orientations.

To employ the FCM algorithm, we first formally define the distance between two orientations. Suppose α and β are two orientations, $\lambda_{cw}(\alpha, \beta)$ and $\lambda_{ccw}(\alpha, \beta)$ denote the minimum angle, one orientation is required to rotate α in the counterclockwise and clockwise sense to be the same as β, i.e.,

$$\lambda_{cw}(\alpha, \beta) = (\alpha - \beta) \bmod 180, \tag{4.9}$$

$$\lambda_{ccw}(\alpha, \beta) = (\beta - \alpha) \bmod 180. \tag{4.10}$$

The relative orientation of α with respect to β is then defined as:

$$\lambda(\alpha, \beta) = \min(\lambda_{cw}(\alpha, \beta), \lambda_{ccw}(\alpha, \beta)). \tag{4.11}$$

Note that $\lambda_{cw}(\alpha, \beta) + \lambda_{ccw}(\alpha, \beta) = 180$ and $\sin(\lambda_{cw}(\alpha, \beta)) = \sin(\lambda_{ccw}(\alpha, \beta))$, then the sine distance between two orientations is

$$d(\alpha, \beta) = |\sin \lambda(\alpha, \beta)| = |\sin(\alpha - \beta)|. \tag{4.12}$$

The value of d is in the range $[0, 1]$. Note that this distance function is specially designed for the orientation data, and it is a periodic function with a period of 180°.

Suppose x_j and w_j, $j = 1, 2, \ldots, n$ are the orientation and its corresponding percentage, respectively. y_i, $i = 1, \ldots, c$ is the center of each cluster. The objective function of the FCM algorithm is defined as follows:

$$J = \sum_{j=1}^{n} \sum_{i=1}^{c} u_{ij}^m w_j d_{ij}^2, \tag{4.13}$$

where $d_{ij} = d(x_j, y_i)$ is the angular distance from data point x_j to the center of the i-th cluster, m is the fuzziness parameter, $1 < m < \infty$. u_{ij} denotes the degree of data points i belonging to cluster j, which is a nonnegative value and subjected to

$$\sum_{i=1}^{c} u_{ij} = 1 \; \forall j = 1, \ldots, n. \tag{4.14}$$

Using the Lagrange multiplier method, minimization of the objective function results in the membership function (after normalization)

$$u_{ij} = \left(\sum_{k=1}^{c} \left(\frac{w_j d_{ij}^2}{w_j d_{kj}^2} \right)^{1/(m-1)} \right)^{-1}, \tag{4.15}$$

and the center of each cluster is obtained as follows:

$$
\begin{aligned}
\frac{\partial J_i}{\partial y_i} &= \sum_{j=1}^{n} u_{ij}^m w_j 2 \sin(y_i - x_j) \cos(y_i - x_j) \\
&= \sum_{j=1}^{n} u_{ij}^m w_j \sin(2y_i - 2x_j) \\
&= \sum_{j=1}^{n} u_{ij}^m w_j (\sin 2y_i \cos 2x_j - \sin 2x_j \cos 2y_i) \\
&= \sum_{j=1}^{n} u_{ij}^m w_j \cos 2x_j \sin 2y_i - \sum_{j=1}^{n} u_{ij}^m w_j \sin 2x_j \cos 2y_i \\
&= A_i \sin 2y_i - B_i \cos 2y_i,
\end{aligned} \tag{4.16}
$$

where

$$A_i = \sum_{j=1}^{n} u_{ij}^m w_j \cos 2x_j, \qquad (4.17)$$

$$B_i = \sum_{j=1}^{n} u_{ij}^m w_j \sin 2x_j. \qquad (4.18)$$

Letting $\frac{\partial J_i}{\partial y_i} = 0$ yields $A_i \sin 2y_i - B_i \cos 2y_i = 0$,

$$\frac{A_i}{\sqrt{A_i^2 + B_i^2}} \sin 2y_i - \frac{B_i}{\sqrt{A_i^2 + B_i^2}} \cos 2y_i = 0. \qquad (4.19)$$

Letting $\sin \alpha = \frac{B_i}{\sqrt{A_i^2 + B_i^2}}$ and $\cos \alpha = \frac{A_i}{\sqrt{A_i^2 + B_i^2}}$, $\alpha \in [0, 360)$, then

$$\sin 2y_i \cos \alpha - \cos 2y_i \sin \alpha = 0, \sin(2y_i - \alpha) = 0, y_i = \frac{\alpha}{2}, \qquad (4.20)$$

where y_i takes a value from 0 to 180°.

After setting the initial cluster centers, the FCM algorithm iterates through the update rule defined in Eqs. (4.15) and (4.20), and finally converges to either a local minimum or saddle point of the objective function (Bezdek et al. 1987). The cluster centers y_i, $i = 1, \ldots, c$, are the orientations best representing the distribution data.

To make the orientations distribute evenly in the circular plane, we integrate a regularization term into the objective function Eq. (4.13). This term measures the cost associated with a function of the solution that embeds the requirement of separation maximization (Poggio and Girosi 1990). Because all of the cluster centers locate at a circular plane, we can simplify it by just considering the neighboring cluster centers. The separation of one cluster center from other cluster centers can be measured by the following cost function:

$$s_i = d^2(y_{i-1}, y_i) + d^2(y_i, y_{i+1}), \qquad (4.21)$$

and the separation of all the cluster centers is given by

$$S = \frac{2}{c} \left(d^2(y_c, y_1) + \sum_{i=1}^{c-1} d^2(y_{i+1}, y_i) \right), \qquad (4.22)$$

subject to

$$\lambda(y_c, y_1) + \sum_{i=1}^{c-1} \lambda(y_{i+1}, y_i) = 180. \qquad (4.23)$$

Integrating this regularization term into the FCM algorithm, the generalized objective function is defined as

$$J = \frac{1}{n} \sum_{j=1}^{n} \sum_{i=1}^{c} u_{ij}^{m} w_j d_{ij}^2 + \lambda S, \tag{4.24}$$

where $\lambda (0 \le \lambda < \infty)$ is a tunable regularization parameter that controls the balance of representation of data and separation of cluster centers. When it equals 0, the objective function Eq. (4.24) is the same as Eq. (4.13), which means that the cluster result only depends on the representation of data and does not consider the separation of cluster centers. When it equals ∞, the cluster result is completely controlled by the separation cost function. The clustering result will be determined by the prior distribution and forced to have the maximum separation cost.

Using the Lagrange multiplier method on objective function Eq. (4.24), we can obtain the update functions of u_{ij} and y_i. Because u_{ij} is independent of S, the update function of u_{ij} is the same as Eq. (4.15). The update function y_i is obtained in a similar way as Eqs. (4.16)–(4.20), while A_i and B_i are defined as follows:

$$A_i = \left(\frac{1}{n} \sum_{j=1}^{n} u_{ij}^{m} w_j \cos 2x_j + \frac{2\lambda}{c} (\cos 2y_{i+1} + \cos 2y_{i-1}) \right), \tag{4.25}$$

$$B_i = \left(\frac{1}{n} \sum_{j=1}^{n} u_{ij}^{m} w_j \sin 2x_j + \frac{2\lambda}{c} (\sin 2y_{i+1} + \sin 2y_{i-1}) \right). \tag{4.26}$$

In conclusion, given the statistical distribution of winning indices and the initialization of the cluster centers, the presented FCM-based method iteratively updates the membership and the cluster centers using Eqs. (4.15) and (4.20) until convergence. The presented modified FCM method is summarized in Fig. 4.6.

4.3.3 Experimental Results

In this section, the presented method and some state-of-the-art coding-based methods, such as ordinal measure (Sun et al. 2005) and RLOC (Jia et al. 2008), are compared using the Hong Kong PolyU palmprint database (version 2). The database consists of 7752 images of 193 individuals (D. Zhang). The samples of each individual were collected in two sessions, and the average interval between the two sessions was around two months. During each session, each person provides about 10 left palmprint images and 10 right palmprint images. Figure 4.7 shows two palmprint images from the Hong Kong PolyU palmprint database.

```
Input :  Statistical distribution of 180 winning indices (xⱼ,wⱼ) and
         c initial cluster centers yᵢ'
Output : c cluster centers yᵢ
Init : Iter_Num = 0, EPS, MAX_ITER_NUM, λ
```

1   DO

2   　FOR i=1 TO c LET $y_i = y_i'$;

3   　FOR i=1 TO c, j=0 TO 179

4   　　$d_{ij} = \left| \sin(x_j - y_i) \right|$;

5   　FOR i=1 TO c, j=0 TO 179

6   　　$u_{ij} = \left(\sum_{k=1}^{c} \left(\frac{w_j d_{ij}^2}{w_j d_{kj}^2} \right)^{1/(m-1)} \right)^{-1}$;

7   　FOR i=1 TO c

8   　　$A_i = \left(\frac{1}{n} \sum_{j=1}^{n} u_{ij}^m w_j \cos 2x_j + \frac{2\lambda}{c} \left(\cos 2y_{i+1} + \cos 2y_{i-1} \right) \right)$;

9   　　$B_i = \left(\frac{1}{n} \sum_{j=1}^{n} u_{ij}^m w_j \sin 2x_j + \frac{2\lambda}{c} \left(\sin 2y_{i+1} + \sin 2y_{i-1} \right) \right)$;

10 　　Find α, $\alpha \in [0, 360)$, satisfy $\sin\alpha = \frac{B_i}{\sqrt{A_i^2 + B_i^2}}$ and $\cos\alpha \frac{A_i}{\sqrt{A_i^2 + B_i^2}}$;

11 　　$y_i' = \frac{\alpha}{2}$;

12 　Iter_Num = Iter_Num + 1;

13 WHILE Iter_Num < MAX_ITER_NUM AND $\sum_{i=1}^{c} \lambda(y_i', y_i) > EPS$.

Fig. 4.6 The modified FCM algorithm. Reprinted from Yue et al. (2009), with permission from Elsevier

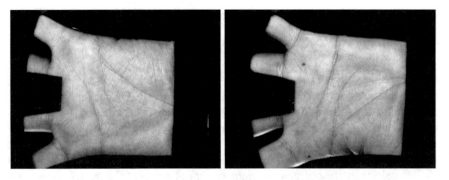

Fig. 4.7 Two typical palmprint images in the PolyU palmprint database. Reprinted from Yue et al. (2009), with permission from Elsevier

4.3.3.1   Preprocessing

Preprocessing is a crucial step in palmprint recognition. The key point of preprocessing is locating stable reference points in the presence of transition and rotation during the capture process. Figure 4.8 shows the main steps of the preprocessing algorithm, which contains five major steps, Gaussian filtering, binarization, morphological operations, boundary tracking, building the coordinate system, and region-of-interest cropping. The morphological operation is used to overcome the broken finger problem caused by shading.

4.3.3.2   Comparison with the Original Competitive Coding Scheme

In this subsection, some experiments are carried out to evaluate the effectiveness of the FCM-based orientation selection strategy. In the experiments, we use the EER value to measure the validity of different palmprint recognition algorithms. The palmprint verification experiment is carried out on the entire palmprint database. All the matching scores of palmprint images are calculated. The matching of palmprint images of different persons is regarded as an impostor matching, while the matching of palmprint images of a person is regarded as a genuine matching. For the PolyU palmprint database, the number of genuine and impostor matchings are 74,068 and 29,968,808, respectively.

First, we tested a wide range of λ values of the FCM-based orientation selection method to examine the influence of regularization parameter λ. The number of clusters was set as six. Each λ can produce six orientations by randomly initialized cluster centers. Figure 4.9 shows the EER value of the FCM-based improved

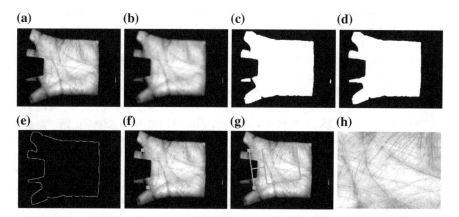

Fig. 4.8 Main preprocessing steps. **a** original image, **b** Gaussian filtering, **c** binarization, **d** morphological operations, **e** boundary tracing, **f** locating reference point, **g** building coordinate system, **h** cropping ROI and rotating. Reprinted from Yue et al. (2009), with permission from Elsevier

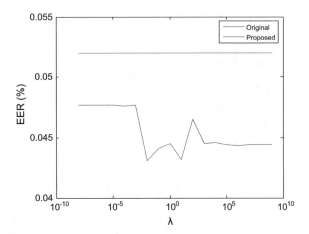

Fig. 4.9 The influence of the parameter λ. Reprinted from Yue et al. (2009), with permission from Elsevier

competitive coding method using Gabor filters with these orientations. When $\lambda \to 0$, the cluster centers are totally dependent on the orientation distribution of palm lines, and the corresponding EER value of the FCM-based orientation selection method is smaller than that of the original competitive code method (0.048 < 0.052 %). When $\lambda \to \infty$, the orientations would be forced to distribute evenly, and the EER value is also smaller (0.044 < 0.052 %). For a wide range of λ values, the orientations selected by the FCM method are consistently better than the original competitive coding scheme, which means that the presented FCM-based method is insensitive to the parameter value. From Fig. 4.9, we set the value of the regularization parameter λ to 10. The EER value of the original competitive coding method is 0.052 %, while the EER value of the FCM-based improved competitive code is 0.043 %, which means about 17.3 % improvement.

Next, we compare the orientations selected by the presented FCM-based method with the original competitive coding scheme. The regularization parameter value is set as $\lambda = 10$. Figure 4.10 shows the orientations selected by the original competitive coding scheme and the presented FCM-based algorithm. Figure 4.10a shows that, for the original competitive code algorithm, the orientations 1, 3, 4, and 5 roughly locate at the valley of the distribution plot. From Fig. 4.10b, after convergence of the FCM algorithm the six cluster centers are 15.174°, 45.171°, 75.170°, 105.170°, 135.170°, and 165.170°. The orientations selected by the presented FCM-based algorithm are significantly different from those of the original competitive coding scheme (average angular distance is 14.83°), and the former orientations are more coincident with the underlying orientation distribution of palmprint lines. The orientations 2, 3, 4, and 5 are very close to the peaks on the distribution plot. In addition, the angular distances between all of the neighbor orientations are almost the same (the standard deviation is 0.0018°), which means that the regularization term we integrated into the classical FCM algorithm works well. Figure 4.11 shows the ROC curves of both methods, which also indicate the improvement of the presented FCM-based orientations selection method. In all

Fig. 4.10 The orientations. Reprinted from Yue et al. (2009), with permission from Elsevier. **a** used by original competitive coding scheme. **b** selected by the presented FCM-based algorithm

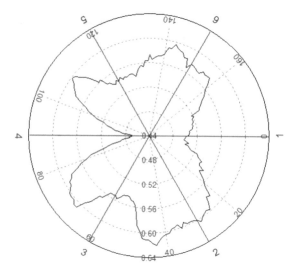

(a) used by original competitive coding scheme

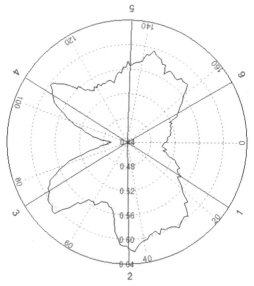

(b) selected by the presented FCM-based algorithm

following experiments, we set the parameter $\lambda = 10$, and name the competitive code method that uses the orientations achieved by this orientation selection strategy as the improved competitive code.

Finally, some experiments were performed to achieve the most suitable number of Gabor filters for competitive coding-based palmprint recognition. In verification

Fig. 4.11 The ROC curves of the original competitive coding scheme and competitive coding scheme with orientations selected by our method. Reprinted from Yue et al. (2009), with permission from Elsevier

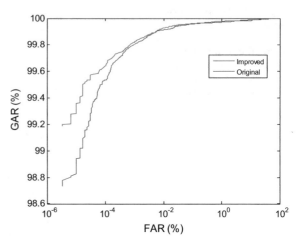

Table 4.1 EER of the competitive code with different numbers of Gabor filters (%)

No. filters	4	6	8	12
EER	0.064	0.043	0.046	0.044

Reprinted from Yue et al. (2009), with permission from Elsevier

experiments, the EER value of the original competitive code with eight filters (orientations start from 0°) is 0.045, which is about 13.46 % less than that for six filters. So we can conclude that for the original competitive code, eight filters perform better than six filters. The probable reason is that the orientations adopted by filters (such as 45°, 67.5°, 112.5°, 135°) are statistically more important according to Fig. 4.5. Thus, these orientations can represent palmprints better and extract more discriminant information. Table 4.1 and Fig. 4.12 show the EER and ROC curves of the improved competitive code, respectively. From Table 4.1 and Fig. 4.12, for the presented modified FCM algorithm, using six orientations can represent palmprints well enough, and increasing the number of filters from six to eight or more will not improve the verification accuracy of the presented FCM-based code scheme. Because the size of competitive code is proportional to the number of filters ($c/2$ bits for each sample point), considering the additional feature size and computational complexity caused by a larger number of filters, six filters would be the best choice.

4.3.3.3 Comparisons with Other Methods

In this subsection, the presented FCM-based competitive coding scheme is compared with several state-of-the-art coding-based palmprint identification methods. Two promising coding-based palmprint recognition methods, i.e., ordinal measure (Sun et al. 2005) and RLOC (Jia et al. 2008), were chosen. The above two

Fig. 4.12 ROC curves of the competitive code with different numbers of Gabor filters. Reprinted from Yue et al. (2009), with permission from Elsevier

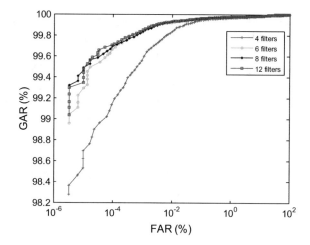

Table 4.2 EER of the improved competitive code and two other palmprint recognition methods (%)

	Ordinal measure	RLOC	FCM-based competitive code
EER (%)	0.097	0.088	0.043

Reprinted from Yue et al. (2009), with permission from Elsevier

Note The EER of the original RLOC algorithm was 0.16 % (Jia et al. 2008), but with our implementation, a much lower value (EER = 0.088 %) was obtained. For fair comparison, we use this better result rather than the published value (Jia et al. 2008)

Fig. 4.13 ROC curves of the improved competitive code and two other palmprint recognition methods. Reprinted from Yue et al. (2009), with permission from Elsevier

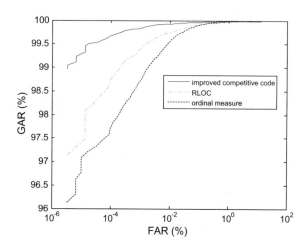

coding-based algorithms both use six filters for palmprint recognition, thus, we also implemented the presented FCM-based competitive code with six Gabor filters.

Table 4.2 and Fig. 4.13 show the EER values and ROC curves, respectively. From Table 4.2 and Fig. 4.13, the presented FCM-based competitive code algorithm is much better than the other two methods for palmprint identification. The EER value obtained by the presented FCM-based competitive code algorithm is 0.043 %, which is much lower than those obtained by the ordinal measure algorithm (0.097 %) and RLOC algorithm (0.088 %). When the false accept rate (FAR) is 10^{-4} %, the genuine accept rate (GAR) obtained by the presented FCM-based competitive code algorithm is 99.67 %, which is also higher than those of the ordinal measure algorithm (98.76 %) and RLOC algorithm (97.54 %).

4.4 Binary Orientation Co-occurrence Vector-Based Palmprint Authentication[1]

The line structures of palmprint images are very complex. Multiple lines may intersect in some regions, so the features extracted by only using one orientation cannot sufficiently represent the local feature of palmprint images. Figure 4.14a, b show an example where two palm lines intersect. Figure 4.14c plots the curve of Gabor filtering response (Kong and Zhang 2004) versus orientation of the local area in Fig. 4.14b. There are two valleys in Fig. 4.14c. This indicates two main orientations in this area. If one orientation is lost, much valuable discriminatory information will also be lost.

In addition, the extracted "dominant" orientation is sensitive to rotation. Figure 4.15 shows an example. If we rotated Fig. 4.15a only by 5° counterclockwise, the extracted orientation of the local area will change from 120° to 90°, i.e., a 30° difference. To overcome the above problems, we present a new feature representation algorithm for palmprint identification, namely the Binary Orientation Co-occurrence Vector (BOCV).

4.4.1 Binary Orientation Co-occurrence Vector

As discussed in the previous section, the Gabor filter can be regarded as a line detector or matched filter to detect palm lines (van Deemter and du Buf 2000). If we normalize the Gabor filtering response vector to L_2-norm unity as in Eq. (4.27), the filter response at each orientation can be treated as a confidence measure of the feature occurring at that orientation (Varma and Zisserman 2005).

---

[1]Parts of this chapter are reprinted from Guo et al. (2009), with permission from Elsevier.

Fig. 4.14 **a** A palmprint image; **b** cropped and enlarged image with two intersected lines; **c** Gabor filtering responses versus orientation. Reprinted from Guo et al. (2009), with permission from Elsevier

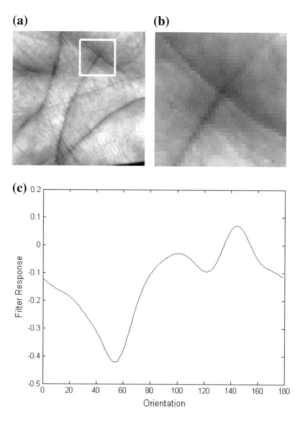

For each local region, a six-dimensional vector is obtained by concatenating the normalized responses along six directions, namely the orientation co-occurrence vector (OCV). Suppose P and Q are the two OCVs of two palmprint images. Then the distance of the two palmprint images is measured by

$$G_j(x,y) = \frac{G'_j(x,y)}{\sqrt{\sum_{i=0}^{5} G'_i(x,y)^2}}, \quad (4.27)$$

$$G'_j(x,y) = I(x,y) * \psi_R(x,y,\omega,\theta_j), \theta_j = j\pi/6, j = \{0,1,2,3,4,5\}$$

For each local region, a six-dimensional vector is obtained by concatenating the normalized responses along six directions, namely the orientation co-occurrence vector (OCV). Suppose P and Q are the two OCVs of two palmprint images. Then the distance of the two palmprint images is measured by

$$D(P,Q) = \frac{\sum_{y=1}^{M}\sum_{x=1}^{N}\sum_{j=0}^{5} |P_j(x,y) - Q_j(x,y)| * (P_M(x,y) \cap Q_M(x,y))}{\sum_{y=1}^{M}\sum_{x=1}^{N} P_M(x,y) \cap Q_M(x,y)}, \quad (4.28)$$

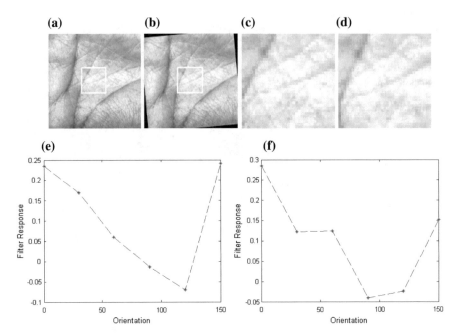

Fig. 4.15 **a** is a palmprint image and **b** is the 5° rotation of it; **c** and **d** are the cropped and enlarged images of **a** and **b**; **e** and **f** are the curves of Gabor filtering responses versus six orientations for **c** and **d**, respectively. Reprinted from Guo et al. (2009), with permission from Elsevier

where P_i and Q_i are the i-th dimension planes of P and Q, respectively. P_M and Q_M are the corresponding palmprint pixel masks (Zhang et al. 2003) of P and Q, respectively.

However, because the orientation features are represented by floating point numbers, it is time consuming to use OCV as a distance measure. To improve the efficiency, for each response of the orientation, we transform it to a binarized vector by using a threshold

$$P_j^b(x, y) = \begin{cases} 1, & if\ G_j'(x, y) < T_j \\ 0, & else \end{cases}. \tag{4.29}$$

The threshold T_j can be simply set as 0. It can also be adaptively set according to the filter response distribution, which could further improve the accuracy. In Sect. 4.4.2, we will present a method to obtain an optimal threshold. In the following, unless stated explicitly, we set $T_j = 0$, $j = \{0, 1, 2, 3, 4, 5\}$. Figure 4.16 shows BOCV features of a palmprint image.

Similar to the competitive code method, the Hamming distance can also be applied to match the two BOCVs of two palmprint images

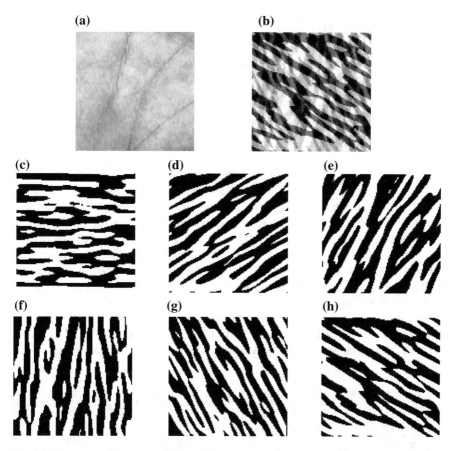

Fig. 4.16 A palmprint image and its BOCV features. **a** Original palmprint image; **b** BOCV feature map; **c–h** are the binarized feature maps by six Gabor filters in six directions. Reprinted from Guo et al. (2009), with permission from Elsevier

$$D(P^b, Q^b) = \frac{\sum\limits_{y=1}^{M} \sum\limits_{x=1}^{N} \sum\limits_{j=0}^{5} \left(P_j^b(x,y) \otimes Q_j^b(x,y)\right) \cap \left(P_M(x,y) \cap Q_M(x,y)\right)}{6 * \sum\limits_{y=1}^{M} \sum\limits_{x=1}^{N} P_M(x,y) \cap Q_M(x,y)}. \tag{4.30}$$

Obviously, D is in the range $[0, 1]$. The smaller the D, the more similar the two palms. In practice, we will shift the BOCV map along different directions in a small range to find the smallest distance between two maps. If the distance is smaller than a certain level, the two palmprints will be classified into the same class.

4.4.2 Experimental Results

These experiments were also performed on the Hong Kong PolyU palmprint database. We again used six Gabor filters to extract the palm features in the following experiments.

4.4.2.1 The Robustness to Rotation

Figure 4.15 shows that the dominant orientation extracted by the competitive code method which is sensitive to small rotations, while the presented BOCV scheme is not so sensitive. To show further that BOCV is more robust to rotation than competitive code, two experiments are described in this subsection. In the first experiment, we used some rotated ROI images to measure the matching distance of the two code methods. Figure 4.17 shows some images that were obtained by rotating a ROI image by 2°, 4°, 6°, 8°, and 10° clockwise. Table 4.3 shows the matching distances between the images by the competitive code method and the presented BOCV method.

Table 4.3 shows that the matching distances by the presented BOCV are smaller than those by competitive code. This indicates that the presented BOCV method is robust to the palmprint images with small alignment or registration errors.

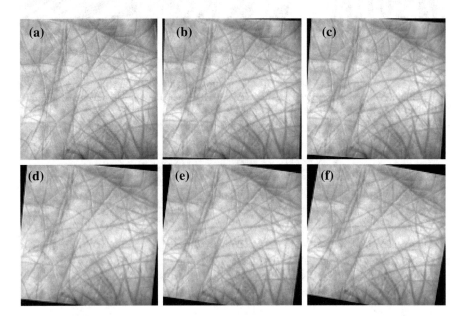

Fig. 4.17 An original image and its rotated images. **a** original image; **b–f** are the rotated images of **a** by 2°, 4°, 6°, 8°, and 10° clockwise, respectively. Reprinted from Guo et al. (2009), with permission from Elsevier

Table 4.3 Matching distances between the images in Fig. 4.17

Competitive code/BOCV	a	b	c	d	e	f
a	0	0.1974/0.1393	0.3337/0.2635	0.4281/0.3744	0.4775/0.4475	0.4959/0.4858
b		0	0.1842/0.1389	0.3243/0.2699	0.4155/0.3688	0.4700/0.4449
c			0	0.1924/0.1398	0.3379/0.2560	0.4333/0.3579
d				0	0.1868/0.1232	0.3465/0.2493
e					0	0.1970/0.1342

Reprinted from Guo et al. (2009), with permission from Elsevier

In the second experiment, each palmprint image in the database was randomly rotated by a degree within a range $[-d, d]$, where $d = \{1, 2, 3, 4, 5, 6\}$. Figure 4.18 shows the EER curves; the EER values of the presented BOCV method are always lower than those by the competitive code method at all rotation angles.

Figure 4.19 and Table 4.7 show the ROC curves and verification accuracy rates by different methods, respectively. In the experiment, some optimizations have been adopted on the ROI extraction and matching, so the experimental results of the

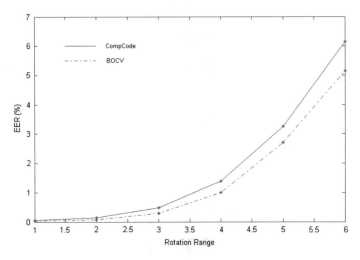

Fig. 4.18 EER versus rotation by competitive code and BOCV. Reprinted from Guo et al. (2009), with permission from Elsevier

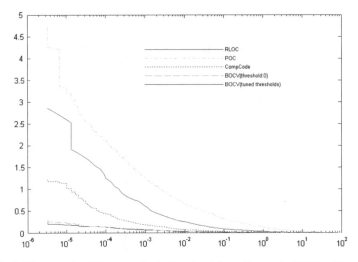

Fig. 4.19 ROC curves by different methods. Reprinted from Guo et al. (2009), with permission from Elsevier

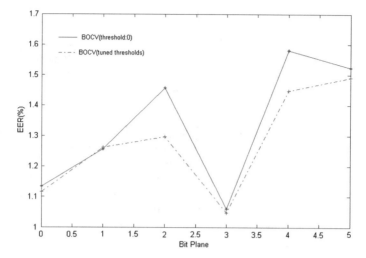

Fig. 4.20 EER versus individual planes. Reprinted from Guo et al. (2009), with permission from Elsevier

RLOC method and competitive code method are better than those reported in previous publications (Jia et al. 2008; Kong and Zhang 2004). Figure 4.19 and Table 4.7 show that the presented BOCV method achieves better performance than the competitive code method. This is because BOCV retains more directional information than the competitive code method, which is helpful in obtaining a higher accuracy. By using tuned thresholds, the EER is lower than using 0 as the threshold, and lower FRR could be achieved in most cases, especially when FAR $\leq 4 \times 10^{-5}$ %. This validates the effectiveness of tuned thresholds in increasing the impostor distance. Figure 4.20 shows the curves of EER versus individual planes. It proves that using tuned thresholds can produce a more even distribution and smaller EER values.

4.4.2.2 Palmprint Verification Results

In the presented BOCV method, some thresholds need to be set for binarization (referring to Eq. (4.29)). The simple method is set as 0, which is widely used in the coding-based method for palmprint (Kong et al. 2006) and iris (Daugman 2003) recognition. However, if we set the threshold as 0, the distribution of the binarized values may not be even. Suppose the probability of 1 in the binarized result is p.

Table 4.4 Exclusive OR output and the associated probability

Exclusive OR output/Possibility	0	1
0	$0/(1 - p) \times (1 - p)$	$1/p \times (1 - p)$
1	$1/(1 - p) \times p$	$0/p \times p$

Reprinted from Guo et al. (2009), with permission from Elsevier

Table 4.5 The average rate of 1 and 0 among six planes by using 0 as threshold

	Plane 0	Plane 1	Plane 2	Plane 3	Plane 4	Plane 5
Rate of 1 (%)	47.6146	47.0470	46.5781	46.2687	46.5260	46.6556
Rate of 0 (%)	52.3854	52.9530	53.4219	53.7313	53.4740	53.3444

Reprinted from Guo et al. (2009), with permission from Elsevier

Table 4.4 shows the exclusive OR outputs and their associated probabilities under different inputs. If we assume the matching score between two BOCV maps from two different palms follows a Bernoulli trial (Daugman 2003), the distance or difference between them will be maximized if and only if $p = 0.5$. When p is not equal to 0.5, the probability of the smaller impostor distance will be increased.

Table 4.5 shows the average rate of 1 and 0 among six planes by using 0 as the threshold. When the threshold is set as 0, the average rates of 1 and 0 in the six planes are not even, and this increases the probability of smaller impostor distance. Thus, if a threshold can result in a more even distribution between 1 and 0 in the binarized plane, the impostor distance could be increased and the accuracy may be increased accordingly.

Because Eq. (4.28) can be rewritten as Eq. (4.31), which is an average distance of six independent planes, the six thresholds for six planes can be tuned based on the first 192 palms, a total of 3849 images. Table 4.6 shows the average percentage of 1 among six planes using tuned thresholds of the presented BOCV method over the whole database. From Table 4.6, we can find that the tuned thresholds can give a more even distribution for each plane.

$$D(P,Q) = \frac{\sum_{y=1}^{M}\sum_{x=1}^{N}\sum_{j=0}^{5}\left(P_j^b(x,y) \otimes Q_j^b(x,y)\right) \cap \left(P_M(x,y) \cap Q_M(x,y)\right)}{6 * \sum_{y=1}^{M}\sum_{x=1}^{N} P_M(x,y) \cap Q_M(x,y)}$$

$$= \frac{1}{6}\sum_{j=0}^{5} D(P_j^b, Q_j^b). \tag{4.31}$$

Table 4.6 The average percentage of 1 and 0 among six planes using tuned thresholds

	Plane 0	Plane 1	Plane 2	Plane 3	Plane 4	Plane 5
Rate of 1 (%)	50.0186	50.0527	50.0505	50.0955	50.0326	50.0496
Rate of 0 (%)	49.9814	49.9473	49.9495	49.9045	49.9674	49.9504

Reprinted from Guo et al. (2009), with permission from Elsevier

Table 4.7 Verification accuracy by different methods

	EER (%)	d'	FRR (when FAR = 3.3×10^{-6} %)
Palmprint Orientation Code (POC) (Wu et al. 2005)	0.2366	3.4549	4.7092
RLOC	0.0905	**6.2768**	2.8594
Competitive code	0.0379	5.4122	1.2273
BOCV (threshold: 0)	0.0220	5.8477	0.3011
BOCV (tuned thresholds)	**0.0189**	5.7575	**0.2525**

Reprinted from Guo et al. (2009), with permission from Elsevier
Note Bold numbers denote the best results with respect to different evaluation indicates

4.5   Summary

In this chapter, we first summarized the coding-based palmprint authentication methods, and then presented two improved coding-based methods for palmprint authentication.

Palm lines have different orientation distributions. To select the most discriminative orientations, an improved orientations selection method based on FCM was presented. Experimental results show that the FCM-based orientations selection method greatly improves the performance of the competitive coding-based palmprint authentication scheme. The FCM-based method achieves higher verification accuracy than some state-of-the-art competitive coding-based methods. Experiments in Sect. 4.3.3.2 also indicate that the competitive code-based methods with six Gabor filters would be a preferable choice for palmprint recognition.

Multiple lines may intersect in some regions; palm line features extracted at one orientation may be lost and insufficiently represent the local features of the palmprint. To retain more orientation information, a novel feature extraction method, binary orientation co-occurrence vector (BOCV), is presented for palmprint verification. Experimental results show that the BOCV scheme is more robust to small rotations than the conventional competitive code-based methods. This BOCV method also can be extended to other binary feature extraction algorithms, such as palmprint orientation code (POC) (Wu et al. 2005), robust line orientation code (RLOC) (Jia et al. 2008), and orthogonal line ordinal feature (OLOF) (Sun et al. 2005).

References

J.C. Bezdek, *Pattern recognition with fuzzy objective function algorithms* (Springer Science & Business Media, 2013)

J.C. Bezdek, R.J. Hathaway, M.J. Sabin, W.T. Tucker, Convergence theory for fuzzy c-means: counterexamples and repairs. IEEE Trans. Syst. Man Cybern. **17**(5), 873–877 (1987)

H. Cheng, J.-R. Chen, J. Li, Threshold selection based on fuzzy c-partition entropy approach. Pattern Recogn. **31**(7), 857–870 (1998)

K.-H. Cheung, A. Kong, D. Zhang, M. Kamel, J. You, *Does eigenpalm work? A system and evaluation perspective*. In Proceedings of International Conference on Pattern Recognition (IEEE, 2006). pp. 445–448

J. Daugman, The importance of being random: statistical principles of iris recognition. Pattern Recogn. **36**(2), 279–291 (2003)

J.G. Daugman, High confidence visual recognition of persons by a test of statistical independence. IEEE Trans. Pattern Anal. Mach. Intell. **15**(11), 1148–1161 (1993)

L.D. Demb, P. Kastner, Fuzzy C-means method for clustering microarray data. Bioinformatics **19**(8), 973–980 (2003)

F. Du, P. Yu, H. Li, L. Zhu, *Palmprint recognition using Gabor feature-based bidirectional 2DLDA*. in Computer Science for Environmental Engineering and EcoInformatics (Springer, 2011)

Z. Guo, D. Zhang, L. Zhang, W. Zuo, Palmprint verification using binary orientation co-occurrence vector. Pattern Recogn. Lett. **30**(13), 1219–1227 (2009)

Z. Guo, W. Zuo, L. Zhang, D. Zhang, A unified distance measurement for orientation coding in palmprint verification. Neurocomputing **73**(4), 944–950 (2010)

D. Hu, G. Feng, Z. Zhou, Two-dimensional locality preserving projections (2DLPP) with its application to palmprint recognition. Pattern Recogn. **40**(1), 339–342 (2007)

D.-S. Huang, W. Jia, D. Zhang, Palmprint verification based on principal lines. Pattern Recogn. **41**(4), 1316–1328 (2008)

W. Jia, D.-S. Huang, D. Zhang, Palmprint verification based on robust line orientation code. Pattern Recogn. **41**(5), 1504–1513 (2008)

A. Kong, D. Zhang, M. Kamel, Palmprint identification using feature-level fusion. Pattern Recogn. **39**(3), 478–487 (2006)

A.W.-K. Kong, D. Zhang, *Competitive coding scheme for palmprint verification*, in Proceedings of International Conference on Pattern Recognition (IEEE, 2004), pp. 520–523

T.S. Lee, Image representation using 2D Gabor wavelets. IEEE Trans. Pattern Anal. Mach. Intell. **18**(10), 959–971 (1996)

D.G. Lowe, Distinctive image features from scale-invariant keypoints. Int. J. Comput. Vision **60**(2), 91–110 (2004)

A. Morales, M. Ferrer, A. Kumar, Towards contactless palmprint authentication. IET Comput. Vision **5**(6), 407–416 (2011)

I. Naseem, R. Togneri, M. Bennamoun, Linear regression for face recognition. IEEE Trans. Pattern Anal. Mach. Intell. **32**(11), 2106–2112 (2010)

D. Özdemir, L. Akarun, Fuzzy algorithms for combined quantization and dithering. IEEE Trans. Image Process. **10**(6), 923–931 (2001)

T. Poggio, F. Girosi, Networks for approximation and learning. Proc. IEEE **78**(9), 1481–1497 (1990)

S. Ribaric, I. Fratric, A biometric identification system based on eigenpalm and eigenfinger features. IEEE Trans. Pattern Anal. Mach. Intell. **27**(11), 1698–1709 (2005)

H. Sang, W. Yuan, Z. Zhang, *Research of palmprint recognition based on 2DPCA*, in Advances in Neural Networks–ISNN 2009 (Springer, 2009)

Z. Sun, T. Tan, Y. Wang, S.Z. Li, *Ordinal palmprint represention for personal identification*, in Proceedings of IEEE Conference on Computer Vision and Pattern Recognition (IEEE, 2005), 279–284

J.H. van Deemter, J.H. du Buf, Simultaneous detection of lines and edges using compound Gabor filters. Int. J. Pattern Recognit Artif Intell. **14**(06), 757–777 (2000)

M. Varma, A. Zisserman, A statistical approach to texture classification from single images. Int. J. Comput. Vision **62**(1–2), 61–81 (2005)

X. Wu, K. Wang, D. Zhang, *Palmprint authentication based on orientation code matching*, in Proceedings of Audio-and Video-Based Biometric Person Authentication (Springer, 2005), pp. 555–562

X. Wu, K. Wang, D. Zhang, *Palmprint texture analysis using derivative of Gaussian filters*, in Proceedings of International Conference on Computational Intelligence and Security (IEEE, 2006), pp. 751–754

Y. Xu, Z. Fan, M. Qiu, D. Zhang, J.-Y. Yang, A sparse representation method of bimodal biometrics and palmprint recognition experiments. Neurocomputing **103**, 164–171 (2013)

Y. Xu, L. Fei, D. Zhang, Combining left and right palmprint images for more accurate personal identification. IEEE Trans. Image Process. **24**(2), 549–559 (2015)

Y. Xu, D. Zhang, J. Yang, J.-Y. Yang, A two-phase test sample sparse representation method for use with face recognition. IEEE Trans. Circuits Syst. Video Technol. **21**(9), 1255–1262 (2011)

F. Yue, W. Zuo, K. Wang, D. Zhang, *A performance evaluation of filter design and coding schemes for palmprint recognition*, in Proceedings of International Conference on Pattern Recognition (IEEE, 2008), pp. 1–4

F. Yue, W. Zuo, D. Zhang, K. Wang, Orientation selection using modified FCM for competitive code-based palmprint recognition. Pattern Recogn. **42**(11), 2841–2849 (2009)

D. Zhang, PolyU palmprint database. Biometric Research Centre, Hong Kong Polytechnic University, (Online). Available from ⟨http://www.comp.polyu.edu.hk/∼bio,etrics/⟩

D. Zhang, W.-K. Kong, J. You, M. Wong, Online palmprint identification. IEEE Trans. Pattern Anal. Mach. Intell. **25**(9), 1041–1050 (2003)

L. Zhang, M. Yang, X. Feng, *Sparse representation or collaborative representation: which helps face recognition?*, in Proceedings of IEEE International Conference on Computer Vision (IEEE, 2011), pp. 471–478

Chapter 5
Orientation Features and Distance Measure of Palmprint Authentication

Abstract Orientation information of palm lines carries much discriminative information and is one of the most promising features for palmprint authentication. For the orientation code-based methods, the orientation extraction and distance measure are two essential issues for palmprint verification. In this chapter, some efficient orientation extraction methods and a novel distance measure method are presented. The chapter is organized as follows. We first give a brief introduction to the orientation code-based methods in Sect. 5.1. In Sects. 5.2 and 5.3, two novel multiscale orientations code-based algorithms are presented. Section 5.4 introduces an improved distance measure method for palmprint authentication.

5.1 Introduction

Coding-based methods, which use some code rule to encode the result of a bank of filters, have been very successful in palmprint recognition. The PalmCode method (Zhang et al. 2003; Kong et al. 2003) is a well-known coding-based method for palmprint authentication, which encodes the phase of the 2-D Gabor filter responses as binary features. The PalmCode method does not have good separability because different palms have a similar filter response when using only a Gabor filter. To overcome this problem, Kong et al. (2006) proposed an improved coding-based algorithm, named the FusionCode method, which encodes the phase of the filter response whose magnitude of filter response is the maximum.

The above two coding-based methods only take into account the phase and magnitude information of the filter response, they ignore the essential traits of the palm, i.e., palm lines of different palms have different orientations. Palm lines are typical features of the palm and carry more discriminative information for personal authentication. To extract the orientation features of a palmprint, several state-of-the-art palmprint identification methods, such as the competitive code (Kong and Zhang 2004), the ordinal code (Sun et al. 2005), and the robust line orientation code (RLOC) (Jia et al. 2008), have been proposed. In this chapter, we name these methods as orientation coding-based methods. The orientation

© Springer Science+Business Media Singapore 2016
D. Zhang et al., *Discriminative Learning in Biometrics*,
DOI 10.1007/978-981-10-2056-8_5

coding-based methods involve three components: the filter for extracting the orientation features, the coding rule, and the matching scheme.

Palm lines are complex, containing three principal lines and many small wrinkles. Both the principal lines and wrinkles contain much discriminative information for palmprint identification. We can generally regard palm lines as typical multiscale features, where the principal lines can be represented at a larger scale while the wrinkles at a smaller scale. Due to the influence of lighting and aging, some wrinkles in the palmprint image may appear or disappear, while the principal lines of the palmprint are robust. However, most coding-based palmprint identification methods only encode the responses of filters at a specific scale. The multiscale characteristics of palm lines are neglected. Thus, the extracted orientation features of palm lines cannot sufficiently represent the palmprint; the performance of these coding-based methods would be degraded for matching palmprint images with poor quality.

To overcome the above problems, several multiscale methods have been proposed for palmprint recognition. For example, the hierarchical matching scheme, which is one of the multiscale methods, was proposed to improve the efficiency of palmprint authentication (You et al. 2004; Li et al. 2005). Some researchers utilize multiscale palmprint features to improve further the recognition performance (Zuo et al. 2008; Han et al. 2008). Zuo et al. (2008) proposed a novel multiscale competitive codes method by the fusion of angular distances of different scales. All the above multiscale methods obtain better performance than using only a scale for palmprint authentication. In this chapter, we will present two novel palmprint identification methods based on multiscale orientations extraction.

The distance measure is another key issue for palmprint identification. The angular distance and orientation equivalence are the most promising algorithms for matching the orientation features. In this chapter, we also present an improved distance measure algorithm for palmprint authentication.

5.2   Multiscale Competitive Code Palmprint Authentication

5.2.1   Multiscale Palmprint Orientation Coding

5.2.1.1   2-D Log-Gabor FilterIng

When implemented in multiresolution, classical Gabor filters yield a nonuniform coverage of the frequency domain (Fischer et al. 2007). In contrast, the 2-D log-Gabor filter has good properties and is widely used to extract multiscale features of palmprint images. Thus, we chose the log-Gabor filter to extract the multiscale features of palmprints in this section. The 2-D Log-Gabor filter is defined as follows:

$$G(\rho, \theta, \rho_0, \theta_0) = \exp\left\{-\frac{1}{2}\left(\frac{\rho - \rho_0}{\sigma_\rho}\right)^2\right\} \exp\left\{-\frac{1}{2}\left(\frac{\theta - \theta_0}{\sigma_\theta}\right)^2\right\}, \tag{5.1}$$

where (ρ, θ) are the coordinates of the log-polar plot, (ρ_0, θ_0) denote the coordinates of the center of the filter, and $(\sigma_\rho, \sigma_\theta)$ are the standard deviations of the Gaussian along the ρ and θ axes.

After defining the log-Gabor filter in the frequency domain, Fourier transformation can be used to transform the frequency filter to the spatial domain. Like the classical Gabor filter, log-Gabor filters also have a real part and an imaginary part. Considering that palm lines are the most salient feature for palmprint images with low resolution, we only select the real part of the log-Gabor filters.

5.2.1.2 Competitive Code

As discussed in the previous chapter (Sect. 4.2.2.1 of Chap. 4), the competitive code method, which was first proposed by Kong, regards the pixel as having the same orientation as the filters whose filtering response is the maximum (sometimes, minimum) among all filtering responses (Kong and Zhang 2004). Given a bank of log-Gabor filters with different orientations, $G(\rho, \theta, \rho_0, \theta_i)$, $\theta_i = i\pi/n_\theta$, $i = \{0, 1, \ldots, n_\theta - 1\}$, suppose $I(x, y)$ is the original palmprint image and $H_i(x, y)$ is the filtering response by using the ith log-Gabor filter $G(\rho, \theta, \rho_0, \theta_i)$. The competitive rule is designed as follows:

$$W(x, y) = \arg\min_i H_i(x, y), \tag{5.2}$$

where $W(x, y)$ is the winning index of pixel (x, y).

To improve the matching speed of palmprint features, we compactly encode each winning index into $n_\theta/2$ bits by using the coding rule as follows. If the number of the orientations n_θ is even, a coding rule is designed as

$$C(x, y, j) = \begin{cases} 1, & j \leq W(x, y) < j + n_\theta/2 \\ 0, & elsewise \end{cases}, j = 1, \ldots, n_\theta/2. \tag{5.3}$$

To further improve the matching efficiency of competitive coding, a downsampling algorithm is adopted to sample a much smaller number of points, e.g., 32×32.

5.2.1.3 Multiscale Orientation Representation

In this subsection, we present a multiscale orientation representation scheme. Suppose $I(x, y)$ denotes an original palmprint image and $G_{s,\theta}(u, v)$ is the log-Gabor filter with orientation θ and scale s in the frequency domain. The filtering response of palm image $I(x, y)$ using log-Gabor $G_{s,\theta}(u, v)$ is

$$H_{s,\theta}(x, y) = \text{real}\{F^{-1}(G_{s,\theta} \cdot F(I(x, y)))\},\tag{5.4}$$

where F and F^{-1} are the Fourier and inverse Fourier transforms, respectively. In the presented method, six orientations are adopted,

$$\theta_i = \begin{cases} i\pi/n_\theta, & \text{if } s \text{ is even} \\ i\pi/n_\theta + \pi/2n_\theta, & \text{if } s \text{ is odd} \end{cases},\tag{5.5}$$

where θ_i is the ith orientation value, $i = \{0, 1, \ldots, n_\theta - 1\}$. s is the number of the scale, $s = 1, 2, \ldots, n_s$. For each scale, we obtain an orientation code of the palmprint by using the coding rule of Eq. (5.3). In this way, multiscale orientation code of the palm image is obtained.

Compared with the classical multisolution Gabor representation, the presented method has several advantages. First, compared with Gabor filters, log-Gabor filters could sufficiently and uniformly cover the whole frequencies, especially the mid frequencies, when implemented in multiresolution. Second, from Fig. 5.1, we can see that by laying the centers of the log-Gabor filters on a uniform hexagonal lattice, the multiscale orientation scheme could achieve a more uniform coverage in the

Fig. 5.1 Schematic contours of the log-Gabor filters in the Fourier domain. © 2008 IEEE. Reprinted with permission, from Zuo et al. (2008)

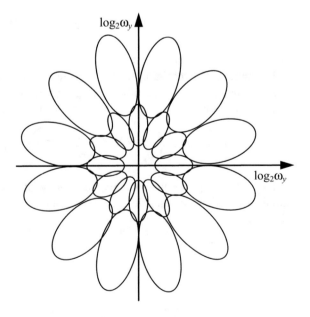

mid-frequency domain. Finally, we adopt the principal orientation information rather than the magnitude or phase information for representation of the palmprint, and thus the presented multiscale orientation coding method is robust to variation in illumination.

A simple downsampling procedure is adopted to improve the efficiency and save stored memory. For the presented multiscale representation, the filtering responses are downsampled by a factor of four at the first scale, and a factor of 8, 16, and $4i$ at the second, third, and ith scales.

5.2.2   Hierarchical Matching Scheme of Palmprint Images

5.2.2.1   Matching of Competitive CodeS

The angular distance, which was proposed by Zuo et al. (2006), is widely used to measure the difference between competitive codes. Considering that the palmprint image may not be aligned absolutely, in palmprint matching, the competitive code of the query palmprint is translated in the horizontal and vertical directions within a specified range, and the minimum distance is used as the final matching score.

5.2.2.2   Hierarchical Matching

In this subsection, we present a hierarchical matching scheme to facilitate fast indexing from a large-scale palmprint database. The presented hierarchical matching schemes are shown in Fig. 5.2. The main steps of the hierarchical matching schemes are as follows. First, two palmprint images are matched at the largest scale n_s (which is faster). If their angular distance d_{n_s} is larger than a specific distance T_{n_s}, we treat this matching as an impostor matching, and will not match them at the remaining scales. If the angular distance d_{n_s} is not larger than threshold T_{n_s}, we will match them at the $(n_s - 1)$th scale d'_{n_s-1}, and use a fusion strategy to combine d_{n_s} and d_{n_s-1} to obtain the final matching score of the $(n_s - 1)$th scale

$$D_{n_s-1} = f(d_{n_s}, d_{n_s-1}). \tag{5.6}$$

Similarly, if the combined angular distance D_{n_s-1} is equal to or smaller than a specific distance T_{n_s-1}, we will further calculate the fusion distance at the lower scale

$$D_s = f(d_{n_s}, d_{n_s-1}, \ldots, d_s), \tag{5.7}$$

until $d_s < T_s$ or $s = 1$.

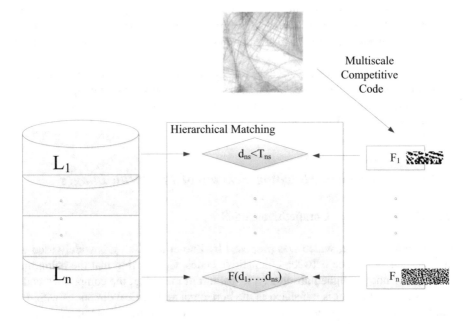

Fig. 5.2 The hierarchical matching scheme. © 2008 IEEE. Reprinted with permission, from Zuo et al. (2008)

You et al. (2004) proposed a hierarchical matching scheme for palmprint authentication. Compared with You et al.'s method, the presented matching scheme has two advantages. First, the orientation features used in the presented hierarchical matching scheme are robust to variations in illumination. Second, at one scale, we use the fusion strategy to combine the distance at the scale and the higher scales, which is able to improve the performance of competitive code for palmprint identification.

5.2.2.3   Fusion of Multiscale Matching Results

In this subsection, we will present a fusion strategy to combine angular distance at different scales. The main steps are as follows. First we use Gaussian distributions to estimate the probabilistic densities of the genuine and scores at each scale. The reason for using Gaussian distributions is that the impostor distribution can be approximated to a Gaussian distribution (Sun et al. 2005). At each scale, given a set of genuine matching distances $M_g = \{d_{i,s}^g \mid i = 1, 2, \ldots, N_g\}$, the mean m_s^g and standard deviation σ_s^g of the Gaussian distributions can be obtained. Similarly, the mean m_s^i and standard deviation σ_s^i of the impostor distribution can also be estimated.

Suppose $\{d_j, d_{j+1}, \ldots, d_{n_s}\}$ denotes a set of angular distances, its joint impostor distribution is approximated as

$$p^i(d_j, d_{j+1}, \ldots, d_{n_s}) = \prod_{j}^{n_s} \frac{1}{\sqrt{2\pi}\sigma_j^i} \exp\left\{\frac{(x - m_j^i)^2}{2\sigma_j^{i\,2}}\right\}, \qquad (5.8)$$

and the joint genuine distribution is approximated as

$$p^g(d_j, d_{j+1}, \ldots, d_{n_s}) = \prod_{j}^{n_s} \frac{1}{\sqrt{2\pi}\sigma_j^g} \exp\left\{\frac{(x - m_j^g)^2}{2\sigma_j^{g\,2}}\right\}. \qquad (5.9)$$

According to $p^i(d_j, d_{j+1}, \ldots, d_{n_s})$ and $p^g(d_j, d_{j+1}, \ldots, d_{n_s})$, the combined angular distance (fusion matching score) is defined as

$$D_j = \frac{1}{n_s - s + 1} \sum_{j=s}^{n_s} \left(w_j^S \left(\frac{(x - m_j^i)^2}{\sigma_j^{i\,2}} - w_g \frac{(x - m_j^g)^2}{\sigma_j^{g\,2}} \right) \right), \qquad (5.10)$$

where w_j^S is the jth scale weight. Compared with the impostor distribution, the genuine distribution usually is not stable and deviates more from the Gaussian. Thus, we introduce a weight w_g $(0 \le w_g < 1)$ to reduce the influence of the inaccurate estimation.

5.2.3   Experimental Results and Discussion

The verification performance of MCC was evaluated on the PolyU palmprint database (version 2) (D. Zhang). In the experiments, each sub-image of the original palmprint image was resized to a 128 by 128 matrix. Two scales are used in the presented MCC algorithm.

First, the presented MCC method is compared with the original competitive code method. Figure 5.3 shows the ROC curves of the MCC algorithm, and the competitive code algorithm at the first and second scales. From Fig. 5.3, we can see that the presented MCC algorithm achieves better performance than the competitive code algorithm at each scale.

To prove the effectiveness of the presented MCC algorithm, the MCC algorithm is further compared with the ordinal code algorithm (Sun et al. 2005; Han et al. 2007) and the RLOC algorithm (Jia et al. 2008). Table 5.1 shows the EER and execution time of the above three algorithms. From Table 5.1, we can see that the presented MCC algorithm not only obtains much lower EER than the other two algorithms, but also has a faster matching speed than the ordinal code and RLOC algorithms. It also indicates that the presented MCC algorithm would be more promising in the case of large-scale palmprint indexing.

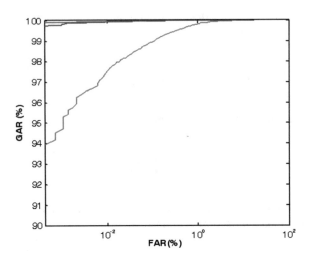

Fig. 5.3 The ROC curves of MCC and competitive code. © 2008 IEEE. Reprinted with permission, from Zuo et al. (2008)

Table 5.1 Execution time and EER of multiscale competitive code, ordinal measure, and RLOC. © 2008 IEEE

Method	Feature extraction (ms)	Matching (ms)	EER (%)
MCC	146	0.03	0.024
Ordinal measure	63	0.05	0.05
RLOC	70	3.9	0.16

Reprinted with permission, from Zuo et al. (2008)

5.3   Integrating Multiscale Competitive Code and Sparse Representation for Palmprint Authentication

5.3.1   Sparse Palmprint Representation

As introduced in the previous section, multiscale features of the palmprint can be extracted by multiscale/multiorientation filter banks. Suppose $\mathbf{D} = [\mathbf{d}_1, \ldots, \mathbf{d}_K] \in \mathbb{R}^{n \times K}$ is a filter bank (dictionary) and $\mathbf{x} \in \mathbb{R}^n$ is an image patch. The convolution method is usually adopted to estimate the filter coefficients, but it suffers from nonorthogonality and crosstalk among the basis filters.

As a palm line patch generally has a specific orientation and scale, the filter coefficients are expected to be sparse, i.e., with only a few nonzero values. As introduced in Chap. 3, a sparse representation has good properties and is widely used in signal processing, machine learning, and face recognition. In this section, we utilize the sparse representation to model the multiscale palmprint representation problem. The multiscale representation model with l_0-regularization is as follows:

$$P0 : \min\|\boldsymbol{\alpha}\|_0, \quad \text{s.t.} \ \|\mathbf{x} - \mathbf{D}\boldsymbol{\alpha}\|_2^2 \le \varepsilon, \ \boldsymbol{\alpha} \in \mathbb{R}^K, \tag{5.11}$$

where $\|*\|_0$ is the l_0-norm, which represents the number of nonzero entries in a vector. Generally speaking, the sparse representation model involves two issues: dictionary learning and sparse coding. The sparse representation model first learns a dictionary from a set of training images, and then uses the learned dictionary to represent the query image.

In the next section, we present an effective palmprint representation method by the combination of sparse representation and multiscale/multiorientation methods. In the presented method, we simply adopt a set of existing second derivatives of Gaussian (sDoG) filters as the dictionary rather than learn a dictionary from a set of training samples. The reason is that sDoG filters have an explicit physical meaning: they are directly related to the local orientation and scale of the palm lines. Therefore, sDoG filters could be utilized to achieve a compact and effective multiscale palmprint representation.

5.3.1.1 The Filter Bank

To represent the palmprint sufficiently, the filter bank used in the presented method consists of 18 sDoG filters at three scales and six orientations. The sDoG filter is defined as

$$F(\delta_x, \delta_y, \theta) = \left((x')^2 - \delta_x^2\right)\frac{A}{\delta_x^4}\exp\left(-\frac{(x')^2}{2\delta_x^2} - \frac{(y')^2}{2\delta_y^2}\right), \tag{5.12}$$

where A is a constant, δ_x and δ_y represent the horizontal and vertical standard deviations, respectively. $x' = (x - x_0)\cos\theta + (y - y_0)\sin\theta$, $y' = -(x - x_0)\sin\theta + (y - y_0)\cos\theta$, (x_0, y_0) denotes the center of the filter, θ is the orientation of the filter. The number of scales s is three and the number of orientations t is six. There are only three parameters to determine the filter bank: average $\bar{\delta}_x$ of δ_x, ratio $\gamma = \delta_y/\delta_x$, and the scale difference is Δ. Then, the filter bank parameters are determined as $(\bar{\delta}_x - \Delta, \gamma\bar{\delta}_x - \gamma\Delta)$, $(\bar{\delta}_x, \gamma\bar{\delta}_x)$, and $(\bar{\delta}_x + \Delta, \gamma\bar{\delta}_x + \gamma\Delta)$. We first determined the values of $\bar{\delta}_x = 2.7$ and $\gamma = 2.5$, and then experimentally determined the value of Δ. The scale parameters (δ_x, δ_y) are (2.4, 6.0), (2.7, 6.75), and (3.0, 7.5), and the window size of the filter is 33×33. Figure 5.4 shows the filter bank used for sparse palmprint representation of the above filters. Each filter is regularized with the mean of 0 and l_1-norm of 1. Finally, all of the regularized filters are adopted to construct the dictionary $\mathbf{D}$ for sparse palmprint representation.

In addition to sDoG, other filters, such as the Gabor filter (Kong and Zhang 2004) and elliptical Gaussian filter (Sun et al. 2005), can also be used to construct

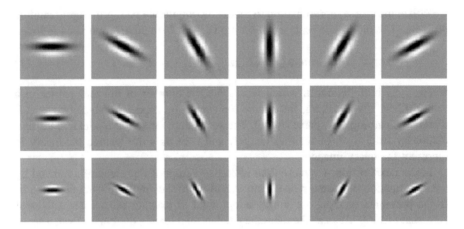

Fig. 5.4 The filter bank used for sparse palmprint representation, which consists of second derivatives of Gaussian filters at three scales and six orientations. © 2010 IEEE. Reprinted with permission, from Zuo et al. (2010)

the dictionary for sparse palmprint representation. Because the Gabor and elliptical Gaussian filters are designed to describe palm line features, it is expected that they will achieve similar performance as orientation coding methods (Yue et al. 2008). Therefore, we only consider the sparse representation by using the sDoG filter rather than Gabor or elliptical Gaussian filters.

5.3.1.2   Sparse Coding

As discussed in the previous subsection, dictionary **D** is constructed by a filter bank of sDoG. For each patch **x** of the palmprint image, a sparse solution can be obtained by solving the sparse representation model defined in Eq. (5.13). As discussed in Chap. 2, the sparse representation model with l_0-regularization is a nonconvex problem and cannot be efficiently solved. In practice, we usually replace the l_0-regularization with the l_1-regularization to translate Problem $P0$ into a convex optimization problem, i.e.,

$$P1 : \min\|\boldsymbol{\alpha}\|_1, \quad \text{s.t. } \|\mathbf{x} - \mathbf{D}\boldsymbol{\alpha}\|_2^2 \leq \varepsilon, \, \boldsymbol{\alpha} \in \mathbb{R}^K. \tag{5.13}$$

Suppose **D** obeys a uniform uncertainty principle. If the solution to $P0$ is sufficiently sparse, then the solution to $P1$ is guaranteed stably to recover the solution to $P0$ (Candes et al. 2006). A sparse solution of Problem $P1$ can be efficiently obtained by several optimization methods, such as the interior point method (Kim et al. 2007) and the iteratively reweighted least-squares method (Gorodnitsky and Rao 1997).

Suppose **I** is a palmprint image, $\mathbf{x}_{ij}$ denotes a sub-image patch with a size of 33×33 and centered at (i, j). We normalized the image patch with a mean of 0 and standard deviation of 1. Then, the sparse solution α_{ij} of the patch image is obtained by solving Problem $P1$.

Problem $P1$ can also be transformed into the following unconstrained optimization problem,

$$P2 : \min \left\| \mathbf{x}_{ij} - \mathbf{D}\alpha_{ij} \right\|_2^2 + \lambda \left\| \alpha_{ij} \right\|_1, \tag{5.14}$$

where λ is a regularization factor with a small value. By choosing an appropriate λ value, Problem $P2$ has the same solution as Problem $P1$. However, the l_1-regularization is non-differentiable when α_{ij} contains zero entries. Several methods have been proposed to obtain the sparse solution of Problem $P2$, such as various subgradient (Garg and Khandekar 2009), unconstrained approximations (Lee et al. 2006), and constrained optimization strategies (Kim et al. 2007).

In the presented method, the fast iterative shrinkage-thresholding algorithm (FISTA) (Beck and Teboulle 2009) is adopted to obtain the sparse solution of the unconstrained optimization problem in Eq. (5.14). Suppose $\mathbf{a}_k$ is the current estimate of α_{ij}, and L denotes the Lipschitz constant of the gradient of the function $f(\alpha) = \left\| \mathbf{x}_{ij} - \mathbf{D}\alpha \right\|_2^2$. FISTA (Beck and Teboulle 2009) uses the following quadratic approximation of $\left\| \mathbf{x}_{ij} - \mathbf{D}\alpha \right\|_2^2 + \lambda \| \alpha \|_1$ at a given point $\mathbf{y}_k$:

$$Q_L(\alpha, \mathbf{y}_k) := f(\mathbf{y}_k) + \langle \alpha - \mathbf{y}_k, \nabla f(\mathbf{y}_k) \rangle + \frac{L}{2} \| \alpha - \mathbf{y}_k \|_2^2 + \lambda \| \alpha \|_1. \tag{5.15}$$

Then, we can obtain an updated solution by solving the following minimization problem,

$$\mathbf{a}_{k+1} = \min_{\alpha} Q_L(\alpha, \mathbf{y}_k). \tag{5.16}$$

Because the l_1-norm is separable, the computation of $\mathbf{a}_{k+1}$ can be efficiently done by solving one 1-D minimization problem for each of its components:

$$\mathbf{a}_{k+1} = \mathcal{T}_{\lambda/L}(\mathbf{y}_k - \nabla f(\mathbf{y}_k)/L), \tag{5.17}$$

where $\mathcal{T}_a$ is the shrinkage operator defined as

$$\mathcal{T}_a(\mathbf{x})_i = (|x_i| - a)_+ \operatorname{sgn}(x_i). \tag{5.18}$$

The detailed steps of the sparse solution are summarized in Algorithm 5.1. In the experiment, the regularization factor λ was set as 0.02. Compared with other methods, in the palmprint authentication experiments, the FISTA method (Beck and Teboulle 2009) is about 13 times faster than l_1 magic (Candes and Romberg 2005) and three times faster than FOCUSS (Gorodnitsky and Rao 1997), yet achieving a comparable verification performance. Thus, the FISTA method is very efficient and suitable for sparse palmprint representation.

Finally, we used an experiment to compare the performance of the regular convolution method and the presented sparse representation method for palmprint orientation representation. From Fig. 5.5, we can see that the representation of the patch palmprint image using the presented sparse representation method is much sparser than that of the convolution method.

Algorithm 5.1: Sparse Palmprint Representation via FISTA

Input: $\mathbf{D}$, $\mathbf{x}_{ij}$, λ, L, $\boldsymbol{\alpha}_0 = \mathbf{D}^T \mathbf{x}_{ij}$, $\mathbf{y}_1 = \boldsymbol{\alpha}_0$, $t_1{=}1$, $k{=}1$

Output: $\boldsymbol{\alpha}_{ij} = \mathbf{a}_k$

1: **while** not converged

2:      $\mathbf{a}_k = \mathcal{T}_{\lambda/L}(\mathbf{y}_k - \nabla f(\mathbf{y}_k)/L)$.

3:      $t_{k+1} = \dfrac{1 + \sqrt{1 + 4t_k^2}}{2}$.

4:      $\mathbf{y}_{k+1} = \mathbf{a}_k + \dfrac{t_k - 1}{t_{k+1}}(\mathbf{a}_k - \mathbf{a}_{k-1})$.

5:      $k = k + 1$.

6: **end while**

5.3.2   Sparse Multiscale Competitive Code for Palmprint Verification

In this subsection, we will extend the general palmprint sparse representation to multiscale palmprint sparse representation for multiscale palmprint verification. We first present an SMCC method for the representation of the sparse multiscale orientation field, and then discuss a fast matching approach to improve the multiscale palmprint verification efficiency.

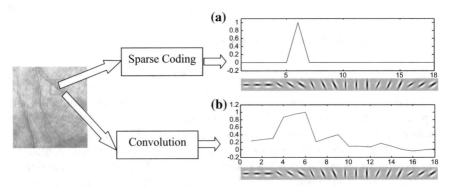

Fig. 5.5 Representation of a palmprint image patch using: **a** sparse coding and **b** regular convolution. © 2010 IEEE. Reprinted with permission, from Zuo et al. (2010)

5.3.2.1 Coding

Figure 5.6 shows the schematic diagram of the feature extraction procedure of the presented SMCC method, which involves three major steps: sparse coding, clipping and summing, and competitive coding. The details of the presented SMCC method are as follows:

(1) Sparse coding: given a 128×128 palmprint image, we uniformly divide it into sample 32×32 patches, where the horizontal and vertical distances between two adjacent centers of patches are three pixels. For each image patch $\mathbf{x}_{ij}$ centered at pixel (i, j), we use the FISTA algorithm (Beck and Teboulle 2009) to obtain the filter coefficients $\boldsymbol{\alpha}_{ij}$ by solving Eq. (5.14). Thus, we obtain 18 coefficient images that correspond to the three scales and six orientations.

(2) Clipping and summing: the response to the correct orientation and scale should be positive. So, after sparse coding, we change all negative values of the sparse multiscale orientation field to zeros, only preserve the sparse coefficients with positive values. Next, we sum the new coefficient images in the same orientation to construct a combined receptive field $\boldsymbol{\omega}_{ij}$ of the palmprint image.

(3) Competitive coding: use the competitive code (Kong and Zhang 2004) method to encode the dominant orientation of the receptive field into a binary representation and adopt the angular distance to calculate the difference between the

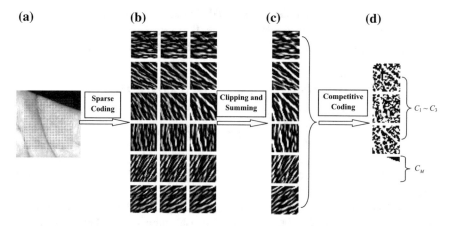

(a)   **(b)**   **(c)**   **(d)**

Fig. 5.6 Schematic diagram of the feature extraction procedure of the sparse multiscale competitive code. First, sparse coding is used to calculate the coefficients of 18 filters in the dictionary that correspond to three scales and six orientations. This is done for all patches centered at the blue pixels in the palmprint image. The sparse codes of all the patches are arranged into 18 coefficient images in, where the images in the same row are in different scales while those in the same column are in different orientations. Second, negative coefficients are replaced with zeros and the coefficient images in the same row are summed to construct a combined receptive field. Finally, the competitive code is generated for the binary palmprint representation, which includes three binary feature matrices and one palmprint mask. © 2010 IEEE. Reprinted with permission, from Zuo et al. (2010)

two palms. For a patch $\mathbf{x}_{ij}$, suppose $\boldsymbol{\omega}_{ij}(\theta)$ denotes the combined receptive field $\boldsymbol{\omega}_{ij}$ in the θ-th direction, then the winning index $W(i, j)$ of the orientation is defined as

$$W(i,j) = \arg \min_{\theta} \boldsymbol{\omega}_{ij}(\theta). \tag{5.19}$$

As discussed in Sect. 5.2.1.2, in the presented SMCC method, we also compactly encode each winning index into $t/2$ bits to improve the matching efficiency of palmprint features. If the number t of orientations is even, a coding rule is defined as

$$C(i,j,k) = \begin{cases} 1, & k \le W(i,j) < k+t/2 \\ 0, & elsewise \end{cases}, \ k = 1,\ldots,t/2. \tag{5.20}$$

In addition, as it is possible that not all pixels in the palmprint image are inside the palm, we further add one mask bit to indicate the palmprint pixels. So, the final SMCC code of a palmprint image consists of $t/2 + 1$ binary matrices $\mathbf{C} = \{C_1, C_2, \ldots, C_{t/2}, C_M\}$, where $C_k = (C(i,j,k))$ and C_M is the palmprint mask.

5.3.2.2 Matching

The angular distance is adopted (Kong and Zhang 2004) to measure the dissimilarity between two SMCC codes. Suppose $\mathbf{P} = \{P_1, P_2, \ldots, P_{t/2}, P_M\}$ and $\mathbf{Q} = \{Q_1, Q_2, \ldots, Q_{t/2}, Q_M\}$ are two SMCC codes, their angular distance is

$$d_A = \frac{\sum\limits_{x=1}^{N} \sum\limits_{y=1}^{N} \sum\limits_{i=1}^{t/2} (P_M(x,y) \wedge Q_M(x,y)) \wedge (P_i(x,y) \otimes Q_i(x,y))}{\dfrac{t}{2} \sum\limits_{x=1}^{N} \sum\limits_{y=1}^{N} (P_M(x,y) \wedge Q_M(x,y))}, \tag{5.21}$$

where $\otimes$ is the bitwise exclusive OR (XOR) operator and $\wedge$ is the bitwise AND operator.

To reduce the adverse effect of palmprint image translation and rotation, we further divide each SMCC binary code into four submatrices. For every combination of translation and rotation, we record the partial angular distance between the training sample and query sample submatrices by submatrices, i.e., the summations in Eq. (5.21) are only for pixels (x, y) that are within the overlapping region of two corresponding submatrices, and then use the average of the four partial angular distances as the mismatching score under the combination of translation and rotation. The minimum mismatching score is recorded as the final mismatching score. Then, the query palmprint is identified to the palmprint that has the smallest mismatching score with the query palmprint.

5.3.3 Experimental Results

In the experiments, some state-of-the-art palmprint authentication algorithms, such as competitive code (Kong and Zhang 2004), ordinal code (Sun et al. 2005), robust line orientation code (RLOC) (Jia et al. 2008), and some multiscale palmprint recognition approaches (Han et al. 2008; Zuo et al. 2008), are compared with the presented SMCC method. All experiments were performed on two popular palmprint databases, PolyU (D. Zhang) and CASIA[1] databases. Three popular evaluation indexes: receiver operating characteristic (ROC) curve, equal error rate (EER), and the false rejection rate (FRR) at a specific false acceptance rate (FAR), were used to evaluate the verification performance of the above palmprint authentication methods.

5.3.3.1 Experimental Results on the PolyU Palmprint Database

For the PolyU palmprint database (version 2), each original palmprint image was also cropped and resized to a 128 by 128 matrix. The total number of matches was 30,042,876, which included 74,068 genuine and 29,968,808 impostor matches.

Figure 5.7 shows the ROC curves of different palmprint identification methods. From Fig. 5.7, we can see that the genuine acceptance rate (GAR) of the presented SMCC method is higher than those of other palmprint identification methods at any given FAR.

Table 5.2 lists the GAR values at several typical FAR values (GAR_{-2} and GAR_{-3}) and the EER values of the presented SMCC method and three popular palmprint authentication methods. In Table 5.2, GAR_{-2} (GAR_{-3}) denotes the GAR values corresponding to FAR $= 10^{-2}$ % (10^{-3} %). Table 5.2 shows that the presented SMCC method achieves the lowest EER value and the highest GAR_{-2} and GAR_{-3} values compared with the other state-of-the-art palmprint authentication methods.

We further demonstrate that the presented SMCC method can greatly improve the error rates of palmprint authentication from the statistical aspect. According to (Guyon et al. 1998), let α be the confidence interval, $\alpha = 0.05$, and e and $\hat{e}$ be the error rate of a classifier C and the estimated error rate obtained by using a test set with limited samples, respectively. Assume that recognition errors are Bernoulli trials. Given a typical value $\beta = 0.2$, Guyon et al. (1998) proposed a simple equation to determine the number of trials, $N \approx 100/e$, to achieve $1 - \alpha$ confidence in that the error rate estimate is within the range $|e - \hat{e}| < \beta e$. For the PolyU palmprint database (version 2), the number of genuine and impostor comparisons are 74,068 and 29,968,808, respectively. Thus, the statistical significance could be guaranteed with an empirical error rate down to 0.33×10^{-3} %. From Table 5.2, one can see that the EER value, the FRR_{-2} ($= 1 - GAR_{-2}$) and FRR_{-3} ($= 1 - GAR_{-3}$) values of the presented SMCC method are both 0.33×10^{-3} %

---

[1]CASIA Palmprint Database, http://www.csbr.ia.ac.cn.

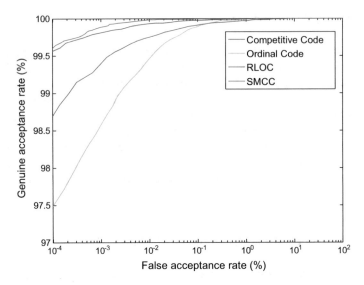

Fig. 5.7 The ROC curves of different palmprint verification methods on the PolyU palmprint database (version 2). © 2010 IEEE. Reprinted with permission, from Zuo et al. (2010)

Table 5.2 Comparison of error rates of different palmprint verification methods on the PolyU palmprint database

	SMCC	Competitive code (Kong and Zhang 2004)	RLOC (Jia et al. 2008)	Ordinal code (Sun et al. 2005)
EER (%)	**0.014**	0.038	0.091	0.104
GAR_{-2} (%)	**99.98**	99.93	99.75	99.46
GAR_{-3} (%)	**99.89**	99.81	99.40	98.58

Note Bold numbers denote the best results with respect to different evaluation indicates (Zuo et al. 2010)

higher and 20 % lower than those of other palmprint identification methods. This proves that the error rates of the presented SMCC method are statistically significantly improved on the PolyU palmprint database.

Table 5.3 lists the computational time and template sizes of the SMCC method and some single-scale palmprint authentication methods. The SMCC method extracts features in several scales, so the feature extraction time of the SMCC method is higher than the other three palmprint authentication methods. From the comparison of matching times, one can see that the SMCC method is much slower than that of the RLOC algorithm, and is only slightly faster than that of the competitive code and ordinal code methods.

Table 5.4 shows a comparison of EER values and template sizes of the SMCC algorithm and two popular multiscale palmprint authentication methods, the multiscale competitive code (MCC) (Zuo et al. 2008) and hierarchical appearance

Table 5.3 Computational time (ms) and template sizes (bytes) of different palmprint verification methods (Zuo et al. 2010)

	SMCC	Competitive Code	RLOC	Ordinal code
Feature extraction (ms)	330	70	2.2	58
Matching (ms)	0.05	0.04	0.85	0.04
Template size (bytes)	384	384	1024	384

Note The experimental environment is: Windows XP Professional, Pentium 4 2.66 GHz, 512 M RAM, VC 6.0

Table 5.4 Comparison of error rate (%) and template sizes (bytes) of different multiscale palmprint verification methods on the PolyU database

	SMCC	MCC	HAS
EER (%)	**0.014**	0.023	0.02
Template size (bytes)	**384**	480	672[*]

Note Bold numbers denote the best values (Zuo et al. 2010)
[*]The number "672" could not be directly obtained from the literature, it is our estimate

statistics (HAS) (Han et al. 2008). From Table 5.4, we can see that the EER value of the SMCC method is lower than that of the two other methods.

Finally, we compare the template sizes of different palmprint identification methods. From Tables 5.3 and 5.4, we can see that the template size of the SMCC method is smaller than those of multiscale methods. Although the SMCC method has the same template size as the competitive code and the ordinal code method, it contains more information than those of two single-scale code methods. It should be noted that the RLOC method can also be stored in 384 bytes, but it is better stored in 1024 bytes for fast matching. In conclusion, the SMCC method is a more compact and effective multiscale palmprint representation method.

5.3.3.2 Experimental Results on the CASIA Palmprint Database

The CASIA palmprint database contains 5239 palmprint images captured from 301 subjects. Each subject provides about eight palmprint images of his/her left and right palms. It should be noted that the individual "101" is the same as individual "19" in this database, so the above two individuals are merged into one individual in the experiments. Thus, the number of individuals is 300 and the number of palms is 600.[2]

For the CASIA palmprint database, the total number of matches is 13,710,466, which includes 20,574 genuine and 13,689,892 impostor matches. Figure 5.8 shows the ROC curves of the SMCC method and different single-scale palmprint identification methods: competitive code, ordinal code, and RLOC. From

---

[2]Two poor quality images were excluded from our experiments because they lack necessary fiducial points for preprocessing.

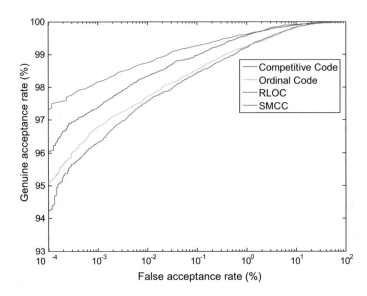

Fig. 5.8 The ROC curves of different palmprint verification methods on the CASIA palmprint database. © 2010 IEEE. Reprinted with permission, from Zuo et al. (2010)

Table 5.5, one can see that the GAR value of the SMCC method is always higher than those of the three other palmprint authentication methods.

Table 5.5 lists the comparison of error rates of the SMCC method and the above single-scale palmprint authentication methods. From Table 5.5, we can see that the SMCC method achieves the lowest EER value and the highest GAR–2 and GAR–3 values of the four methods. For the CASIA palmprint database, we can also discuss the performance improvement of error rates of the SMCC method from the statistical significance aspect by using the same method as that described in Sect. 5.3.3.1. The results also prove that the SMCC method obtains better performance of palmprint verification than other methods.

From Tables 5.2 and 5.5, one can find that the EER values obtained using the CASIA palmprint database are all much higher than those obtained using the PolyU palmprint database. This may be caused by three reasons. First, the quality of palm print images of the CASIA palmprint database is lower than those from the PolyU

Table 5.5 Comparison of error rates of different palmprint verification methods on the CASIA palmprint database		SMCC	Competitive code	RLOC	Ordinal code
	EER (%)	**0.48**	0.55	0.81	0.84
	GAR$_2$ (%)	**98.74**	98.34	97.60	97.74
	GAR$_3$ (%)	**98.16**	97.38	96.31	96.80

Note Bold numbers denote the best results with respect to different evaluation indicates

© 2010 IEEE. Reprinted with permission, from Zuo et al. (2010)

palmprint database. Second, the palmprint images of the PolyU palmprint database restricted registration by using some pegs, while palmprint images of the CASIA palmprint database brought a large degree of freedom. Finally, the number of palms in the CASIA palmprint database is larger than in the PolyU palmprint database, which leads to a bad performance of palmprint verification.

5.4   An Improved Distance Measure for Palmprint Authentication

Distance measure plays an important role in palmprint authentication. Thus, in this section, we will compare different distance measure methods for palmprint authentication. Moreover, we also present an accurate orientation extraction method by using a for palmprint authentication.

5.4.1   Steerable Filter-Based Accurate Orientation Extraction

5.4.1.1   Steerable Filter

A steerable filter can also be viewed as an oriented filter in which a filter of arbitrary orientation is synthesized as a linear combination of a small number of basic filters (Freeman and Adelson 1991). After the filter response of basic filters is obtained, the response at an arbitrary orientation also can be obtained analytically as a function of orientation. Compared with the filter bank-based approach, such as Gabor filters and Gaussian filters, a steerable filter is flexible and provides an alternative to obtain a more accurate result rather than increasing the number of filters. Thus, use of the steerable filter for orientation extraction gives more possibilities to improve the efficiency of the palmprint authentication.

A steerable filter is defined as follows (Jacob and Unser 2004):

$$h(x, y) = \sum_{k=1}^{M} \sum_{i=0}^{k} \alpha_{k,i} \frac{\partial^{k-i}}{\partial x^{k-i}} \frac{\partial^{i}}{\partial y^{i}} g(x, y), \tag{5.22}$$

where $g(x, y)$ denotes an arbitrary isotropic window function, and M represent the order of the steerable filter. For a signal $f(x, y)$, its filter response by using any rotated version of $h(x, y)$ is

$$f(\mathbf{x}) * h(\mathbf{R}_{\theta}\mathbf{x}) = \sum_{k=1}^{M} \sum_{i=0}^{k} b_{k,i}(\theta) f_{k,i}(\mathbf{x}), \tag{5.23}$$

where $\mathbf{x} = (x, y)$, and $\mathbf{R}_\theta$ is the rotation matrix

$$\mathbf{R}_\theta = \begin{bmatrix} \cos(\theta) & \sin(\theta) \\ -\sin(\theta) & \cos(\theta) \end{bmatrix}, \tag{5.24}$$

and the functions $f_{k,i}(x, y)$ are the filter response of the signal $f(x, y)$ with $g_{k,i}(x, y)$

$$f_{k,i}(x, y) = f(x, y) * \underbrace{\left(\frac{\partial^{k-i}}{\partial x^{k-i}} \frac{\partial^i}{\partial y^i} g(x, y) \right)}_{g_{k,i}(x,y)}. \tag{5.25}$$

The orientation-dependent weights $b_{k,i}(\theta)$ are given by

$$b_{k,i}(\theta) = \left(\sum_{j=0}^{k} \alpha_{k,j} \sum_{l,m \in S(k,j,i)} \binom{k-j}{l} \binom{j}{m} (-1)^m \cos(\theta)^{j+(l-m)} \sin(\theta)^{(k-j)-(l-m)} \right), \tag{5.26}$$

where $S(k, j, i)$ is the set

$$S(k, j, i) = \{l, m | 0 \leq l \leq k - j; \quad 0 \leq m \leq j; \quad k - (l + m) = i\}. \tag{5.27}$$

Once $f_{k,i}(x, y)$ are determined, $f(\mathbf{x}) * h(\mathbf{R}_\theta \mathbf{x})$ can be efficiently evaluated via a weighted sum with its coefficients that are trigonometric polynomials of θ (Jacob and Unser 2004). After the image is convolved by basic steerable filters, the filter results at arbitrary orientation can be obtained

$$f * h_\theta = q_0 \cos(\theta)^M + q_1 \cos(\theta)^{M-1} \sin(\theta) + \cdots + q_M \sin(\theta)^M, \tag{5.28}$$

where h_θ denotes the rotated version of filter $h(x, y)$, and $q_0, \ldots, q_M$ can be determined by the filter response of basic filters and coefficient $\alpha_{k,i}$. Eq (5.28) is a function with only one variable—θ. So at the local maxima and minima of $(f * h_\theta)$, we have

$$\frac{\partial}{\partial \theta} (f * h_\theta) = 0. \tag{5.29}$$

Because a palm line is a typical dark line, the final orientation feature of the palm line is defined as

$$\theta^* = \arg \min_\theta (f * h_\theta). \tag{5.30}$$

To determine the optimal steerable filter for orientation extraction of the palm line, some parameters need to be determined, such as the isotropic window function

$g(x, y)$, coefficient $\alpha_{k,i}$, and the order of the steerable filter M in Eq. (5.22). As for the isotropic function, we choose the Gaussian because it is optimally localized in the sense of the uncertainty principle. Coefficient $\alpha_{k,i}$ can be determined based on the Canny-like optimal criterion proposed in (Jacob and Unser 2004). If we choose the idealized palm line model as

$$f_0(x, y) = \delta(y), \tag{5.31}$$

where δ is the Dirac delta function, the filter maximizing the optimal criterion is regarded as the optimal filter for orientation extraction of the palm line. In addition, we prefer to use a high-order steerable filter because it has more degrees of freedom and better orientation selectivity. Because the number of basic filters increases with the order M, to provide the best compromise between computational complexity and detection accuracy, we adopt $M = 4$ in the presented method. Then, the optimal steerable filter is

$$h = -0.204\sigma g_{yy} + 0.059\sigma g_{xx} + 0.063\sigma^3 g_{yyyy} - 0.194\sigma^3 g_{xxyy} + 0.024\sigma^3 g_{xxxx}, \tag{5.32}$$

where $g_x = \partial g/\partial x$, $g_y = \partial g/\partial y$, σ is the Gaussian function parameter.

As shown in Fig. 5.9a–h are eight basic filters; Fig. 5.9i is the optimal steerable filter synthesized from these basic filters. Obviously, if more than eight orientations are adopted for accurate orientation extraction, the high-order steerable filter-based approach will be more computationally efficient than other filter bank-based approaches for palmprint authentication.

5.4.1.2 Discrete Orientation Feature Representation

The orientation feature obtained by Eq. (5.30) is a continuous value in the range [0, 180], as shown in Fig. 5.10a. This representation needs much more space to store and more time to calculate the distance. Compared with the continuous representation, the discrete representation has good properties and can overcome the above problems. Suppose N denotes the quantization number, the resolution (or minimum resolvable angle) of quantization representation is defined as the width of the quantization bin

$$r_D = 180/N. \tag{5.33}$$

The discrete representation of the continuous orientation α is then defined as

$$\alpha_D = [\alpha/r_D], \tag{5.34}$$

where $[\cdot]$ denotes the round function. Angles $\alpha_i = i \times r_D$, $i = 0, 1, \ldots, N - 1$ are known as quantization borders.

(a)   **(b)**   **(c)**   **(d)**   **(e)**   **(f)**   **(g)**   **(h)**   **(i)**

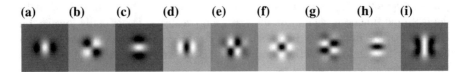

Fig. 5.9 The appearance of basic filters **a** g_{xx}, **b** g_{xy}, **c** g_{yy}, **d** g_{xxxx}, **e** g_{xxxy}, **f** g_{xxyy}, **g** g_{xyyy}, **h** g_{yyyy}, and **i** optimal steerable filter for palm line orientation feature extraction. Reprinted from Zuo et al. (2011), with permission from Elsevier

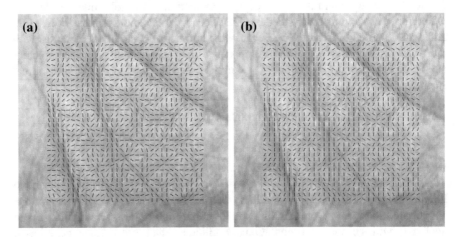

Fig. 5.10 Orientation maps of one palmprint image using: **a** continuous and **b** discrete representation. Reprinted from Zuo et al. (2011), with permission from Elsevier

Figure 5.10b shows an example of an orientation map of one palmprint image using a discrete representation with six quantization numbers. From Fig. 5.10a, b, the discrete representation can be viewed as an approximation of a continuous representation, and the error of approximation (also known as quantization error) decreases with the increase of quantization number N.

It should be noted that different orientations will have the same output after quantization when they are in the same quantization bin. Thus, the difference between them will disappear if we use a discrete representation. On the other hand, if two orientations have small angular distance but fall into different bins, their distance will be enlarged by quantization.

5.4.2   Generalized Angular Distance

In the previous section, we discussed the continuous orientation features and discrete orientation features of palm lines. In this section, we first present a generalized angular distance for matching continuous orientation features, and then extend it to the discrete representation cases for palmprint authentication.

5.4.2.1   Continuous Cases

Suppose α and β are two orientations, d_{cw} and d_{ccw} are the minimum angle one requires to rotate α in the clockwise and counterclockwise sense to be the same as β, respectively,

$$d_{cw}(\alpha, \beta) = (\alpha - \beta) \mod 180, \tag{5.35}$$

$$d_{ccw}(\alpha, \beta) = (\beta - \alpha) \mod 180. \tag{5.36}$$

As shown in Fig. 5.11a, the angular distance between α and β is

$$d_{C\_A}(\alpha, \beta) = \min(d_{cw}, d_{ccw}). \tag{5.37}$$

To deal with the adverse effect of rotation caused by palmprint preprocessing and the deformation caused by finger movement, the distance measure should have some tolerance for small angular differences and can be defined as

$$d_{C\_L}(\alpha, \beta) = \begin{cases} 0, & \text{if } d_{C\_A}(\alpha, \beta) \leq T_l \\ \frac{d_{C\_A}(\alpha,\beta) - T_l}{90 - T_l}, & \text{otherwise} \end{cases}, \tag{5.38}$$

where T_l denotes the lower threshold for angular tolerance. On the other hand, we also can form a distance measure to penalize large angular distance, which is unusual for genuine palmprint matching. We define

$$d_{C\_U}(\alpha, \beta) = \begin{cases} \frac{d_{C\_A}(\alpha,\beta)}{T_u} & \text{if } d_{C\_A}(\alpha, \beta) \leq T_u \\ 1 & \text{otherwise} \end{cases}, \tag{5.39}$$

where T_u denotes the upper threshold for angular penalization.

By taking both tolerance for small angular difference and penalty for large angular distance into account, a generalized angular distance is defined as

$$d_{C\_G}(\alpha, \beta) = \begin{cases} 0 & d_{C\_A}(\alpha, \beta) \leq T_l \\ \frac{d_{C\_A}(\alpha,\beta) - T_l}{T_u - T_l} & T_l < d_{C\_A}(\alpha, \beta) \leq T_u \\ 1 & d_{C\_A}(\alpha, \beta) > T_u \end{cases}, \tag{5.40}$$

where T_l and T_u are lower and upper thresholds, $T_l \leq T_u$. When $T_l = T_u$, it becomes a simple threshold function, we denote it as d_{C_T}

$$d_{C\_T}(\alpha, \beta) = \begin{cases} 0 & \text{if } d_{C\_A}(\alpha, \beta) \leq T_l \\ 1 & \text{otherwise} \end{cases}. \tag{5.41}$$

Figure 5.11 shows a graphical comparison of the above five distance measures using a continuous representation. Obviously, when $T_l = 0$ and $T_u = 90$, the presented generalized angular distance is a typical conventional angular distance, while d_{C_L} and d_{C_U} correspond to the cases of d_{C_G} with $T_u = 90$ and $T_l = 0$.

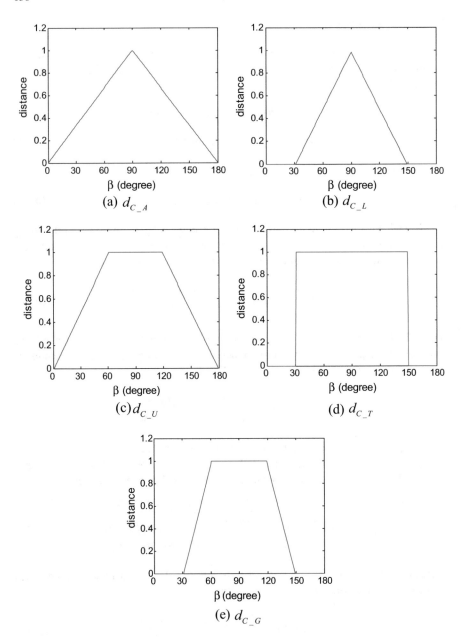

Fig. 5.11 Five distance measures for comparing orientations α and β using a continuous representation. We set $\alpha = 0$ and calculate the distance between α and β when β varies from 0 to 180 degrees using: **a** angular distance, **b** angular distance with lower threshold $T_l = 30$, **c** angular distance with upper threshold $T_u = 60$, **d** generalized angular distance with $T_l = T_u = 30$, and **e** generalized angular distance with $T_l = 30$ and $T_u = 60$. Reprinted from Zuo et al. (2011), with permission from Elsevier

5.4.2.2   Discrete Cases

In this subsection, the above five angular distances of the continuous cases are extended to the discrete versions. Suppose d_{D_A}, d_{D_L}, d_{D_U}, d_{D_T}, and d_{D_G} are angular distances of discrete cases. It should be noted that when applied to discrete data, thresholds T_l and T_u are restricted by the resolution of quantization representation. The valid threshold must be an integer in the range $[0, N/2]$, which corresponds to the angular distance of integral multiple of resolution, r_D.

When $T_l = 0$ and $T_u = 1$, the generalized angular distance is the same as the orientation equivalence proposed in (Jia et al. 2008), which simply matches the two orientations whether they are the same or not. We denote it as d_{D_O}. Figure 5.12 shows all six distance measures for discrete representation when the quantization number $N = 6$. In Fig. 5.12, the distance measures in the first row belong to d_{D_L}, those in the first column belong to d_{D_U}, and those in the diagonal line belong to d_{D_T}. Thus, the orientation equivalence (as shown in Fig. 5.12f) can be viewed as special cases of both d_{D_U} and d_{D_T}, while the angular distance (as shown in Fig. 5.12a) can be viewed as special cases of both d_{D_L} and d_{D_U}.

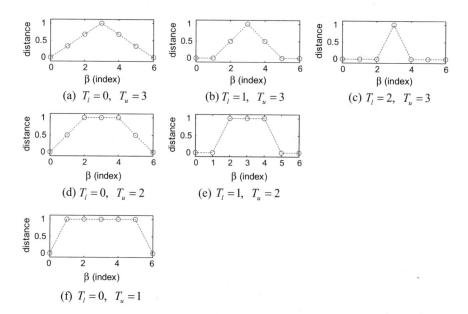

(a) $T_l = 0$, $T_u = 3$ (b) $T_l = 1$, $T_u = 3$ (c) $T_l = 2$, $T_u = 3$

(d) $T_l = 0$, $T_u = 2$ (e) $T_l = 1$, $T_u = 2$

(f) $T_l = 0$, $T_u = 1$

Fig. 5.12 All six distance measures for a discrete representation when the quantization number $N = 6$. We set $\alpha_D = 0$ and calculate the distance between α_D and β_D when β_D varies from 0 to 5, using different thresholds T_l and T_u. **a, b, c** belong to d_{D_L}, **a, d, f** belong to d_{D_U}, and **c, e, f** belong to d_{D_T}. Moreover, **a** and **f** are also known as the angular distance (Kong and Zhang 2004) and orientation equivalence (Jia et al. 2008), respectively. Reprinted from Zuo et al. (2011), with permission from Elsevier

5.4.3 Experimental Results and Discussion

In this section, we again use the PolyU and CASIA palmprint databases to evaluate the presented orientation extraction and distance measure algorithms. In the experiments, different distance measures are compared for matching of continuous and discrete orientation features. The continuous orientation feature is extracted by steerable filters described in Sect. 5.4.1, and the discrete representation is obtained using Eq. (5.36).

5.4.3.1 Experimental Results on PolyU Database

Similar to the previous experiment, each palmprint image of the PolyU database was also cropped and resized to the 128 by 128 matrix (Zhang et al. 2003). To reduce the influence of imperfect ROI extraction, the features are vertically and horizontally translated in a small range in the matching stage, and the ranges of the vertical and horizontal translations are defined from −4 to +4. A minimal distance obtained by translated matching is regarded as the final distance. In the following experiments, we also used the EER value to evaluate different palmprint authentication methods.

(1) **Continuous cases**

We first compare different angular distances for matching of continuous orientation features on the PolyU database. We test d_{C_A}, d_{C_L} with different T_l values, d_{C_U} with different T_u values, and d_{C_T} with different $T_l = T_u$ values. Figure 5.13 shows the EER values of different angular distances using a continuous representation. From Fig. 5.13, we can find that, using small T_l values, the EER value of d_{C_T} is much higher than that of d_{C_A}. However, with an increase in T_l, the EER value of d_{C_T} drops quickly and becomes smaller than that of d_{C_A}. For most cases, the EER values of d_{C_L} are much higher than the other three distance measures. The EER value of d_{C_L} grows with the increase of T_l, which indicates that pure tolerance for angular difference cannot efficiently improve the palmprint identification performance. Thus, in the following experiments we will set $T_l = 0$ or $T_l = T_u$ and do not consider other values of T_l. Figure 5.13 also shows that the EER value of d_{C_U} drops quickly from $T_u = 3$ to $T_u = 21$ and then smoothly to its minimum when $T_u = 30$, which indicates that an appropriate penalty for large angular distance is helpful for improving the palmprint identification performance.

(2) **Discrete cases**

Discrete representations have the characteristics of small feature size and fast matching speed. To get an appropriate discrete representation, such as the quantization number N and the values of T_l and T_u, we give an analysis of the properties of different distance measures and their performance using a continuous representation. First, because d_{C_T} has the advantages of large angular

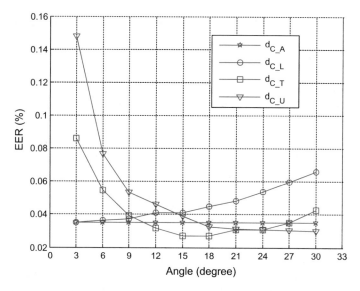

Fig. 5.13 Comparisons of the EER values on the PolyU palmprint database using a continuous representation and different distance measures. Reprinted from Zuo et al. (2011), with permission from Elsevier

penalty and small angular tolerance, its results can suggest an appropriate angular threshold. To make this threshold valid for a discrete representation, the resolution of quantization representation should be equal to or smaller than the optimal threshold of d_{C_T}. Figure 5.13 shows that when $T_1 = T_u = 15$, the EER value of d_{C_T} reaches the minimum value. Thus, we can set the resolution of quantization to $15°$ and the quantization number $N = 180/15 = 12$. In this case, the values of T_l and T_u can be taken in the range of [0, 6], each of which corresponds to an angle of a multiple of $15°$. Second, as discussed in the previous section, the EER values of d_{C_L} suggest that tolerance for angular difference cannot improve the identification performance, so in the discrete representation we set T_l to 0. Finally, the EER value of d_{C_U} drops to its minimum value with the increase of the angle, thus we set $T_u = 2$ because the resolution of quantization is 15 degrees. Using the parameters obtained above, i.e., $N = 12$, $T_l = 0$, and $T_u = 2$, the optimal discrete representation and distance measure are obtained. Table 5.6 shows a comparison of EER values of different distance measures using the above optimal discrete representation. From Table 5.6, one can see that using the generalized distance measure can achieve the smallest EER value. Table 5.7 lists the EER value using the generalized distance measure, the competitive code method, and the RLOC method. From Table 5.7, we can see that the discrete representation with the generalized distance measure achieves a better performance than the other two methods for palmprint authentication.

Table 5.6 Comparison of EER of different distance measures using a discrete representation with $N = 12$

	$T_l = 0, T_u = 2$	$T_l = 0, T_u = 6$ (d_{D_A})	$T_l = 0, T_u = 1$ (d_{D_o})
EER (%)	**0.031**	0.035	0.045

Note Bold numbers denote the best values

Reprinted from Zuo et al. (2011), with permission from Elsevier

Table 5.7 Comparison of EER of the proposed method with competitive code and RLOC

	Presented method	Competitive code	RLOC
EER (%)	**0.031**	0.038	0.082

Note Bold numbers denote the best values

Reprinted from Zuo et al. (2011), with permission from Elsevier

If we use 12 Gabor filters to extract the orientation features, and use generalized distance measure to match orientation features, the EER value is 0.029 %. Compared with the EER value of the presented method listed in Table 5.7, in terms of verification accuracy, a high-order steerable filter-based approach is a little lower than the filter bank-based approach. However, the presented method is more efficient than using the filter bank-based approach with 12 Gabor filters because only the presented method involves the convolution with eight steerable filters, while the latter involves 12 convolution operations.

(3) **Space and time requirements**

For the designed algorithm, the recognition accuracy, space, and efficiency are all very important in real applications. The competitive code and RLOC methods both use six filters to extract features, then save the extracted feature with three bits in a bitwise way, and use a feature matching method by bitwise operations to identify the unknown palm. Thus, the template size of the two methods is 384 bytes, and the matching time of two templates is 0.25 ms. For the above two methods, if we use 12 filters to extract orientation features, the template size will become 768 bytes, and the matching time of the two templates will become 0.5 ms. For the presented generalized distance measure, the bitwise matching method cannot be applied directly, so we present utilization of a look up table for the storage of the distance between orientations, and its space requirement is 256×256 bytes. By using this table, we only need $\lceil \log_2 12 \rceil = 4$ bits to store one orientation feature. Thus, the template size of the presented method is 512 bytes, and the average matching time of the presented generalized distance measure is about 0.3 ms. Thus, in both template size and matching speed, the generalized distance measure is superior to angular distance and orientation equivalence. Although the efficiency of the presented method is a little lower than that of the competitive code method and RLOC method, it is still fast enough for practical small-scale and medium-scale palmprint recognition applications.

5.4.3.2   Experimental Results on the CASIA Database

In this section, we use the CASIA database[3] to evaluate the presented method. A detailed introduction to the CASIA palmprint database is in Sect. 5.3.2. In the following experiments, we also use the same test protocol described in Sect. 5.4.3.1 to compare different algorithms.

(1) **Continuous cases**

Figure 5.14 shows comparisons of the EER values on the CASIA palmprint database using a continuous representation and different distance measures. From Fig. 5.14, we can see that the EER value of d_{C_L} grows with the increase of the degree, which is similar to that on the PolyU palmprint database. However, d_{C_T} and d_{C_U} can obtain much smaller EER than d_{C_A} even for a small degree, which is slightly different from that on the PolyU palmprint database. Furthermore, the T_u thresholds when they obtain the minimum EER are much smaller than those on the PolyU palmprint database. When $T_l = T_u = 9$ degrees, d_{C_T} obtains the minimum EER value 0.380 %, while d_{C_U} obtains the minimum EER value of 0.392 % when the threshold is $T_u = 15$.

(2) **Discrete cases**

For the CASIA palmprint database, we use the same manner described in Sect. 5.4.3.1 to achieve the optimal parameters of the generalized distance measure for discrete representation. Thus, in the following experiment, some parameters of the presented method are set as follows, the quantization number $N = 180/9 = 20$, lower threshold $T_l = 0$ and upper threshold $T_u = 2$. Table 5.8 shows the comparison of EER of different distance measures using discrete representation with the above parameters. From Table 5.8, we can find that the performance of d_{D_O} is much better than that of d_{D_A}, which is consistent with the results in (Guo et al. 2010). The presented distance measure achieves the best performance on the CASIA palmprint database. The EER is 0.407 % when we use 20 Gabor filters to replace the steerable filter for feature extraction of the presented method, which is comparable to that of the steerable filter-based approach. However, the presented method only needs eight steerable filters for feature extraction, which is roughly 2.5 times faster than using 20 Gabor filters in feature extraction.

Table 5.9 lists a comparison of EER of the presented method, competitive code method, and RLOC method. Table 5.9 also shows that the presented method achieves a better performance than the other two methods for palmprint identification. From Tables 5.7 and 5.9, we can see that using an appropriate distance measure and more precise orientation representation makes it possible to improve the performance of palmprint identification.

---

[3]CASIA Palm print Database, [Online]. http://www.cbsr.ia.ac.cn/PalmDatabase.htm.

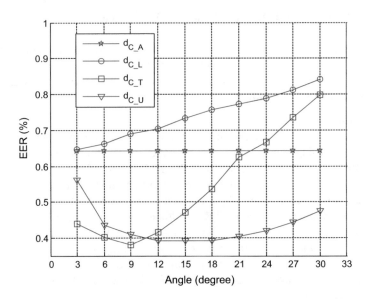

Fig. 5.14 Comparisons of EER values on the CASIA palmprint database using a continuous representation and different distance measures. Reprinted from Zuo et al. (2011), with permission from Elsevier

Table 5.8 Comparison of EER of different distance measures using discrete representation with $N = 20$

	$T_l = 0, T_u = 2$	$T_l = 0, T_u = 10 \ (d_{D\_A})$	$T_l = 0, T_u = 1 \ (d_{D\_o})$
EER (%)	**0.412**	0.643	0.441

Note Bold numbers denote the best values
Reprinted from Zuo et al. (2011), with permission from Elsevier

Table 5.9 Comparison of EER of presented method with competitive code and RLOC

	Presented distance measure	Competitive code	RLOC
EER (%)	**0.412**	0.548	0.714

Note Bold numbers denote the best values
Reprinted from Zuo et al. (2011), with permission from Elsevier

(3) **Discussion**

Intuitively, a good genuine matching can be achieved with an increase in the lower threshold, T_l. However, it may lead to many impostor matchings be falsely accepted, and thus leads to a bad palmprint recognition performance. The above experiments also show that the verification performance cannot be efficiently improved using the angular difference with pure tolerance.

In contrast, the upper threshold, T_u, may cause some genuine matchings to fail. However, it can also eliminate many falsely accepted impostor matchings, and thus improves the performance of palmprint authentication. Compared with

d_{D_A}, the use of an appropriate upper threshold T_u is helpful to improve the verification performance of d_{D_G}.

When using a discrete representation, the orientations in the same quantization bin will have the same discrete value, thus the orientations will also have the same value after quantization. In addition, if two orientations have a small angular distance but fall into different bins, the distance of the two orientations will be increased, which is helpful to obtain a good performance. As a result, the best performance of d_{D_G} for discrete representation is a little worse than that of d_{C_U} when we use a continuous representation. For example, on the PolyU palmprint database, the minimum EER value of d_{C_U} is 0.029 %, while the minimum EER value of d_{D_G} is 0.031 % when $T_l = 0$ and $T_u = 2$. On the CASIA database, the minimum EER values of the above two methods are 0.392 and 0.412 %, respectively.

The experimental results also demonstrate that although the quantization numbers on the two palmprint databases are different, the optimal low and high thresholds for the generalized distance measures are the same, i.e., $T_l = 0$ and $T_u = 2$. This indicates that the orientations are treated as the same in the same quantization bin, as "similar" in the adjacent bins, and as totally different for other conditions. This is a little different from orientation equivalence, which only contains two selections, where the orientations are treated as the same in the same bin, and as totally different for other conditions. We should point out that two orientations with small angular distance may fall into adjacent bins and will have an increased distance by quantization, the presented distance measure is more robust against this type of quantization error, and thus can obtain better performance than d_{D_O}.

5.5   Summary

Orientation code-based methods are one of the most promising algorithms for palmprint authentication. For the orientation code-based method, the used orientation extraction and distance measure algorithms have a great influence on the performance of palmprint authentication. In this chapter, we presented two novel orientation extraction algorithms, and a novel distance measure algorithm for palmprint authentication. Experimental results on PolyU and CASIA palmprint databases prove that the presented multiscale competitive code methods and the distance measure are all beneficial to improve the performance of palmprint recognition.

References

A. Beck, M. Teboulle, A fast iterative shrinkage-thresholding algorithm for linear inverse problems. SIAM J. Imaging Sci. **2**(1), 183–202 (2009)

E. Candes, J. Romberg, *l1-magic: recovery of sparse signals via convex programming*. URL: www.acm.caltech.edu/l1magic/downloads/l1magic.pdf. **4**, 14 (2005)

E.J. Candes, J.K. Romberg, T. Tao, Stable signal recovery from incomplete and inaccurate measurements. Commun. Pure Appl. Math. **59**(8), 1207–1223 (2006)

S. Fischer, F. Šroubek, L. Perrinet, R. Redondo, G. CRIST BAL, Self-invertible 2D log-Gabor wavelets. Int. J. Comput. Vision **75**(2), 231–246 (2007)

W.T. Freeman, E.H. Adelson, The design and use of steerable filters. IEEE Trans. Pattern Anal. Mach. Intell. **9**, 891–906 (1991)

R. Garg, R. Khandekar, *Gradient descent with sparsification: an iterative algorithm for sparse recovery with restricted isometry property*, in Proceedings of the 26th Annual International Conference on Machine Learning (ACM, 2009), pp. 337–344

I.F. Gorodnitsky, B.D. Rao, Sparse signal reconstruction from limited data using FOCUSS: a re-weighted minimum norm algorithm. IEEE Trans. Signal Process. **45**(3), 600–616 (1997)

Z. Guo, W. Zuo, L. Zhang, D. Zhang, A unified distance measurement for orientation coding in palmprint verification. Neurocomputing **73**(4), 944–950 (2010)

I. Guyon, J. Makhoul, R. Schwartz, V. Vapnik, What size test set gives good error rate estimates? IEEE Trans. Pattern Anal. Mach. Intell. **20**(1), 52–64 (1998)

Y. Han, Z. Sun, T. Tan, *Combine hierarchical appearance statistics for accurate palmprint recognition*, in Proceedings of International Conference on Pattern Recognition (IEEE, 2008), pp. 1–4

Y. Han, T. Tan, Z. Sun, *Palmprint recognition based on directional features and graph matching* (Springer, Advances in Biometrics, 2007)

M. Jacob, M. Unser, Design of steerable filters for feature detection using canny-like criteria. IEEE Trans. Pattern Anal. Mach. Intell. **26**(8), 1007–1019 (2004)

W. Jia, D.-S. Huang, D. Zhang, Palmprint verification based on robust line orientation code. Pattern Recogn. **41**(5), 1504–1513 (2008)

S.-J. Kim, K. Koh, M. Lustig, S. Boyd, D. Gorinevsky, An interior-point method for large-scale l 1-regularized least squares. IEEE J. Sel. Topics Sign. Proces. **1**(4), 606–617 (2007)

A. Kong, D. Zhang, M. Kamel, Palmprint identification using feature-level fusion. Pattern Recogn. **39**(3), 478–487 (2006)

A.W.-K. Kong, D. Zhang, *Competitive coding scheme for palmprint verification*, in Proceedings of International Conference on Pattern Recognition (IEEE, 2004), pp. 520–523

W.K. Kong, D. Zhang, W. Li, Palmprint feature extraction using 2-D Gabor filters. Pattern Recogn. **36**(10), 2339–2347 (2003)

S.-I. Lee, H. Lee, P. Abbeel, A.Y. Ng, *Efficient l ∼ l regularized logistic regression*, in Proceedings of National Conference on Artificial Intelligence (Menlo Park, CA; Cambridge, MA; London; AAAI Press; MIT Press; 1999, 2006), pp. 401

W. Li, J. You, D. Zhang, Texture-based palmprint retrieval using a layered search scheme for personal identification. IEEE Trans. Multimedia **7**(5), 891–898 (2005)

Z. Sun, T. Tan, Y. Wang, S.Z. Li, *Ordinal palmprint representation for personal identification*, in Proceedings of IEEE Conference on Computer Vision and Pattern Recognition (IEEE, 2005), pp. 279–284

J. You, W.-K. Kong, D. Zhang, K.H. Cheung, On hierarchical palmprint coding with multiple features for personal identification in large databases. IEEE Trans. Circuits Syst. Video Technol. **14**(2), 234–243 (2004)

F. Yue, W. Zuo, K. Wang, D. Zhang, *A performance evaluation of filter design and coding schemes for palmprint recognition*, in Proceedings of International Conference on Pattern Recognition (IEEE, 2008), pp. 1–4

D. Zhang. PolyU palmprint database. Biometric Research Centre, Hong Kong Polytechnic University, (Online). Available from http://www.comp.polyu.edu.hk/~bio,etrics/

D. Zhang, W.-K. Kong, J. You, M. Wong, Online palmprint identification. IEEE Trans. Pattern Anal. Mach. Intell. **25**(9), 1041–1050 (2003)

W. Zuo, Z. Lin, Z. Guo, D. Zhang, *The multiscale competitive code via sparse representation for palmprint verification*, in IEEE Conference on Proceedings of Computer Vision and Pattern Recognition (CVPR), 2010 (IEEE, 2010), pp. 2265–2272

W. Zuo, F. Yue, K. Wang, D. Zhang, *Multiscale competitive code for efficient palmprint recognition*, in Proceedings of International Conference on Pattern Recognition (IEEE, 2008), pp. 1–4

W. Zuo, F. Yue, D. Zhang, On accurate orientation extraction and appropriate distance measure for low-resolution palmprint recognition. Pattern Recogn. **44**(4), 964–972 (2011)

W. Zuo, D. Zhang, K. Wang, Bidirectional PCA with assembled matrix distance metric for image recognition. IEEE Trans. Syst. Man Cybern. B Cybern. **36**(4), 863–872 (2006)

Chapter 6
Multifeature Palmprint Authentication

Abstract A 2D-based palmprint authentication system is easily fooled by spoof attacks, such as a fake palmprint. To solve that problem, we present a multifeature palmprint authentication system using both 2D and 3D palmprint features in this chapter. This chapter is organized as follows: Sect. 6.1 briefly introduces the background of 2D- and 3D-based palmprint authentication systems. Section 6.2 presents a multifeature palmprint authentication system and the 2D and 3D palmprint image acquisition device. In Sect. 6.3, 2D and 3D feature extraction algorithms are presented. In Sect. 6.4, we present a 2D features matching algorithm for 2D palmprint verification, and then present a 3D features matching algorithm for 3D palmprint authentication. Some experiments are reported to illustrate the robustness of the presented algorithm in Sect. 6.5. The chapter is concluded in Sect. 6.6.

6.1 Introduction

In recent years, various techniques for automatic palmprint authentication have been proposed. From the viewpoint of the information used, available palmprint authentication methods can be categorized into three general groups (Kumar and Zhang 2005): texture-based, line-based, and appearance-based methods. Most existing palmprint authentication methods, including the methods presented in previous chapters, are all proposed for 2D palmprint authentication (Hennings-Yeomans et al. 2007; Connie et al. 2005; Kumar et al. 2003; Li et al. 2002). Experiments show that 2D palmprint authentication methods have some merits, such as fast implementation, simplicity in extracting the features and achievement of high accuracy. However, 2D image-based methods suffer from the problem of various illuminations, colors and strains. Moreover, the 2D palmprint is easy to copy. For example, someone could make his (her) palmprint like that of another person by drawing some lines on his (her) palm. Thus, a 2D-based palmprint verification system is not the best choice for high-security applications.

© Springer Science+Business Media Singapore 2016
D. Zhang et al., *Discriminative Learning in Biometrics*,
DOI 10.1007/978-981-10-2056-8_6

To overcome the above problems associated with the 2D palmprint image, a good solution is to use 3D palmprint images for personal verification. Compared with a 2D palmprint image, the 3D palmprint image is stable to various illuminations and colors, and provides more discriminative features, such as depth information and curvature of the palm surface.

There are few studies reporting the use of 3D features for hand geometry recognition. Typical 3D image-based hand geometry recognition systems (Ross and Jain 1999; Sanchez-Reillo et al. 2000) extract some 3D features such as height of the finger and the palm from 3D hand images. Kumar and Zhang (2007) proposed a 3D-based hand geometry recognition system using a simple peg free imaging setup for personal verification. However, their algorithm does not make use of any 3D features of the hand. Woodard and Flynn (2005) presented a 3D-based personal identification method by extracting surface features of a finger as a biometric feature. In their method, a curvature-based shape index is extracted to represent the finger's surface. Chen et al. (2009) designed a 3D image acquisition system using multiple cameras and light projection for the collection of 3D finger and palmprint images. Malassiotis et al. (2006) proposed a 3D-based biometric identification system using 3D finger geometry features. The hand segmentation, localization and 3D feature measurement were all discussed in their personal authentication system (Malassiotis et al. 2006).

In addition to using the 3D images for personal identification, the fusion methodologies of multiple instances have received much attention in recent years. For example, Singh et al. (2004) proposed a face recognition algorithm by the combination of infrared and visible images, which performed well in reducing the influence of various illuminations. Some researchers proposed to combine 2D and 3D features for face recognition (Chang et al. 2005; Lu et al. 2006). Yan and Bowyer (2005) showed that ear recognition performance can be greatly improved by the fusion of 2D and 3D ear images. The above references all proved that use of multi-biometrics is helpful to improve the recognition performance. Thus, in this chapter, we will present a palmprint verification algorithm by the combination of 2D and 3D palmprint images.

6.2 Multifeature Palmprint Authentication System

To improve the robustness of existing 2D image-based palmprint authentication systems, we present a novel palmprint verification system by utilizing both 2D and 3D palmprint features in this chapter. Figure 6.2 shows the block diagram of the presented palmprint verification system. Figure 6.4 shows the 2D and 3D palmprint image acquisition device, which was designed by the Biometric Research Center of the Hong Kong Polytechnic University and is based on the principle of structured light. Figure 6.1 shows the block diagram of the image acquisition module. In the

Fig. 6.1 Block diagram of
the image acquisition module.
Reprinted from Zhang et al.
(2010), with permission from
Elsevier

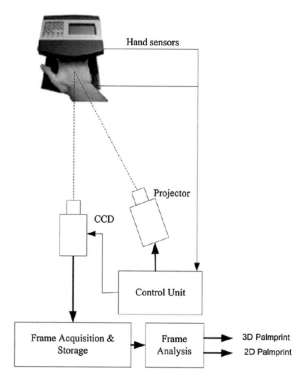

palmprint image acquisition system, some infrared sensors are used to detect the
presence of the hand. When a hand is detected, the palmprint image acquisition
device projects multiple light patterns onto the palm surface and acquires depth
information of the palm using active triangulation. In the device, depth information
is coded with different levels of brightness to distinguish between stripes, and a
computer-controlled liquid crystal display (LCD) projector is employed to generate
arbitrary stripe patterns. A charge-coupled device (CCD) camera is used to capture
the 2D and 3D palmprint images of the hand. The 3D palmprint data are obtained in
point cloud form and are well registered with the corresponding 2D image. The size
of these 2D and 3D palmprint images acquired by this device is 768 × 576.

For each 2D palmprint image, we first use the algorithm proposed by Zhang
et al. (2003) to extract the region of interest (ROI) of the palmprint. Zhang et al.
(2003) presented a robust ROI extraction method by using the gaps between the
fingers as reference points. These ROI subimages have the same size and are all
located at the central part of the 2D palmprint. In fact, when the acquired 2D and
3D palmprint images are well registered by the device, the 2D and 3D palmprint
images have the same ROI. Thus, when the ROI is extracted from 2D palmprint
images, the ROI of 3D palmprint images can be easily located.

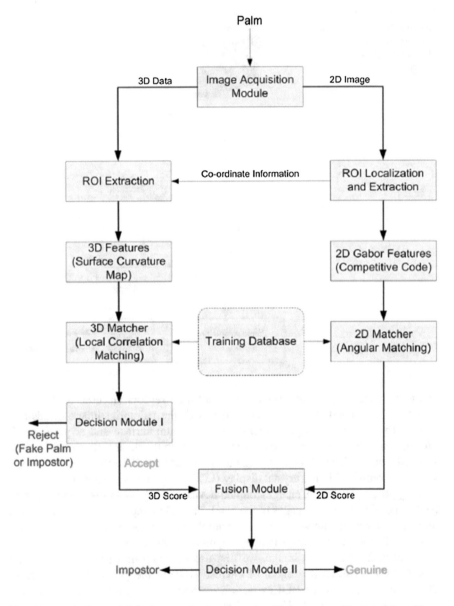

Fig. 6.2 Block diagram of the presented palmprint authentication system. Reprinted from Zhang et al. (2010), with permission from Elsevier

Figure 6.2 shows the detailed information of the presented multilevel palmprint authentication system. Some samples of 3D and the corresponding 2D subimages in the palmprint database are shown in Fig. 6.3. For 3D palmprint subimages, the surface curvature features are further extracted for 3D palmprint verification.

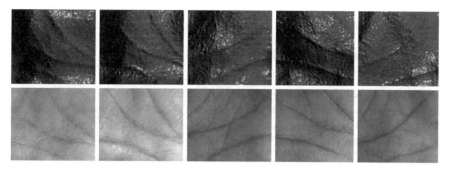

Fig. 6.3 Samples of 3D (*first row*) and 2D (*second row*) subimages in the palmprint database. Reprinted from Zhang et al. (2010), with permission from Elsevier

Fig. 6.4 Data acquisition using the developed device. Reprinted from Zhang et al. (2010), with permission from Elsevier

For each 2D subimage, we adopt the competitive code method (Kong and Zhang 2004) to extract its code features for 2D palmprint matching. For 3D features matching, we use the local correlation method to measure the similarity of two 3D palmprints in this chapter. If the matching score is higher than the threshold of Decision Module I, the unknown palmprint is regarded as a fake palmprint and the process is terminated. This verification step can be viewed as Level 1 of the presented multilevel palmprint authentication system. On the other hand, if the matching score is less than the threshold of Level 1, matching proceeds to Level 2 where a fusion Module is further used to identify the unknown palmprint. In Level 2, 2D and 3D matching scores are fused to make a final decision.

6.3 Feature Extraction

6.3.1 Extraction of 2D Palmprint Features

In the previous chapter, some typical palmprint features-extraction algorithms were introduced in detail. In this chapter, we adopt a typical coding-based method, the competitive coding method (Kong and Zhang 2004), to extract the 2D palmprint features. As described in Sect. 4.2.2.1 of Chap. 4, the competitive coding method utilizes several Gabor filters to extract orientation features of the palm lines. The Gabor filter is defined as

$$
\psi(x, y, \omega_0, \theta) = \frac{\omega_0}{\sqrt{2\pi}\kappa} e^{\left(-\omega_0^2/8\kappa^2\right)\left(4(x\cos\theta + y\sin\theta)^2 + (-x\sin\theta + y\cos\theta)^2\right)}
$$
$$
\times \left[e^{i(\omega_0 x\cos\theta + \omega_0 y\sin\theta)} - e^{-k^2/2} \right],
\tag{6.1}
$$

where ω_0 is the radial frequency in radians per unit length and θ is the filter orientation in radians. κ is a constant and defined by $\kappa = \sqrt{2\ln 2}\left(\frac{2^\delta + 1}{2^\delta - 1}\right)$, δ is the half-amplitude bandwidth of the frequency response. The center frequency ω_0 can be calculated as κ/σ.

In this chapter, we also adopt six orientations to extract the palmprint features. The competitive coding method chooses the filter orientation with minimum filter response as the dominant orientation, and the competitive rule is defined as

$$
P = \arg\min_{j} \left(I(x, y) * \psi_R(x, y, \omega, \theta_j) \right),
\tag{6.2}
$$

where I is a 2D palmprint image, ψ_R is the real part of the Gabor filter, and $*$ denotes the convolution operator. Orientations $\theta_j = j\pi/6, j = \{0, 1, \ldots, 5\}$. After that, the winning orientation p is coded with three bits. The competitive code method uses these binary codes to represent the palmprint features for palmprint authentication. Refer to Sect. 4.2 for a detailed introduction to the code rule of the competitive coding method.

6.3.2 Extraction of 3D Palmprint Features

The extraction of stable and discriminative features is very important for palmprint verification. 3D palmprint images contain rich local structural features. Surface curvature maps, which have good characteristics on representing the local shape of a surface, are typical local features and widely used as 3D features for 3D image classification. In this chapter, we adopt the mean and Gaussian curvatures to represent the surface of a 3D palmprint image (Cantzler and Fisher 2001).

For an image patch centered at a pixel, represented by $X(u, v) = (u, v, f(u, v))$, the Gaussian curvature (K) and mean curvature (H) are defined as (O'neill 2006):

$$K(X) = \frac{f_{uu}f_{vv} - f_{uv}^2}{\left(1 + f_u^2 + f_v^2\right)^2}$$

and

$$H(x) = \frac{\left(1 + f_u^2\right)f_{vv} + \left(1 + f_v^2\right)f_{uu} - 2f_u f_v f_{uv}}{\left(1 + f_u^2 + f_v^2\right)^{3/2}}, \tag{6.3}$$

where f_u, f_v and f_{uu}, f_{vv}, f_{uv} are first- and second-order partial derivatives of $f(u, v)$, respectively. For a 3D surface, the principal curvatures $k1$ and $k2$ can be calculated using

$$k_1, k_2 = H \pm \sqrt{H^2 - K}. \tag{6.4}$$

In practice, these principal curvature values are calculated by fitting a surface over a local neighborhood and then estimating first and second derivatives of the surface at the center pixel (Flynn and Jain 1989). The key issue is to choose a 2D polynomial of appropriate order (at least twice differentiable, since we have to estimate its second-order derivatives). While a higher-order polynomial, such as a bicubic, better approximates the local surface shape, it can make the surface fit more sensitive to noise or outliers in the data. Therefore, we performed local surface fitting with a biquadratic polynomial

$$f(u, v) = a_{00} + a_{10}u + a_{01}v + a_{11}uv + a_{20}u^2 + a_{02}v^2. \tag{6.5}$$

For the center of the image patch ($u = 0, v = 0$), the first and second derivatives of the fitted polynomial are

$$f_u = a_{10}, f_v = a_{01}, f_{uv} = a_{11}, f_{uu} = 2a_{20}, f_{vv} = 2a_{02}. \tag{6.6}$$

Polynomial coefficients can be obtained by solving Eq. (6.5) with a least squares procedure. Then an image filter such as a rectangular window operator can also be obtained. Some specific examples of these window operators are discussed in (Yokoda and Levine 1989; Besl and Jain 1988).

It should be noted that the estimated curvature values with a second-order derivate are also sensitive to noise, which is bad for palmprint authentication. This problem can be solved by increasing the window size of the local patch used for fitting the surface. However, a large window size will excessively smooth the image, which leads to loss of much detailed information of the 3D palmprint image.

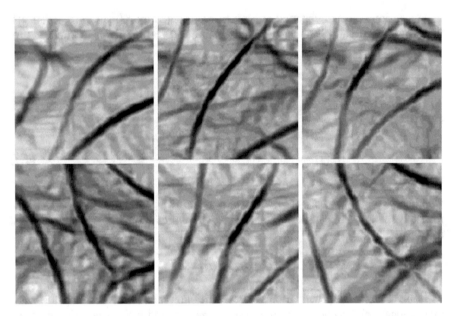

Fig. 6.5 Surface curvature maps for six different subjects. Reprinted from Zhang et al. (2010), with permission from Elsevier

Thus, choosing a suitable fitting size is very important for curvature extraction. In this chapter, we empirically adopt the fitting window size as 13 × 13.

To represent the curvature of every point of the 3D palmprint image by a scalar value, we utilized the curvedness (C) introduced in (Koenderink and van Doorn 1992). The positive value C denotes the degree of sharpness or gentleness of the curve of a pixel of 3D palmprint image (Cantzler and Fisher 2001). The positive value C is defined as

$$C = \sqrt{(k_1^2 + k_2^2)/2}. \tag{6.7}$$

Thus, for a 3D palmprint image, a scalar value of curvature of each pixel is obtained. The set of such curvature scalar values can be viewed as a surface curvature map. This curvature can be stored in a 2D matrix for matching. Samples of curvature maps of some 3D palmprint images are shown in Fig. 6.5. From Fig. 6.5, one can find that the surface curvature maps obtained by the presented 3D features extraction algorithm closely resemble the palm lines, especially the strong principal lines.

6.4 Feature Matching

6.4.1 Matching 2D Features

For 2D palmprint images, the angular distance (Kong and Zhang 2004) is used to match 2D palmprint features in this chapter. Suppose P and Q are two feature matrices of two palmprints. P_M and Q_M are masks of palmprints P and Q used for indicating the nonpalm print pixels. Angular distance $D(P, Q)$ is defined as

$$D(P,Q) = \frac{\sum_{y=0}^{N} \sum_{x=0}^{N} \sum_{i=1}^{3} (P_M(x,y) \otimes Q_M(x,y)) \cap \left(P_i^b(x,y) \cap Q_i^b(x,y)\right)}{3 \sum_{y=0}^{N} \sum_{x=0}^{N} P_M(x,y) \otimes Q_M(x,y)},$$

(6.8)

where $\cap$ and $\otimes$ represent the bitwise AND and XOR operations, respectively. $P_i^b(Q_i^b)$ represents the ith bit plane of palmprint $P(Q)$. Taking into account that palmprint images may be not well registered by the image acquisition device, multiple matches of two palmprints are implemented with one of the features translated in horizontal and vertical directions. We adopt the minimum of the resulting matching scores as the final matching score of two palmprints.

6.4.2 Matching 3D Features

In this subsection, we will present a 3D feature-matching algorithm to measure the similarity of two 3D palmprints. As discussed in Sect. 6.3.2, we use a curvature map to represent the 3D palmprint. The size of the extracted curvature map is 128×128. In the presented algorithm, we use the normalized local correlation of two curvature maps to represent the similarity of two corresponding 3D palmprints. We take the average value of these local correlation values as the final matching score of two 3D palmprints. For 3D features, the matching score is defined as

$$C = \frac{\sum_{i=-N}^{N} \sum_{j=-N}^{N} (P_{ij} - \bar{P})(Q_{ij} - \bar{Q})}{\sqrt{\left[\sum_{i=-N}^{N} \sum_{j=-N}^{N} (P_{ij} - \bar{P})^2\right] \times \left[\sum_{i=-N}^{N} \sum_{j=-N}^{N} (Q_{ij} - \bar{Q})^2\right]}},$$

(6.9)

where P_{ij} and Q_{ij} are curvature values in the local area centered at point (i, j) of the 3D palmprint P and Q, respectively, and $\bar{P}$ and $\bar{Q}$ are the mean curvature values in those local areas. N denotes the radius of the local square area. Clearly, the value of C lies in the range $[-1, 1]$; $C = 1$ and -1 mean a perfect match and mismatch, respectively. Figures 6.6 and 6.7 show a comparison of 3D features matching of the same and different subject by using the presented normalized local correlation method. Red (dark) colored pixels in the correlation map represent high values of

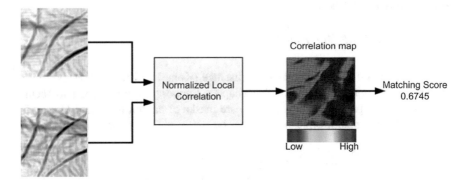

Fig. 6.6 Matching curvature maps from the same subject. Reprinted from Zhang et al. (2010), with permission from Elsevier

correlation while blue (light) represents low correlation of the two curvature maps. The final matching score of two 3D palms is the mean of the correlation map. From Figs. 6.6 and 6.7, one can find that the higher the matching score, the more similar the two 3D palmprints.

6.5 Experimental Results and Discussion

In this section, some experiments are described to evaluate the performance of the presented system. The database used in this section contains 648 palmprint images from 108 individuals and was collected at the Biometric Research Center, the Hong Kong Polytechnic University. The image acquisition device, as shown in Fig. 6.4, was used to capture the 2D and corresponding 3D palm images of the database. For the database, each subject was asked to provide six samples of 2D and 3D palmprint images.

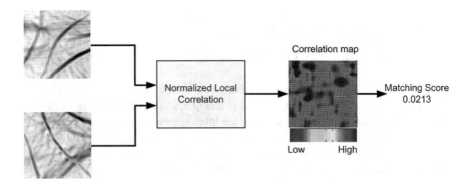

Fig. 6.7 Matching curvature maps from two different subjects. Reprinted from Zhang et al. (2010), with permission from Elsevier

6.5.1   Verification Experiments

A superior palmprint recognition algorithm not only achieves high accuracy in a real palmprint database, but also is robust to spoof attacks. Thus, in this subsection, we will focus on the comparison of different algorithms on real 2D and 3D palmprint images. In the next subsection, we will use some fake palmprint images to test the robustness of the 3D palmprint features against spoof attacks.

In experiments, each palmprint image is matched with all other palmprint images in the database. The total number is 209,628, which includes 1620 genuine and 208,008 impostors. Figure 6.8 shows the genuine and impostor matching score distributions using 2D and 3D palmprint features, respectively. From Fig. 6.8, one can find that the genuine and impostor matching score distributions are well separated and can be easily separated by a linear classifier.

We first use the receiver operating characteristic (ROC) curve, false acceptance rate (FAR) and false rejection rate (FRR), to evaluate the individual palmprint verification performance using the 2D and 3D palmprint features. The FAR and FRR plots of 2D and 3D features are shown in Fig. 6.9a, b, respectively. Table 6.1 shows a comparison of the equal error rate (EER) using 2D, 3D and the (2D+3D) palmprint features. From Table 6.1 and Fig. 6.9, one can find that the verification performance of 2D palmprint features is better than that of 3D features.

We further use some experiments to prove the effectiveness of the combination of 2D and 3D palmprint features. In the Decision Module I, the point at which no genuine users are rejected at Level 1 is chosen as the threshold. In other words, we set the threshold to the value at which FRR obtained using 3D palmprint features becomes zero. From Fig. 6.9, one can find that at point 61.03 the FRR is zero; thus, we set the threshold of Decision Module I as 61.03. Figure 6.10 also shows that all

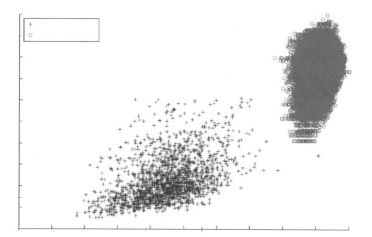

Fig. 6.8 Genuine and impostor scores in 2D space. Reprinted from Zhang et al. (2010), with permission from Elsevier

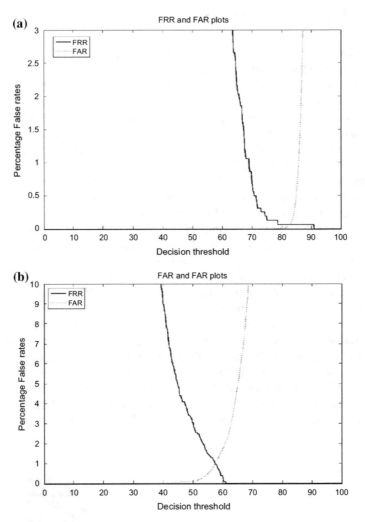

Fig. 6.9 **a** FAR and FRR plots for 2D features. **b** FAR and FRR plots for 3D features. Reprinted from Zhang et al. (2010), with permission from Elsevier

Table 6.1 Performance indices for 2D, 3D and the (2D+3D) palmprint representations

Palmprint matcher	EER (%)	Decidability index (d')
2D	0.0621	6.50
3D	0.9914	5.97
Multilevel (2D+3D)	0.0022	7.45

Reprinted from Zhang et al. (2010), with permission from Elsevier

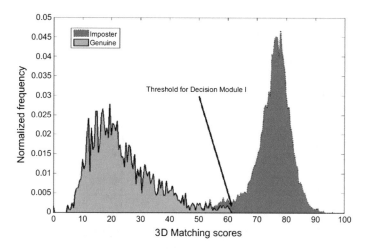

Fig. 6.10 Selection of threshold for Decision Module I. Reprinted from Zhang et al. (2010), with permission from Elsevier

3D matching scores (genuine as well as impostor) above this threshold are rejected at Level 1. After rejection at Level 1, these scores are further used in the next level (Level 2). At Level 2 there are 205,287 matches which include 1620 genuine and 203,667 impostor matches for each of the two modalities. From Fig. 6.10, we can find that the distribution of genuine and impostor matching scores can be well separated by a simple linear classifier. Inspired by this observation, we utilize a simple weighted sum rule to combine the 2D and 3D matching scores at Level 2 for palmprint authentication. The combined matching score of 2D and 3D scores is defined as

$$S_{2D+3D} = w_1 S_{2D} + w_2 S_{3D}, \tag{6.10}$$

where S_{2D} and S_{3D} denote the normalized 2D and 3D matching scores, respectively. S_{2D} is normalized to the (0, 100) range. Because the original 3D matching score denotes the dissimilarity of the two palmprints, so we first normalize it to the range (0, 100), and then transform the normalized score to a similarity score and regard the final score as S_{3D}. w_1 and w_2 are two weights used to balance the contribution of the 2D and 3D matching scores. In the experiments, w_1 and w_2 were empirically chosen as 0.56 and 0.44, respectively.

To prove the effectiveness of the presented multifeature palmprint method, a decidability index (d') is used to quantify the improvement in the separability of impostor and genuine matching score distributions. The decidability index is defined as

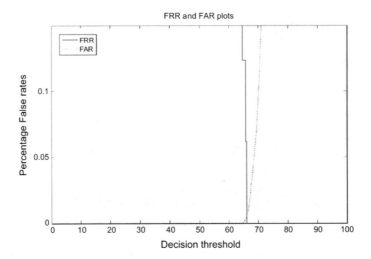

Fig. 6.11 FAR, FRR plots for (2D+3D) features. Reprinted from Zhang et al. (2010), with permission from Elsevier

$$d' = \frac{|\mu_1 - \mu_2|}{\sqrt{\frac{\sigma_1^2 + \sigma_2^2}{2}}}, \tag{6.11}$$

where μ_1 and μ_2 are the mean values and σ_1^2 and σ_2^2 are the variances of the genuine and impostor matching score distributions, respectively.

A comparison of decidability indexes by using different features is shown in Table 6.1. From Table 6.1, one can find that the presented multifeature method achieves the highest decidability index and the lowest EER. Figure 6.11 shows the FAR and FRR plots of the presented multifeature palmprint authentication method. Figure 6.12 shows comparative ROC curves by using 2D, 3D and the presented multifeatures method.

Table 6.1 and Fig. 6.11 both show that the palmprint verification performance can be greatly improved by the combination of 2D and 3D features. In addition, the combination of 2D and 3D palmprint features outperforms each individual 2D and 3D scheme for palmprint verification.

6.5.2 Spoof Experiments

In this subsection, we use some experiments to demonstrate the robustness of the 3D palmprint features against spoof attacks. The database used in the experiments should include some fake palmprint images. The database has five subjects and is captured in two stages by the presented image capture system. In the first stage, the

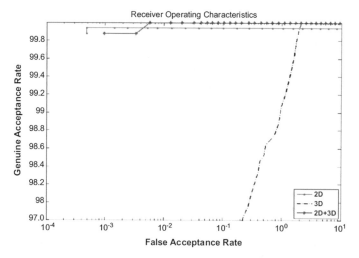

Fig. 6.12 The ROC curves for 2D, 3D and the proposed multilevel (2D+3D) features. Reprinted from Zhang et al. (2010), with permission from Elsevier

"real" palmprint image of each volunteer was captured, while in the second stage, palmprint images of the same person's hand (palm side) shown in Fig. 6.13e were presented to the images capture device. Figure 6.13 shows fake palmprint images used in the experiments. Fake palmprint images were captured from genuine users' palmprints (Fig. 6.13a–d). In other words, for a person, the real 2D and corresponding 3D images were acquired in the first stage, and the fake 2D images and real 3D images were captured in the second stage.

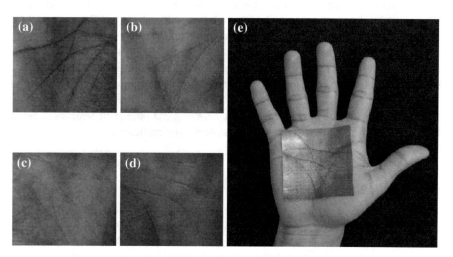

Fig. 6.13 Fake palmprints. **a–d** Show the palmprint images printed on paper to use as spoofs. **e** Shows a fake palmprint pasted on the hand to spoof the system. Reprinted from Zhang et al. (2010), with permission from Elsevier

Table 6.2 Matching scores from fake palmprints (spoof attack analysis)

User ID	2D matching score (threshold = 82.69)	3D matching score (threshold = 58.19)	2D+3D matching score (threshold = 66.01)
1	63.75	72.42	67.56
2	66.69	75.68	70.65
3	67.09	81.89	73.60
4	59.46	74.59	66.10
5	60.26	76.79	67.50

Reprinted from Zhang et al. (2010), with permission from Elsevier

In the verification experiments, for a subject, the palmprint image captured in the first stage is matched to the palmprint image captured in the second stage. If the matching score of the two palmprint images is less than the system threshold, the two palmprint images will be identified to the same class or person. In the experiments, the threshold was chosen as the operating point of EER. A comparison of spoof attacks by using individual 2D, 3D and 2D+3D palmprint features is shown in Table 6.2.

From Table 6.2, one can find that all matching scores obtained using only 2D palmprint features are much less than the threshold, which indicates that all matches are correct by using the 2D palmprint features. In other words, using only 2D palmprint features for palmprint authentication cannot automatically separate the real and fake palmprint samples. On the other hand, matching scores obtained by using 3D and (2D+3D) palmprint features are all higher than the corresponding system threshold. So these matches will be regarded as incorrect. This illustrates that using 3D or 2D+3D features for palmprint verification can separate the real and fake palmprints. From Table 6.2, one sees that the matching scores by using only 3D palmprint features are much higher than the threshold, while the matching scores using 2D+3D features are closer to the threshold. This also shows that the discriminative ability against spoof attacks is entirely reliant on 3D palmprint features. It should be noted that the threshold of Decision Module I is 61.03, and all of the 3D matching scores in Table 6.2 are much higher than this threshold. This indicates that all fake palmprints will be rejected at Level 1 of the presented palmprint algorithm. Thus, in conclusion, utilizing 3D palmprint features is beneficial for improving the robustness for palmprint authentication.

6.6 Summary

In this chapter, we presented a robust palmprint authentication system using both 2D and 3D palmprint features. Experimental results reported in Sect. 6.5.1 show that the presented multifeature palmprint algorithm achieves better verification performance than the individual 2D and 3D palmprint authentication algorithm. Experimental results in Sect. 6.5.2 demonstrate that the palmprint verification system using 3D features has the ability to detect a fake palmprint, while 2D features cannot. All of the experimental results show that the presented 2D+3D palmprint authentication system is superior to the individual 2D and 3D palmprint authentication systems, and is robust against spoof attacks.

References

P.J. Besl, R.C. Jain, Segmentation through variable-order surface fitting. IEEE Trans. Pattern Anal. Mach. Intell. **10**(2), 167–192 (1988)

H. Cantzler, R.B. Fisher, in *Comparison of HK and SC curvature description methods*, Proceedings of International Conference on 3D Digital Imaging and Modeling (IEEE, 2001), 285–291

K.I. Chang, K.W. Bowyer, P.J. Flynn, An evaluation of multimodal 2D+3D face biometrics. IEEE Trans. Pattern Anal. Mach. Intell. **27**(4), 619–624 (2005)

F. Chen, 3D fingerprint and palm print data model and capture devices using multi structured lights and cameras. Google Patents, 2009

T. Connie, A.T.B. Jin, M.G.K. Ong, D.N.C. Ling, An automated palmprint recognition system. Image Vis. Comput. **23**(5), 501–515 (2005)

P.J. Flynn, A.K. Jain, in *On reliable curvature estimation*, Proceedings of IEEE Conference on Computer Vision and Pattern Recognition (1989), pp. 110–116

P.H. Hennings-Yeomans, B. Kumar, M. Savvides, Palmprint classification using multiple advanced correlation filters and palm-specific segmentation. IEEE Trans. Inf. Forensics Secur. **2**(3), 613–622 (2007)

J.J. Koenderink, A.J. van Doorn, Surface shape and curvature scales. Image Vis. Comput. **10**(8), 557–564 (1992)

A.W.-K. Kong, D. Zhang, in *Competitive coding scheme for palmprint verification*, Proceedings of International Conference on Pattern Recognition (IEEE, 2004), pp. 520–523

A. Kumar, D. Zhang, Personal authentication using multiple palmprint representation. Pattern Recogn. **38**(10), 1695–1704 (2005)

A. Kumar, D. Zhang, Hand-geometry recognition using entropy-based discretization. IEEE Trans. Inf. Forensics Secur. **2**(2), 181–187 (2007)

A. Kumar, D.C. Wong, H.C. Shen, A.K. Jain, in *Personal verification using palmprint and hand geometry biometric*, Proceedings of Audio-and Video-Based Biometric Person Authentication (Springer, 2003), pp. 668–678

W. Li, D. Zhang, Z. Xu, Palmprint identification by Fourier transform. Int. J. Pattern Recognit Artif Intell. **16**(04), 417–432 (2002)

X. Lu, A.K. Jain, D. Colbry, Matching 2.5 D face scans to 3D models. IEEE Trans. Pattern Anal. Mach. Intell. **28**(1), 31–43 (2006)

S. Malassiotis, N. Aifanti, M.G. Strintzis, Personal authentication using 3D finger geometry. IEEE Trans. Inf. Forensics Secur. **1**(1), 12–21 (2006)

B. O'neill, *Elementary differential geometry* (Academic Press, 2006)

A. Ross, A. Jain, in *A prototype hand geometry-based verification system*, Proceedings of 2nd Conference on Audio and Video Based Biometric Person Authentication (1999), pp. 166–171

R. Sanchez-Reillo, C. Sanchez-Avila, A. Gonzalez-Marcos, Biometric identification through hand geometry measurements. IEEE Trans. Pattern Anal. Mach. Intell. **22**(10), 1168–1171 (2000)

S. Singh, A. Gyaourova, G. Bebis, I. Pavlidis, in *Infrared and visible image fusion for face recognition*, Proceedings of Defense and Security. International Society for Optics and Photonics (2004), pp. 585–596

D.L. Woodard, P.J. Flynn, Finger surface as a biometric identifier. Comput. Vis. Image Underst. **100**(3), 357–384 (2005)

P. Yan, K.W. Bowyer, in *Multi-biometrics 2D and 3D ear recognition*, Proceedings of Audio-and Video-based Biometric Person Authentication. Springer (2005), pp. 503–512

N. Yokoda, M. Levine, Range image segmentation based on differential geometry. IEEE Trans. Pattern Anal. Mach. Intell. **11**(6), 643–649 (1989)

D. Zhang, W.-K. Kong, J. You, M. Wong, Online palmprint identification. IEEE Trans. Pattern Anal. Mach. Intell. **25**(9), 1041–1050 (2003)

D. Zhang, V. Kanhangad, N. Luo, A. Kumar, Robust palmprint verification using 2D and 3D features. Pattern Recogn. **43**(1), 358–368 (2010)

Part IV
Sparse Representation for Face Recognition

Chapter 7
Discriminative Learning via Encouraging Virtual Face Images

Abstract A limited number of available training samples have become one bottleneck of face recognition. In real-world applications, the face image might have various changes owing to varying illuminations, facial expressions, and poses. However, non-sufficient training samples cannot comprehensively convey these possible changes, so it is hard to obtain very high accuracy for real-world face recognition. In this chapter, we present some effective schemes based on competent virtual face images to overcome the above problems. The adopted schemes and algorithms also seem to be applicable for some other applications.

7.1 Introduction

In the past, various face recognition algorithms have been devised (Feng et al. 2012; Jiang et al. 2005; Shan et al. 2006; Sim and Kanade 2001). However, up to now, face recognition is still faced with a number of challenges such as varying illumination, facial expression, and poses (Wang et al. 2012a, b; Zhang 2009; Zhang and Gao 2009). It seems that more training samples are able to reveal more possible variation of the illumination, facial expression, and poses and are consequently beneficial for correct classification of the face. However, in real-world applications, there are usually only a limited number of available training samples. This is mainly because a face recognition system usually has limited storage space and captures training samples in a short time. In some special cases such as the personal identity card based face recognition, there is even only one training sample per subject. Non-sufficient training samples indeed have become one bottleneck of face recognition (Naseem et al. 2004, 2012; Yang et al. 2005, 2011).

In order to obtain better face recognition result, the literatures have proposed to synthesize new samples from the true face images. For example, Bin et al. (2003) used prototype faces and an optic flow and expression ratio image based method to generate 'virtual' facial expression. Thian et al. (2003) used simple geometric transformations to generate virtual samples. Ryu and Oh (2002) exploited the distribution of the given training set to generate virtual training samples. Beymer

© Springer Science+Business Media Singapore 2016
D. Zhang et al., *Discriminative Learning in Biometrics*,
DOI 10.1007/978-981-10-2056-8_7

and Poggio (1995) and Vetter (1998) synthesized new face samples with virtual views. Jung et al. (2004) exploited the noise to synthesize new face samples. Sharma et al. (2010) synthesized multiple virtual views of a person under different poses and illumination from a single face image and exploited extended training samples to classify the face. In order to overcome the small sample size problem of face recognition, Liu et al. (2007) represented each single image as a subspace spanned by its synthesized (shifted) samples. From the viewpoint of applications, the ways to generate virtual face images can be categorized into two kinds, i.e., the way to generate two-dimensional virtual face images and the way to construct three-dimensional virtual face images (Hu et al. 2004).

Among a variety of face recognition methods, the representation-based classification (RBC) method can achieve a very high accuracy and has received much attention (Shi et al. 2009; Wright et al. 2009, 2010; Yang et al. 2012). In this chapter, the presented algorithms are also based on it.

7.2   The Representation-Based Classification Method

In this section, we first introduce representation-based classification (RBC) briefly, and then present an improved RBC algorithm based on two-step face recognition. Because LRC has a distinct characteristic, we describe it in Sect. 7.2.1 and present other RBCs in Sect. 7.2.2. We assume that there are c classes and each class has n original training samples. Let $x_1, \ldots, x_N$ be all N original training samples in the form of column vectors $(N = cn)$. Column vector $x_{(i-1)n+k}$ $(k = 1, \ldots, n)$ stands for the kth original training sample of the ith subject, $i = 1, 2, \ldots, c$. Let column vector z stand for the test sample.

7.2.1   LRC

LRC establishes an equation for each class. The equation of the ith class is

$$z = X_i A_i, \tag{7.1}$$

where $A_i = [a_1^i \ldots a_n^i], X_i = [x_{(i-1)^*n+1} \ldots x_{i^*n}]..$ The solution of Eq. (7.1) is obtained using

$$\widehat{A}_i = (X_i^T X_i)^{-1} X_i^T z. \tag{7.2}$$

The deviation between the ith class and the test sample is defined as $d_i = \left\| z - X_i \widehat{A}_i \right\|$. If $k = \arg \min_i d_i$, then the test sample is assigned to the kth class.

7.2.2   Brief Introduction to Other RBCs

For the representation-based classification methods, all the methods except for LRC first exploit a linear combination of all the training samples to represent the test sample.

RBC with the l_2 norm minimization constraint can be briefly described as follows. We first take collaborative representation classification (CRC) as an example to show the basic characteristics of this kind of method. CRC assumes that Eq. (7.3) is approximately satisfied

$$z = XB, \tag{7.3}$$

where $B = [b_1 \ldots b_N]^{\mathrm{T}}, X = [x_1 \ldots x_N]$. The solution of Eq. (7.3) is usually obtained using

$$\widehat{B} = (X^{\mathrm{T}}X + \mu I)^{-1}X^{\mathrm{T}}z, \tag{7.4}$$

μ is a small positive constant and I is the identity matrix. Let $\widehat{B} = [\hat{b}_1 \ldots \hat{b}_N]^{\mathrm{T}}$. Of course, if $X^{\mathrm{T}}X$ is not singular, the solution of Eq. (7.3) can be also obtained using

$$\widehat{B} = (X^{\mathrm{T}}X)^{-1}X^{\mathrm{T}}z. \tag{7.5}$$

CRC calculates the residual of the test sample with respect to the ith class using $r_i = \left\| z - X_i\widehat{B}_i \right\|$, where $X_i = [x_{(i-1)^*n+1} \ldots x_{i^*n}]$ and $\widehat{B}_i = [\hat{b}_{(i-1)^*n+1} \ldots \hat{b}_{i^*n}]^{\mathrm{T}}$. If $k = \arg\min_i r_i$, then CRC assigns the test sample to the kth class.

The main difference between CRC and the other RBCs with the l_2 norm minimization constraint is that other RBCs might have extra constraints or steps. For example, the improvement to the nearest neighbor classifier (INNC) (Gao et al. 2012) has the same equation and solution scheme as CRC but uses a simpler classifier. The two-phase sparse representation (TPSR) method (Xu et al. 2011) has the same first step as CRC but exploits an extra step to obtain a sparse linear combination of all the training samples to represent the test sample.

SRC, i.e., RBC with the l_1 norm minimization constraint can be briefly described as follows. SRC attempts to solve the following problem

$$\min_{B} \|B\|_1 \quad \text{s.t. } \|z - XB\|_2 \le \varepsilon, \tag{7.6}$$

where $\varepsilon > 0$ is a constant. SRC has no a closed solution and should be iteratively solved. The original SRC algorithm is very computationally inefficient and recently some efficient algorithms for SRC have been proposed (Huang and Yang 2010; Peng and Li 2012).

7.2.3　Two-Step CRC (TSCRC) Face Recognition Algorithm

In this subsection we present the algorithm of two-step face recognition in detail. This algorithm first coarsely determines a small number of candidate classes of the test sample and then finely identifies the class that the test sample is the most similar to.

As introduced in Sect. 7.2, for CRC algorithm, the effect on representing the test sample of the kth class can be evaluated using

$$d_i = \left\| z - X_i \widehat{B}_i \right\|. \tag{7.7}$$

It is clear that X_i are training samples of the ith class and $\widehat{B}_i$ are the corresponding coefficients. We would like to point out that the effect on representing the test sample of the ith class is somewhat similar to the distance between the test sample and the ith class.

If $d_{r_1} \leq d_{r_2} \cdots \leq d_{r_c}$, then we say that the r_1th, r_2th, …, r_tth classes are the first t candidate classes of the test sample. In other words, we can consider that the ultimate class label of the test sample should be one element of $D = \{c_{r_1}, c_{r_2}, \ldots, c_{r_t}\}$. $c_{r_1}, c_{r_2}, \ldots, c_{r_t}$ are the class labels of the first t candidate classes, respectively. As the above steps roughly determine that the test sample is from a small number of classes, we refer to them as coarse classification.

The algorithm then uses a linear combination of the training samples of the first t candidate classes to represent the test sample. In other words, if the training samples of the first t candidate classes are denoted by $\tilde{x}_1', \ldots, \tilde{x}_{tm}'$, respectively, then the algorithm assumes that the following equation is approximately satisfied:

$$z = f_1 \tilde{x}_1' + \cdots + f_{tm} \tilde{x}_{tm}', \tag{7.8}$$

where f_i is the coefficient. We rewrite Eq. (7.8) as

$$\tilde{z} = X'F, \tag{7.9}$$

where $F = [f_1 \ldots f_{tm}]^{\mathrm{T}}, X' = [\tilde{x}_1', \ldots, \tilde{x}_{tm}']$. F is calculated using

$$\overline{F} = (X'^{\mathrm{T}} X' + \gamma I)^{-1} X'^{\mathrm{T}} \tilde{z}. \tag{7.10}$$

$\overline{F} = [\bar{f}_1 \ldots \bar{f}_{tm}]^{\mathrm{T}}$. γ is a small positive constant and I also denotes the identity matrix.

Suppose that $\tilde{x}_g', \ldots, \tilde{x}_h'$ stand for all the training samples of the rth class ($r \in \{c_{r_1}, c_{r_2}, \ldots, c_{r_t}\}$) and the coefficients are $\bar{f}_g, \ldots, \bar{f}_h$, respectively. The ultimate effect on representing the test sample of the rth class can be evaluated using

$$u_r = \left\| z - \sum_{i=g}^{h} \overline{f_i} \tilde{x}'_i \right\|. \tag{7.11}$$

If $k = \arg\min_r u_r$, then test sample z is ultimately assigned to the kth class, which is also referred to as the result of fine classification.

7.3   Face Recognition Using 'Symmetrical Face'

7.3.1   Symmetrical Face

The face has a symmetrical structure. Not only the facial structure but also the facial expression is symmetry (Ekman et al. 1981). The symmetry property has been successfully applied to face detection (Saber and Tekalp 1998; Saha and Bandyopadhyay 2007; Su and Chou 1999). In face detection, the symmetry property of the human face is very useful to quickly locate the candidate faces (Su and Chou 1999).

For a face image, it is easy to obtain two virtue faces based on the symmetrical structure of the face. Let a face image $x = [a_1, a_2, \ldots, a_n, a_{n+1}, \ldots, a_{2n}]$, then the two "symmetrical faces" are

$$y^1 = [a_1, a_2, \ldots, a_n, a_n, a_{n-1}, \ldots, a_1], \tag{7.12}$$

$$y^2 = [a_{2n}, a_{2n-1}, \ldots, a_{n+1}, a_{n+1}, \ldots, a_{2n-1}, a_{2n}]. \tag{7.13}$$

Figure 7.1 shows some original training samples from the ORL face database and the 'symmetrical face' training samples generated from the original training samples. Figure 7.2 shows some original training samples from the FERET face database and the corresponding 'symmetrical face' training samples. Figure 7.3 shows some original training samples from the AR face database and the corresponding 'symmetrical face' training samples. The 'symmetrical face' training samples not only seem to be different from the original training samples, but also indeed somewhat reflect the possible variation of the face in image scale, pose and illumination. Thus, 'symmetrical face' training samples are very useful to overcome the issue of non-sufficient training samples.

Fig. 7.1 Some original training samples from the ORL face database and the corresponding 'symmetrical face' training samples. The *first row* shows the original training samples. The *second* and *third rows,* respectively, show the *first* and *second* 'symmetrical face' training samples generated from the original training sample. Reprinted from Xu et al. (2013b), with permission from Elsevier

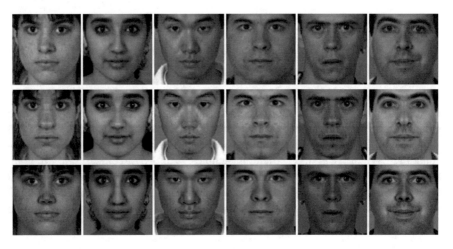

Fig. 7.2 Some original training samples from the FERET face database and the corresponding 'symmetrical face' training samples. The *first row* shows the original training samples. The *second* and *third* rows, respectively, show the *first* and *second* 'symmetrical face' training samples generated from the original training sample. Reprinted from Xu et al. (2013b), with permission from Elsevier

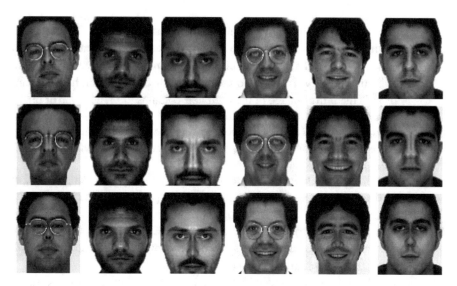

Fig. 7.3 Some original training samples from the AR face database and the corresponding 'symmetrical face' training samples. The *first row* shows the original training samples. The *second* and *third rows,* respectively, show the *first* and *second* 'symmetrical face' training samples generated from the original training sample. Reprinted from Xu et al. (2013b), with permission from Elsevier

7.3.2   Using the Original and 'Symmetrical Face' Training Samples to Perform TSCRC Face Recognition

In this section we present a novel face recognition method by using the original and 'symmetrical face' training samples to perform TSCRC face recognition. We will first briefly present the main steps of this method, and then we analyze the rationale of the presented method.

7.3.2.1   Main Steps of the Method

The proposed method includes the following main steps. The first step generates 'symmetrical face' training samples. The second and third steps use the original and 'symmetrical face' training samples to perform two-step face recognition, respectively. The fourth step combines the scores obtained using the second and third steps to conduct weighted score level fusion, getting the ultimate classification result. The main steps of the present algorithm are as follows.

Step 1.   Use every original training sample to generate two 'symmetrical face' training samples. Let $x_i \in \Re^{p \times q}$ be the ith training sample in the form of image matrix. Let y_i^1 and y_i^2 respectively stand for the first and second 'symmetrical face' training samples generated from x_i. The left half columns of y_i^1 is set to the same as that of x_i and the right half columns of y_i^1 is the mirror image of the left half columns of y_i^1. However, the right half columns of y_i^2 is set to the same as that of x_i and the left half columns of y_i^2 is the mirror image of the right half columns of y_i^2. The mirror image S of an arbitrary image R is defined as $S(i,j) = R(i, V - j + 1), i = 1, \ldots,$ $U, j = 1, \ldots, V$. U and V stand for the numbers of the rows and columns of R, respectively. $S(i,j)$ denotes the pixel located in the ith row and jth column of S.

Step 2.   Use the original training samples to perform two-step face recognition. Let s_j^1 denote the score of test sample z with respect to the jth class. For the algorithm, please see Sect. 7.2.2.

Step 3.   Use the 'symmetrical face' training samples to perform two-step face recognition. Let s_j^2 denote the score of test sample z with respect to the jth class. This step shares the same algorithm as Step 2.

Step 4.   Combine the scores obtained using the second and third steps to conduct weighted score level fusion. For test sample z, we use $s_j = w_1 s_j^1 + w_2 s_j^2$ to calculate the ultimate score with respect to the jth class. w_1 and w_2 are the weights. Let $w_1 + w_2 = 1$ and w_2 be smaller than w_1.

7.3.2.2   Analysis of the Proposed Method

From Figs. 7.1, 7.2 and 7.3, we can find that the 'symmetrical face' is a front face which is able to reduce the influence of the various poses. And using the 'symmetrical face' the training samples can increase the number of the training samples which is able to sufficiently represent the test sample via the RBC method.

The second rationale of the presented method is that it, respectively, uses the 'symmetrical face' training samples and the original training samples to obtain the scores of the test sample with respect to different classes and properly exploits a weighted fusion scheme to combine them for ultimate face recognition. As the 'symmetrical face' training samples contain less information than the original training samples, it is very reasonable for the proposed method to assign a smaller weight to the 'symmetrical face' training samples.

The third rationale of the proposed method is that it uses the two-step face recognition, which is able to reduce the side effect on classification, of the test sample, of the classes that are very dissimilar to the test sample. Actually, the literature has shown that the test sample is usually not from these classes (Xu et al. 2011). As a result, by eliminating these classes the fine recognition can increase the probability of the test sample being correctly classified and can achieve a higher accuracy. The significance of every step of the proposed method can be briefly described in Fig. 7.4.

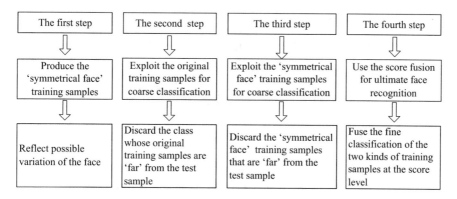

Fig. 7.4 The significance of each step of the proposed method. Reprinted from Xu et al. (2013b), with permission from Elsevier

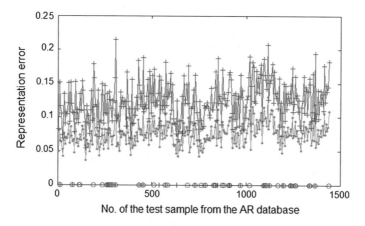

Fig. 7.5 The representation errors of the test sample obtained using the coarse classification and fine classification based on the original training samples. The *blue* and *red lines,* respectively, depict the representation errors obtained using the coarse classification and fine classification. In the horizontal axis, the *red circle* and *blue* '+', respectively, means that the corresponding test sample is erroneously classified by the coarse classification and fine classification based on the original training samples. Reprinted from Xu et al. (2013b), with permission from Elsevier

Figures 7.5 and 7.6 show the representation errors of the test sample obtained using the coarse classification and fine classification based on the original training samples and 'symmetrical face' training samples, respectively. These figures are obtained under the condition that the first 14 face images of each subject in the AR face database are used as original training samples and the remaining face images are taken as test samples. We see that the coarse classification based on the original training samples and 'symmetrical face' training samples always leads to a lower representation error than the corresponding fine classification. However, these two figures show that the fine classification produces fewer classification errors than the

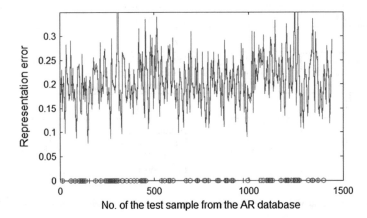

Fig. 7.6 The representation errors of the test sample obtained using the coarse classification and fine classification based on the 'symmetrical face' training samples. The *green* and *purple lines,* respectively, depict the representation errors obtained using the coarse classification and fine classification. In the horizontal axis, the *red circle* and *blue* '+', respectively, means that the corresponding test sample is erroneously classified by the coarse classification and fine classification based on the 'symmetrical face' training samples. Reprinted from Xu et al. (2013b), with permission from Elsevier

coarse classification. Actually, as shown in the experimental section, the fine classification always obtains a lower rate of classification errors. This tells us that for a RBC, the key is not to produce a low representation error but to make the class that the test sample is truly from the most similar with the test sample, having the minimum deviation from the test sample among all the classes. Though the fine classification is not optimal for providing a good representation for the test sample, it performs very well in making the test sample more similar with the test sample. As shown early, it achieves this by discarding the classes that are 'far' from the test sample. Usually, there is also a large probability of the test sample being not truly from these classes.

7.3.3   Experimental Results

We used the FERET, AR and ORL face databases to conduct experiments. For the FERET and ORL databases, we show the experimental results under the conditions that the weights of the score fusion were set to $w_1 = 0.85$ and $w_2 = 0.15, w_1 = 0.75$ and $w_2 = 0.25, w_1 = 0.65$ and $w_2 = 0.35$, respectively. For the AR database, because the experiment is very time-consuming, we conduct only the experiment on $w_1 = 0.75$ and $w_2 = 0.25$. Both μ and γ were set to 0.01. Each sample was converted into a unit vector with length of 1 in advance. Tables 7.1, 7.2, and 7.3 show the rate of classification errors under the condition that $0.3 * c$ candidate classes were used. Besides our proposed method was tested, several state-of-the-art face

Fig. 7.7 Six test samples and six training samples from the SCface database (Grgic et al. 2011) as well as the mirror images of these training samples. The *first* and *second rows* show six test samples and six training samples, respectively. The *third row* shows the mirror images of the six training samples shown in the *second row*. The images in the same column are generated from a same face. Reprinted from Xu et al. (2014b), with permission from Elsevier [available: http://www.scface.org/ (Online)]

recognition methods such as two-phase test sample sparse representation (TPTSSR) (Xu et al. 2011), collaborative representation (CR) proposed in Zhang et al. (2011), the feature space-based representation method proposed in Xu et al. (2012), sparse representation classification (SRC) proposed in Koh et al. (2008) and linear regression classification (LRC) (Naseem et al. 2010) were also tested. As the performance of the feature space-based representation method is directly related to parameter σ, we set it to different values and show the best classification result and the corresponding value in the table. In the experiments, we performed 'coarse score fusion' as follows: CR was, respectively, first implemented for the original and 'symmetrical face' training samples and then the scores generated from the original and 'symmetrical face' training samples were fused for ultimate face recognition by using the same weight fusion scheme as our proposed method. When implementing TPTSSR, we set parameter $M = N/2$, where N is the number of all the original training samples. We also tested the combination of two-step classification and the feature space-based representation method proposed in Xu et al. (2012). Specifically, the feature space-based representation method first, respectively, uses the original and 'symmetrical face' training samples to perform coarse classification and then, respectively, uses them to conduct fine classification. The fine classification was also implemented under the condition that $0.3 * c$ candidate classes were exploited. Finally, the weighted fusion scheme ($w_1 = 0.75$ and $w_2 = 0.25$) in our method was used to combine the scores generated from the fine classification on the original and 'symmetrical face' training samples and the combined score was used to ultimately classify the test sample.

Table 7.1 Experimental results on the AR database

Number of the original training samples per class	13 (%)	14 (%)	15 (%)	16 (%)
The proposed method ($w_1 = 0.75$)	23.72	9.93	8.03	6.83
CR on the original training samples	28.97	14.86	11.82	9.83
CR on the 'symmetrical face' training samples	36.15	27.15	22.27	18.83
Coarse score fusion	28.33	14.44	11.74	9.58
SRC	32.37	16.74	16.82	17.42
TPTSSR	24.81	9.72	8.33	7.17
LRC	34.36	13.13	12.58	13.25
Feature space-based representation method ($\sigma = 1.0e6$) (Xu et al. 2012)	39.36	25.07	24.47	25.42
Combination of two-step classification and the feature space-based representation method ($\sigma = 1.0e6$)	39.23	25.07	24.47	25.33

Reprinted from Xu et al. (2013b), with permission from Elsevier

7.3.3.1 Experiments the AR Face Database

From the AR face database[1], we used 3120 gray images from 120 subjects, each providing 26 images. These images were taken in two sessions. Every image was resized to a 50 × 40 image. We, respectively, took the first 13, 14, 15, and 16 face images of each subject as the original training samples and treated the remaining face images as the test samples. The experimental results were shown in Table 7.1. We see that our method obtains a lower rate of classification errors than all the other methods. For example, when the first 13 face images of each subject were used as the original training samples and the remaining face images were taken as the test samples, the rates of classification errors of our method, CR on the original training samples, SRC, TPTSSR, LRC, and the feature space-based representation method are 23.72, 28.97, 32.37, 24.81, 34.36 and 39.36 %, respectively. The fact that coarse score fusion also obtains a higher rate of classification errors than our method also means that to discard the classes that are 'far' from the test sample is really beneficial for the correct classification of the test sample. Moreover, we see that the combination of two-step classification and the feature space-based representation method also performs worse than our method.

7.3.3.2 Experiments the ORL Face Database

The ORL database[2] includes 400 face images taken from 40 subjects, each providing 10 face images. For some subjects, the images were taken at different times, with varying lighting, facial expressions (open/closed eyes, smiling/not smiling),

---

[1]http://www2.ece.ohio-state.edu/~aleix/ARdatabase.html.

[2]http://www.cl.cam.ac.uk/research/dtg/attarchive/facedatabase.html.

Table 7.2 Experimental results on the ORL database

Number of the original training samples per class	1 (%)	2 (%)	3 (%)
The proposed method ($w_1 = 0.85$)	24.72	10.31	10.00
The proposed method ($w_1 = 0.75$)	24.17	10.31	8.93
The proposed method ($w_1 = 0.65$)	24.72	10.63	9.29
CR on the original training samples	31.39	16.56	15.00
CR on the 'symmetrical face' training samples	34.72	23.13	20.71
Coarse score fusion	30.28	16.25	13.57
SRC	26.67	15.00	14.29
TPTSSR	26.39	13.44	11.43
LRC	32.50	20.94	18.21
Feature space-based representation method ($\sigma = 1.0e7$) (Xu et al. 2012)	27.22	11.87	10.71
Combination of two-step classification and the feature space-based representation method ($\sigma = 1.0e7$)	27.22	11.25	10.71

Reprinted from Xu et al. (2013b), with permission from Elsevier

and facial details (glasses/no glasses). Each image was also resized to an image with one-half of the original size by using the downsampling algorithm. We, respectively, took the first 1, 2, and 3 face images of each subject as the original training samples and treated the remaining face images as the test samples. The experimental results were shown in Table 7.2. It shows again that our method performs better than all the other methods. For example, when the first face image of each subject and the remaining face images were, respectively, used as the original training samples and the test samples, the rates of classification errors of our method ($w_1 = 0.75$ and $w_2 = 0.25$), CR on the original training samples, SRC, TPTSSR, LRC and the feature space-based representation methods are 24.17, 31.39, 26.67, 26.39, 32.50 and 27.22 %, respectively. We also see that the combination of two-step classification and the feature space-based representation method obtains a higher rate of classification errors than our method.

7.3.3.3   Experiments the FERET Face Database

We used a subset of the FERET face database[3] to test our method. This subset consists of 1400 images from 200 individuals each providing seven images. This subset was composed of images whose names are marked with two-character strings: 'ba', 'bj', 'bk', 'be', 'bf', 'bd', and 'bg'. We resized each image to a 40×40 image using the downsampling algorithm. We, respectively, took the first 1, 2, and 3 face images of each subject as the original training samples and treated the remaining face images as the test samples. Table 7.3 shows the rate of

---

[3]http://www.itl.nist.gov/iad/humanid/feret/feret_master.html.

Table 7.3 Experimental results on the FERET database

Number of the original training samples per class	1 (%)	2 (%)	3 (%)
The proposed method ($w_1 = 0.85$)	50.42	35.30	41.88
The proposed method ($w_1 = 0.75$)	48.75	34.80	41.63
The proposed method ($w_1 = 0.65$)	48.08	32.80	38.25
CR on the original training samples	55.67	41.60	55.63
CR on the 'symmetrical face' training samples	58.33	39.20	41.38
Coarse score fusion	55.67	40.00	52.25
SRC	50.25	35.20	40.00
TPTSSR	52.17	38.70	46.88
LRC	55.08	36.80	42.88
Feature space-based representation method ($\sigma = 1.0e6$) (Xu et al. 2012)	56.25	43.40	50.50
Combination of two-step classification and the feature space-based representation method ($\sigma = 1.0e6$)	54.25	41.70	48.50

Reprinted from Xu et al. (2013b), with permission from Elsevier

classification errors. This table shows that in most cases our method outperforms all the other methods. Table 7.3 also shows that the combination of two-step classification and the feature space-based representation method obtains a higher rate of classification errors than our method.

7.3.3.4　Variation of the Performance of Our Method with the Number of Candidate Classes

In order to comprehensively show the performance of our method, we use Table 7.4 to briefly indicate the variation of the rate of classification errors of our method with the number of candidate classes. We see that when the number of candidate classes is smaller than that of all the classes, our method almost always

Table 7.4 Variation of the rate of classification errors of our method ($w_1 = 0.75$ and $w_2 = 0.25$) with the number of candidate classes

The ORL database (3 training sample per subject)			
Number of candidate classes	10	20	30	40
The rate of classification errors (%)	10.00	9.29	8.93	12.50
The FERET database (3 training sample per subject)			
Number of candidate classes	50	100	150	200
The rate of classification errors (%)	40.75	45.25	47.13	51.25
The AR database (13 training sample per subject)			
Number of candidate classes	30	60	90	120
The rate of classification errors (%)	23.40	24.42	25.64	28.21

Reprinted from Xu et al. (2013b), with permission from Elsevier

obtains a lower rate of classification errors. This clearly shows that to discard the classes that are 'far' from the test sample is really beneficial for the improvement of the accuracy of our method.

7.4 Face Recognition Using Face Mirror Images

7.4.1 Mirror Face

Suppose that the original face image matrix has P rows and Q columns. The mirror image of an original face image has the same size. For a face image x, its mirror image y $(k = 1, \ldots, n)$ is generated using

$$y(p, q) = x(p, Q - q + 1), \quad p = 1, \ldots, P, \ q = 1, \ldots, Q, \tag{7.14}$$

$x(p, q)$ and $y(p, q)$ denote the pixels located in the pth row and qth column of x and y, respectively.

Figure 7.7 shows six test samples and six training samples from the SCface database[4] (Grgic et al. 2011) as well as the mirror images of these training samples. They have the same size but have different poses. Table 7.5 shows the original and mirror distances of the same subject. We see that for the same face the mirror distance is greatly smaller than the original distance. This implies that the simultaneous use of both the original face image and mirror image will enable us to more accurately classify the face image.

The following example shows that the proposed scheme can somewhat overcome the variation of the illumination of the original face image. Figure 7.8 shows several test samples and training samples of the same face from the Yale B database. They have the same size but different illuminations. For the test sample, the right face has stronger illumination than the left face. For the training sample, the right face has weaker illumination than the left face. Table 7.6 shows the original and mirror distances on the samples shown in Fig. 7.8. The mirror distance is also much smaller than the original distance. This again implies that the use of the mirror image is beneficial for correctly recognizing the face.

Table 7.5 The original and mirror distances of the samples shown in Fig. 7.7

No. of the subject	1	2	3	4	5	6
Original distance ($\times 10^3$)	9.94	8.33	8.72	8.61	9.90	8.82
Mirror distance ($\times 10^3$)	4.05	6.62	3.57	4.08	4.47	4.01

Each sample has the size of 75×75. Reprinted from Xu et al. (2014b), with permission from Elsevier

---

[4]Available: http://www.scface.org/ (Online).

Fig. 7.8 Six test samples and six training samples from the Yale B database as well as the mirror images of these training samples. The *first* and *second* rows show six test samples and six training samples, respectively. The *third row* shows the mirror images of the six training samples shown in the *second row*. The images in the same column are generated from a same face. Reprinted from Xu et al. (2014b), with permission from Elsevier

Table 7.6 The original and mirror distances on the samples shown in Fig. 7.8

No. of the column	1	2	3	4	5	6
Original distance ($\times 10^4$)	2.47	2.16	3.23	2.30	2.07	1.36
Mirror distance ($\times 10^4$)	2.34	2.01	3.10	2.15	1.95	1.21

Reprinted from Xu et al. (2014b), with permission from Elsevier

7.4.2   Integrating the Original Face Image and Its Mirror Image for Face Recognition

7.4.2.1   Main Steps of the Method

Though the used mirror image is simply generated from the original face image, it also appears to be a natural image and properly reflects possible variation of the original face image in pose and illumination. Moreover, the mirror image is also sufficiently different from the original face image in terms of the distance metric, so the use of the mirror image does enable the face recognition method to exploit more available information of the face.

In this section we describe the RBC method by integrating the original face image and its mirror image for face recognition in detail. The scheme works as follows. It first generates the mirror image of each original face image for training.

It then exploits both the original face image of a face for training and the corresponding mirror image as training samples of this face. As a result, a face has $2n$ training samples in total. The algorithm of the presented scheme can be presented as follows.

Step 1.   Generate mirror face images via Eq. (7.14) for each original training sample, and then convert each original training sample and the corresponding mirror face to a column vector, respectively. Suppose $x_{(i-1)n+k}$ is a column vector of the kth original training sample of the ith class, and $y_{(i-1)n+k}$ denotes the vector of the corresponding mirror sample.

Step 2.   For the ith face $(i = 1, \ldots, c)$, let $X_i = [x_{(i-1)^*n+1} \cdots x_{i^*n} \, y_{(i-1)n+1} \cdots y_{i^*n}]$. Actually, $X_1, \ldots, X_c$ are, respectively, the matrices consisting of all training samples including the original face images and mirror images of the first to the ith faces. $x_{(i-1)^*n+1} \cdots x_{i^*n} \, y_{(i-1)n+1} \cdots y_{i^*n}$ are all column vectors. c stands for the number of the faces, i.e., number of the subjects. Then X is defined as $X = [X_1 \ldots X_c]$. A RBC method (LRC or an ordinary RBC method) is applied to each test sample and corresponding training samples, respectively. For an ordinary RBC method, the equation on test sample z is expressed as $z = XB$ and the solution is denoted by $\widehat{B}$. If the applied method is LRC, then test sample z has c equations and the ith equation is expressed as $z = X_i A_i$. Let $\widehat{A}_i$ denote the solution of $z = X_i A_i$.

Step 3.   For LRC, after solutions $\widehat{A}_1, \ldots, \widehat{A}_c$ are obtained, the deviation between the test sample and the ith subject is calculated using $d_i = \left\| z - X_i \widehat{A}_i \right\|$. If $k = \arg \min_i d_i$, then LRC assigns the test sample to the kth class. For other RBC methods, solution $\widehat{B}$ is a vector and has $2cn$ entries. It is clear that each entry of $\widehat{B}$ is associated with one column of X (i.e., one training sample). We refer to an entry of $\widehat{B}$ as coefficient of the corresponding training sample. Let $\widehat{B}_i$ be the vector consisting of $2n$ entries of $\widehat{B}$, i.e., the coefficients of $x_{(i-1)^*n+1}, \ldots, x_{i^*n}, y_{(i-1)n+1}, \ldots, y_{i^*n}$, respectively. In other words, $\widehat{B}_i$ is associated with the ith subject. The residual of the test sample with respect to the ith class is calculated using $r_i = \left\| z - X_i \widehat{B}_i \right\|$. If $j = \arg \min_i r_i$, then test sample z is assigned to the jth subject.

7.4.2.2   Analysis of the Proposed Method

In this section, we will give more interpretation of the proposed scheme. As we know, RBC exploits the deviation or residual of each class to classify the test sample. RBC assigns the test sample to the class with the minimum deviation or

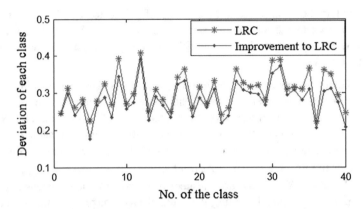

Fig. 7.9 The deviations between a test sample and all the classes of the ORL face database. The deviations are obtained by using LRC and the improvement to LRC, respectively. The test sample is from the fifth class. Reprinted from Xu et al. (2014b), with permission from Elsevier

residual. The deviation and residual indeed somewhat reflect the ability, to well represent the test sample, of the training samples of a class. The smaller the deviation or residual is, the greater ability to well represent the test sample the corresponding class has.

Figure 7.9 shows the deviations between a test sample and all the classes of the ORL face database. The deviations obtained using LRC and the improvement to LRC (i.e., the integration of our proposed scheme and LRC) are both shown in Fig. 7.9. This test sample is from the fifth class. From Fig. 7.9, we see that LRC will lead to erroneous classification of the test sample, since the corresponding deviation between the test sample and the fifth class is not the smallest. However, the improvement to LRC will obtain the correct classification result, because the corresponding deviation between the test sample and the fifth class is the smallest. Figure 7.9 also implies that the improvement to LRC has stronger ability to represent the test sample than LRC.

Figure 7.10 shows the deviations between a test sample and all the classes of the FERET face database. This test sample is from the nineteenth class. From Fig. 7.10, we see that LRC will lead to erroneous classification for this test sample, but the improvement to LRC will obtain the correct classification result. Shan (2013) also exploited the mirror image of the face image in recognizing the face, but the performance of his method is associated with the size of the blocks generated from the original face image.

The rationale of the proposed scheme can also be presented from the viewpoint of numerical analysis. For simplicity of presentation, we just take LRC and the improvement to LRC as an example. Suppose that the test sample is from the ith class. As the improvement to LRC has more available training samples than LRC, it is easy to know that the deviation between the ith class and the test sample obtained using the improvement to LRC is usually smaller than that obtained using LRC.

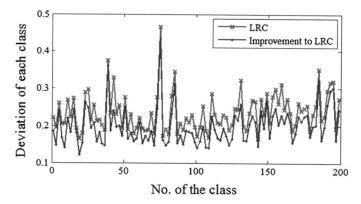

Fig. 7.10 The deviations between a test sample and all the classes of the FERET face database. The deviations are obtained by using LRC and the improvement to LRC, respectively. The test sample is from the nineteenth class. Reprinted from Xu et al. (2014b), with permission from Elsevier

7.4.3 Experimental Results

7.4.3.1 Experiments on the FERET Face Database

The method introduced in this section is also tested on the FERET face database. We, respectively, took the first 1, 2, 3, and 4 face images of each subject as original training samples and treated the remaining face images as test samples. Table 7.7 shows the rates of classification errors of different methods. We see that our proposed scheme can improve LRC, CRC, SRC, INNC and coarse to fine k nearest neighbor classifier (CFKNNC) (Xu et al. 2013a). Hereafter, the integrations of our proposed scheme and LRC, CRC, SRC, INNC as well as KNNC are referred to as the improvements to LRC, CRC, SRC, INNC as well as KNNC, respectively. When each subject provided two training samples, the rates of classification errors of LRC, CRC, INNC, and CFKNNC are 35.9, 41.6, 41.7 and 36.70 %, respectively. However, the rates of classification errors of the improvements to LRC, CRC, INNC, and CFKNNC are 22.4, 34.5, 33.5 and 27.70 %, respectively. When CFKNNC and improvement to CFKNNC were implemented, we set parameter n and K to $n = N/4$ and $K = 1$. N stands for the number of all the original training samples. $K = 1$ means that the nearest neighbor classification is indeed performed.

7.4.3.2 Experiments on the ORL Face Database

For ORL database, each image was also resized to a 56 by 46 image matrix by using the downsampling algorithm. We, respectively, took the first 1, 2, 3, and 4 face images of each subject as original training samples and treated the remaining

Table 7.7 The rates of classification errors (%) of different methods on the FERET database

Number of the training samples of each subject	4	3	2	1
LRC	21.50	42.88	36.80	55.08
Improvement to LRC	14.17	22.13	22.40	50.83
INNC	42.67	49.50	41.70	56.50
Improvement to INNC	35.50	35.75	33.50	54.08
CRC	44.67	55.63	41.60	55.67
Improvement to CRC	36.50	36.88	34.50	53.25
SRC	23.33	40.00	35.20	49.75
Improvement to SRC	21.00	39.75	34.70	49.00
CFKNNC	38.50	45.12	36.70	52.17
Improvement to CFKNNC	25.50	29.00	27.70	51.17

Reprinted from Xu et al. (2014b), with permission from Elsevier

Table 7.8 The rates of classification errors (%) of different methods on the ORL database

Number of the training samples of each subject	4	3	2	1
LRC	13.75	18.57	20.62	32.50
Improvement to LRC	12.08	12.14	17.81	28.89
INNC	12.50	17.86	18.44	28.33
Improvement to INNC	14.17	14.64	16.56	28.06
CRC	11.50	13.93	16.56	31.94
Improvement to CRC	13.33	12.14	14.69	28.89
SRC	10.00	14.29	15.00	27.50
Improvement to SRC	8.33	12.14	14.06	26.67
CFKNNC	14.58	19.29	17.81	26.39
Improvement to CFKNNC	12.50	14.29	15.00	26.67

Reprinted from Xu et al. (2014b), with permission from Elsevier

face images as test samples. The experimental results were shown in Table 7.8. We see again that proposed scheme can improve all the methods.

7.4.3.3 Experiments on the Yale B Face Database

In this subsection we use the Yale B (Georghiades et al. 2001) and the Extended Yale B[5] face databases to conduct experiments. There are 10 subjects in the Yale B database, and 28 subjects in the extended Yale B database. Each subject has 64 images under different illumination conditions. The facial portion of each original

---

[5]Available: http://vision.ucsd.edu/leekc/ExtYaleDatabase/ExtYaleB.html (Online).

Table 7.9 The rates of classification errors (%) of different methods on the Yale B database

Number of the training samples of each subject	24	20	16
LRC	16.51	23.33	24.73
Improvement to LRC	12.76	20.93	24.07
INNC	33.29	31.04	31.96
Improvement to INNC	23.95	27.15	31.03
CRC	22.57	24.70	26.86
Improvement to CRC	19.54	21.77	24.01
SRC	40.86	43.18	46.27
Improvement to SRC	35.20	37.20	37.06
CFKNNC	29.28	29.61	31.03
Improvement to CFKNNC	28.68	27.57	29.77

Reprinted from Xu et al. (2014b), with permission from Elsevier

image was cropped to a 192 X 168 image. We resized the cropped image to a 96 by 84 matrix. In order to computationally efficiently perform improvement to CFKNNC and CFKNNC, we did as follows. Before improvement to CFKNNC and CFKNNC were implemented, the face image was further resized to 48 by 42. We, respectively, took the first 16, 20, and 24 face images of each subject as original training samples and treated the remaining face images as test samples. Table 7.9 shows the rates of classification errors (%) of different methods on the Yale B database. The experimental results show again that our proposed scheme can improve all the methods.

7.5 Face Recognition Using Mean Faces

In this section, we will present another approach by using the mean faces to improve the performance of the face recognition with various poses and illuminations in detail. We assume that $X_i \in \Re^{m \times n}$ represents the training sample set of the ith class, and each column of X_i is a training sample of ith class. Suppose that we have c classes of subjects, and let $A = [X_1, X_2, \ldots, X_c]$.

7.5.1 Mean Face

Suppose that X_i have l training samples, and let $X_i = [x_i^1, x_i^2, \ldots, x_i^l]$. If each two samples of these l samples are used for synthesizing virtual training samples, there are $C_l^2 = (l(l-1)\ldots(l-1))/2$ possible combinations. If two samples from these l samples are x_i^s and x_i^t, then a virtual training sample will be

$$x_v^j = \left(x_i^t + x_i^s\right)/2, \tag{7.15}$$

where $x_v^j (j = 1, 2, \ldots, C_l^2)$ is the synthesized virtual training sample. So, the ith class has C_l^2 virtual training samples. We take i as the label of these synthesized virtual training samples. If each class of c classes of subjects synthesizes virtual training samples in accordance with the same way, the blend training sample set (BTSS) includes all original and the synthesized virtual training samples each class.

Figure 7.11 shows five original training samples of the fourteenth subject from the ORL database and the corresponding ten synthesized virtual training samples. We can see that the synthesized virtual training samples and original training sample have proper difference in lighting and expression (especially in the position of the mouth).

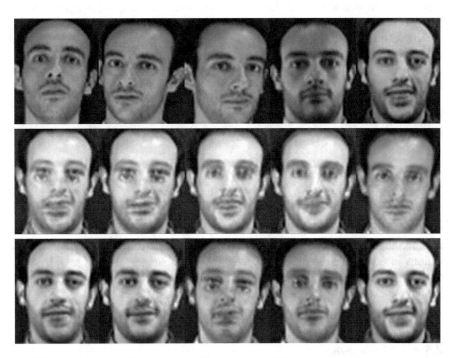

Fig. 7.11 Five original training samples (the *first row*) of the fourteenth subject from the ORL database and the corresponding synthesized virtual training samples (the *second* and the *third rows*). © 2014 IEEE. Reprinted with permission, from Xu et al. (2014a)

7.5.2   Using the Original Face Image and Mean Face for Face Recognition

7.5.2.1   Main Steps of the Method

Our proposed approach includes three steps. The first step is to generate mean faces by Eq. (7.15). The second step devises a good scheme to determine the most 'useful' training samples from the set of all the original and synthesized virtual training samples. The key of this step is to make the determined 'useful' training samples helpful for correctly classifying the test sample. The third step applies the CRC algorithm to classify the test sample.

In the second step, the Euclidean distance is used to select the useful training samples. We assume that the blend training sample set has n training samples that from c classes and we denote by $x_i^j (i = 1, 2, \ldots, c; \ j = 1, 2, \ldots, n)$ a training sample of the blend training sample set. Once a test sample $y \in \Re^m$ comes, we calculate distance between x_i^j and y by using

$$\mathrm{dist}_j = \left\| y - x_i^j \right\|^2. \tag{7.16}$$

Equation (7.16) can be somewhat viewed as a measurement of similarity between x_i^j and y. We consider that a small dist_j means that the x_i^j is very similar to the test sample y. We exploit dist_j to identify the K useful training samples that have the K smallest dist_j. We refer to these samples as the K nearest neighbors of the test sample. Let $H = (h_1, h_2, \ldots h_d)$, a set of some numbers, stand for the set of class labels of the K nearest neighbors.

In the third step, the K nearest training samples are used to perform the CRC algorithm for identifying the test sample.

7.5.2.2   Analysis of the Proposed Method

Now we demonstrate that to use a weighted sum of the original training samples to generate new training samples will not bring truly new representation information of the subject. The main reason is that the rank of matrix A will not change. Actually, for high-dimensional image data, we usually have the following theorem.

Theorem 7.1 *If a virtual training sample is a linear combination of original training samples and we add the virtual training sample into matrix A as a new column, then the new matrix has the same rank as the previous matrix.*

Proof Let the virtual training sample be $b = \sum_{j=1}^{n} v_j A'_j, n \leq N$, where $A'_j \in \{A_1, \ldots, A_N\}$, Let $B = [A \quad b]$. Suppose that A and B are $p \times q$ and $p \times (q+1)$ matrices, respectively. For high-dimensional image data, we usually have $p \gg q$. So, we can obtain $r_A = \text{rank}(A) \leq q \ll p$. If we transform the last column of $B(i, e.b)$ into $b - \sum_{j=1}^{n} v_j A'_j$, then the last column of B will become zero vector! If we denote the transformation result of B by B', then we have $B' = [A' \quad 0]$. It is sure that $\text{rank}(B') = \text{rank}(A')$. Since the above transformation is an elementary transformation, we also know that $\text{rank}(B) = \text{rank}(B')$ and $\text{rank}(A) = \text{rank}(A')$. As a result, we have $\text{rank}(B) = \text{rank}(A)$!

As a result, we say that if the virtual training sample is a weighted sum of the original training samples, then it will not be able to provide complementary representation information of the subject.

From the viewpoint of numerical computation, we can also show that if virtual training sample b is a weighted sum of the original training samples, then it is not useful. Let $Ax = t$ and $Bx' = t(x' = \begin{pmatrix} x \\ y \end{pmatrix}, B = [A \quad b])$ denote the problem models of the original method and the method based on the original and virtual training samples. t stands for the test sample. According to the proof of Theorem 7.1, $Bx' = t$ can be converted into $[A' \quad 0]x' = t'$. As a result, we have $A'x + 0y = t'$. means that y, i.e., the weight corresponding to virtual training sample b indeed can be set to arbitrary value and x will be same as the solution of $Ax = t$. Thus, we can say that though virtual training sample b is used, it does not bring any certain information for determining the problem model of the method. Actually, arbitrary means totally 'uncertain'. Moreover, when we use an algorithm to solve $Bx' = t$, y will also be assigned a value by the rule of the algorithm. As the solution is somewhat 'uncertain', the classification procedure based on the solution usually cannot obtain a good result. In this sense, it is reasonable to select as many as the original training samples from all the samples including the original and virtual training samples and to use the selected training samples to represent and classify the test sample. Furthermore, as among the original and virtual training samples the samples that are very 'far' from the test sample usually have side effect on the classification of the test sample, we propose to select and exploit fewer samples to represent and classify the test sample.

Moreover, we have the following conclusion: only if a virtual training sample is not a linear combination of original training samples, it can provide complementary representation information of the subject.

The proof of Theorem 7.1 also shows that because of $q < p$, representation-based face recognition is usually an overdetermined problem. This implies that in linear system $Au = y$ the equations are more that the unknown variables, i.e., the components of u. As a result, it is very reasonable to obtain the least-squares solution of $Au = y$.

7.5.3   *Experimental Results*

We conducted a number of experiments on the AR[6] and GEORGIA TECH (GT)[7] face databases. The codes are available at http://www.yongxu.org/lunwen.html. We also conducted experiments of PCA, LDA, KNN, CRC (Zhang et al. 2011), LRC (Naseem et al. 2010), NNLS (Li and Ngom 2013) and some sparse methods proposed in (Wright et al. 2009; Yang et al. 2010) with the original training sample set. In all experiments, we compare the running time and recognition rate of different methods and the regularization parameters λ were set to 0.01.

7.5.3.1   AR Database

For the AR database, we tested different methods in two evaluation protocols. Evaluation Protocol 1 (EP1) takes the first eight images of each subject as the training samples, while the remaining images are designated as test samples. For Evaluation Protocol 2 (EP2), for each subject, the seven images (with only illumination and expression changes) from Session 1 were used for training samples, with the other seven images from Session 2 for test samples (Wright et al. 2009). All images were resized to 40×50 by using the downsampling algorithm (Xu and Jin 2008). Figure 7.12 shows some of the face images of a subject from the AR database.

Figure 7.13 shows the recognition rate for the AR database with respect to the scale of K in two cases of the EP1 and EP2. For EP 1, with the scale of K decreases, the recognition rate gradually improves until the scale of the K reaching $0.9 * \text{scale}(A)$. In EP 2, the curve of the recognition rate increases at first until the scale of the K reaching $0.4 * \text{scale}(A)$ and then decreases.

Table 7.10 shows the recognition rate of different approaches in the AR database. The SRC (l_1_ls) achieves the best recognition rate yet with the most running time in the EP 1 and EP 2. In EP 1, our approach achieves the third highest recognition rate (only 3.14 and 0.18 % lower than the SRC (l_1_ls) and SRC (DALM), respectively), but the speed are 9.79 and 4.00 times than the SRC (l_1_ls) and SRC (DALM), respectively. In EP 2, our approach also achieves a comparable recognition rate without lower than the SRC (l_1_ls) and SRC (DALM) approaches but it is significantly faster than them. In an overall sense, it is shown to be fairly comparable to all other approaches, including the latest SRC approaches.

In this research, we address a fundamental challenge of face recognition, i.e., contiguous occlusion. Commonly used objects, such as caps, sunglasses, and scarves, tend to obstruct facial features, causing recognition errors (Naseem et al. 2010). The AR database consists of two models of contiguous occlusion, i.e., images with a pair of sunglasses and a scarf. Figure 7.14 reflects these two

---

[6]Available: http://cobweb.ecn.purdue.edu/?aleix/aleix?face?DB.html.

[7]Available: http://www.anefian.com/facereco.htm.

Fig. 7.12 Some face images of a subject from the AR database

Fig. 7.13 Recognition rate
for the AR database with
respect to the scale of the
nearest neighbor set K being
chosen for the test sample

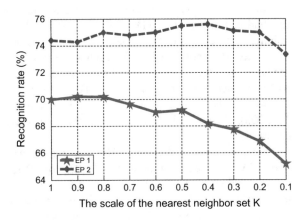

Table 7.10 The recognition rate and running time of different methods on the AR database

Experiment protocol	EP 1		EP 2	
	Classification rate (%)	Time (s)	Classification rate (%)	Time (s)
CRC	69.95	0.0521	73.93	0.0454
PCA	56.30	0.0054	64.76	0.0052
LDA	59.30	0.0136	61.07	0.0219
KNN ($K = 5$)	57.08	0.0045	64.88	0.0046
SRC (l_1_ls)	**73.38**	**10.5338**	**78.21**	**8.7744**
SRC (DALM)	**70.42**	**4.3012**	**76.55**	**4.2657**
SRC (DALM_fast)	55.23	0.6698	61.90	0.6765
SRC (FISTA)	58.19	0.3824	66.31	0.3055
SRC (Homotopy)	68.00	0.3062	73.00	0.2986
Our approach	**70.24**	**1.0757**	**75.60**	**0.4745**

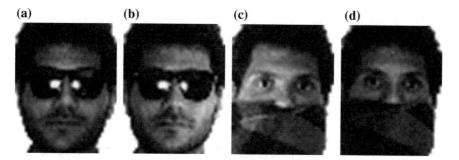

Fig. 7.14 Examples of contiguous occlusion of a subject from the AR database

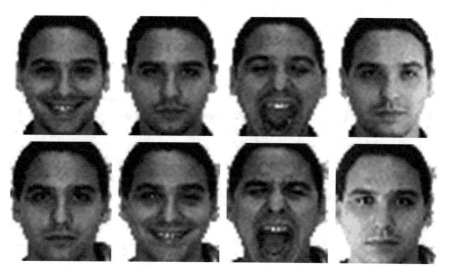

Fig. 7.15 Gesture variations of a subject from the AR database. The *top row* shows the changing position of the head with different poses. The *bottom row* shows two sessions incorporating neutral, happy, angry, and screaming, respectively

scenarios for two different sessions. The test system is designed that we take these images that are shown in Fig. 7.15 as the original training sample set for each subject. The test sample set consists of Fig. 7.14a, b for sunglass occlusion and Fig. 7.14c, d for scarf occlusion. The experimental results are shown in Table 7.10. As the sparse approach is too time-consuming, we selected two best sparse approaches SRC (l_1_ls) and SRC (DALM) to participate our experiment. Our approach achieves the second highest recognition rate [only 0.42 % lower than SRC (DALM)] for the case of sunglass occlusion. In the case of scarf occlusion, our approach is the third best with lagging the CRC and SRC (l1_ls) approaches by margin of 13.75 and 13.33 %, respectively. From the results in Table 7.11, we can see that our approach is more advantageous in practical contiguous occlusion.

Table 7.11 Recognition rate for occlusion

Approach	Recognition rate	
	Sunglass (%)	Scarf (%)
Our method	**90.83**	43.75
CRC	87.92	**57.50**
LRC	87.08	29.58
SRC (l1_ls)	90.42	**57.08**
SRC (DALM)	**91.25**	41.67
NNLS	90.00	41.25
KNN (k = 5)	82.08	29.58
PCA (90.00 % energy)	83.33	26.25
LDA (PCA + LDA + NN)	70.00	42.92

7.5.3.2   Georgia Tech (GT) Database

Similarly, we tested different methods in two cases. We used the first seven images of each subject as the training samples and took the remaining images as test samples in the first case (Case 1). In the second case (Case 2), we used the first eight images of each subject as the training samples and took the remaining images as test samples. All images were cropped and resized to 50×60 pixels. Figure 7.16 shows some face images from the GT database. The recognition rate curve with respect to the scale of the nearest neighbor set for the test sample is shown in Fig. 7.17. We can see that, in the two cases, recognition rate of our approach increases with the decreasing of the scale of the nearest neighbor set K and achieves the peak of the curve under the scale of $0.2 * \text{scale}(A)$. Table 7.12 shows the recognition results and running time of different of approaches. Our approach achieves the best recognition rate (under the scale of $0.2 * \text{scale}(A)$ in the case 1 and

Fig. 7.16 Some face images from the GT database

Fig. 7.17 Recognition rate for the GT database with respect to the scale of the nearest neighbor set K being chosen for the test sample

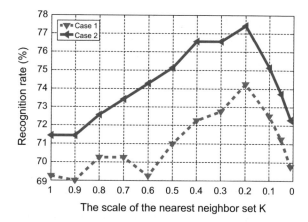

Table 7.12 The recognition rate and running time of different methods on the GT database

Experiment protocol	Case 1		Case 2	
	Recognition rate (%)	Time (s)	Recognition rate (%)	Time (s)
CRC	65.00	0.0209	67.71	0.0254
PCA	62.75	0.0030	66.29	0.0030
LDA	57.00	0.0214	59.14	0.0252
KNN ($K = 2$)	64.50	0.0026	65.43	0.0027
SRC (l1_ls)	71.00	3.1643	72.57	3.7345
SRC (DALM)	72.50	12.1705	73.71	12.2367
SRC (DALM_fast)	72.00	0.9017	74.00	1.3752
SRC (FISTA)	65.00	0.1152	66.00	0.1441
SRC (Homotopy)	68.75	0.1009	70.29	0.1011
Our approach	**74.25**	**0.2232**	**77.43**	**0.2905**

2, respectively) in the two cases with 1.75 % higher than SRC (DLAM) in the case 1 and 3.43 % higher than SRC (DALM_fast) in the case 2. For the running time, the speed of our approach is 54.53 times faster than SRC (DLAM) in the case 1 and 4.7 times faster than SRC (DALM_fast) in the case 2. Overall, our approach outperforms the classical PCA, LDA, KNN and the latest CRC, SRC approaches.

7.6   Summary

In this chapter, we have presented several schemes using the virtual face for face recognition, and three types of virtual faces are introduced. Using the virtue faces as training samples is very helpful for overcoming the drawback of limited training samples in the real-world face recognition system. The virtue face image is easy to be generated, and can be exploited to simulate possible variation of the face image and is able to reduce the side effect of the pose and illumination difference between the training and test samples of the same face. The experimental results also prove the rationales of the proposed scheme.

References

D. Beymer, T. Poggio, in *Face recognition from one example view*. Proceedings of International Conference on Computer Vision (IEEE, 1995), pp. 500–507

T. Bin, L. Siwei, H. Hua, in *High performance face recognition system by creating virtual sample*. Proceedings of the 2003 International Conference on Neural Networks and Signal Processing (IEEE, 2003), pp. 972–975

P. Ekman, J.C. Hager, W.V. Friesen, The symmetry of emotional and deliberate facial actions. Psychophysiology **18**(2), 101–106 (1981)

Q. Feng, J.-S. Pan, L. Yan, Restricted nearest feature line with ellipse for face recognition. J. Inf. Hiding Multimedia Signal Process. **3**(3), 297–305 (2012)

X. Gao, K. Zhang, D. Tao, X. Li, Image super-resolution with sparse neighbor embedding. IEEE Trans. Image Process. **21**(7), 3194–3205 (2012)

A.S. Georghiades, P.N. Belhumeur, D.J. Kriegman, From few to many: illumination cone models for face recognition under variable lighting and pose. IEEE Trans. Pattern Anal. Mach. Intell. **23**(6), 643–660 (2001)

M. Grgic, K. Delac, S. Grgic, SCface–surveillance cameras face database. Multimedia Tools Appl. **51**(3), 863–879 (2011)

Y. Hu, D. Jiang, S. Yan, L. Zhang, H. Zhang, in *Automatic 3D reconstruction for face recognition*. Proceedings of IEEE International Conference on Automatic Face and Gesture Recognition (IEEE, 2004), pp. 843–848

J.-B. Huang, M.-H. Yang, in *Fast sparse representation with prototypes*. Proceedings of IEEE Conference on Computer Vision and Pattern Recognition (IEEE, 2010), pp. 3618–3625

D. Jiang, Y. Hu, S. Yan, L. Zhang, H. Zhang, W. Gao, Efficient 3D reconstruction for face recognition. Pattern Recogn. **38**(6), 787–798 (2005)

H.-C. Jung, B.-W. Hwang, S.-W. Lee, in *Authenticating corrupted face image based on noise model*. Proceedings of IEEE International Conference on Automatic Face and Gesture Recognition (IEEE, 2004), pp. 272–277

K. Koh, S. Kim, S. Boyd, *l1 ls: A Matlab Solver for Large-Scale ℓ1-Regularized Least Squares Problems* (2008)

Y. Li, A. Ngom, Classification approach based on non-negative least squares. Neurocomputing **118**, 41–57 (2013)

J. Liu, S. Chen, Z.-H. Zhou, X. Tan, Single image subspace for face recognition, *Analysis and Modeling of Faces and Gestures* (Springer, Berlin, 2007)

I. Naseem, R. Togneri, M. Bennamoun, Linear regression for face recognition. IEEE Trans. Pattern Anal. Mach. Intell. **32**(11), 2106–2112 (2010)

I. Naseem, R. Togneri, M. Bennamoun, Robust regression for face recognition. Pattern Recogn. **45**(1), 104–118 (2012)

C. Peng, J. Li, Fast sparse representation model for l1-norm minimisation problem. Electron. Lett. **48**(3), 162–164 (2012)

Y.-S. Ryu, S.-Y. Oh, Simple hybrid classifier for face recognition with adaptively generated virtual data. Pattern Recogn. Lett. **23**(7), 833–841 (2002)

E. Saber, A.M. Tekalp, Frontal-view face detection and facial feature extraction using color, shape and symmetry based cost functions. Pattern Recogn. Lett. **19**(8), 669–680 (1998)

S. Saha, S. Bandyopadhyay, in *A symmetry based face detection technique*. Proceedings of Proceedings of the IEEE WIE National Symposium on Emerging Technologies (2007), pp. 1–4

G. Shan, Virtual sample generating for face recognition from a single training sample per person. Sci. Technol. Eng. **13**(14), 3908–3911 (2013)

T. Shan, B.C. Lovell, S. Chen, in *Face recognition robust to head pose from one sample image*. Proceedings of International Conference on Pattern Recognition (IEEE, 2006), pp. 515–518

A. Sharma, A. Dubey, P. Tripathi, V. Kumar, Pose invariant virtual classifiers from single training image using novel hybrid-eigenfaces. Neurocomputing **73**(10), 1868–1880 (2010)

Y. Shi, D. Dai, C. Liu, H. Yan, Sparse discriminant analysis for breast cancer biomarker identification and classification. Prog. Nat. Sci. **19**(11), 1635–1641 (2009)

T. Sim, T. Kanade, in *Combining models and exemplars for face recognition: an illuminating example*. Proceedings of the CVPR 2001 Workshop on Models Versus Exemplars in Computer Vision (2001)

M.-C. Su, C.-H. Chou. in *Application of associative memory in human face detection*. Proceedings of International Joint Conference on Neural Networks (1999), pp. 3194–3197

N.P.H. Thian, S. Marcel, S. Bengio. in *Improving face authentication using virtual samples*. Proceedings of IEEE International Conference on Acoustics, Speech, and Signal Processing, vol. 3 (IEEE, 2003), pp. III-233–236

T. Vetter, Synthesis of novel views from a single face image. Int. J. Comput. Vis. **28**(2), 103–116 (1998)

J. Wang, J. You, Q. Li, Y. Xu, Orthogonal discriminant vector for face recognition across pose. Pattern Recogn. **45**(12), 4069–4079 (2012a)

S.-J. Wang, J. Yang, M.-F. Sun, X.-J. Peng, M.-M. Sun, C.-G. Zhou, Sparse tensor discriminant color space for face verification. IEEE Trans. Neural Netw. Learn. Syst. **23**(6), 876–888 (2012b)

J. Wright, A.Y. Yang, A. Ganesh, S.S. Sastry, Y. Ma, Robust face recognition via sparse representation. IEEE Trans. Pattern Anal. Mach. Intell. **31**(2), 210–227 (2009)

J. Wright, Y. Ma, J. Mairal, G. Sapiro, T.S. Huang, S. Yan, Sparse representation for computer vision and pattern recognition. Proc. IEEE **98**(6), 1031–1044 (2010)

Y. Xu, Z. Jin, in *Down-sampling face images and low-resolution face recognition*. Proceedings of International Conference on Innovative Computing Information and Control (IEEE, 2008), pp. 392–392

Y. Xu, D. Zhang, J. Yang, J.-Y. Yang, A two-phase test sample sparse representation method for use with face recognition. IEEE Trans. Circuits Syst. Video Technol. **21**(9), 1255–1262 (2011)

Y. Xu, Z. Fan, Q. Zhu, Feature space-based human face image representation and recognition. Opt. Eng. **51**(1), 017205-1–017205-7 (2012)

Y. Xu, Q. Zhu, Z. Fan, M. Qiu, Y. Chen, H. Liu, Coarse to fine K nearest neighbor classifier. Pattern Recogn. Lett. **34**(9), 980–986 (2013a)

Y. Xu, X. Zhu, Z. Li, G. Liu, Y. Lu, H. Liu, Using the original and 'symmetrical face' training samples to perform representation based two-step face recognition. Pattern Recogn. **46**(4), 1151–1158 (2013b)

Y. Xu, X. Fang, X. Li, J. Yang, J. You, H. Liu, S. Teng, Data uncertainty in face recognition. Trans. Cybern. IEEE **44**(10), 1950–1961 (2014a)

Y. Xu, X. Li, J. Yang, D. Zhang, Integrate the original face image and its mirror image for face recognition. Neurocomputing **131**, 191–199 (2014b)

J. Yang, D. Zhang, A.F. Frangi, J.-Y. Yang, Two-dimensional PCA: a new approach to appearance-based face representation and recognition. IEEE Trans. Pattern Anal. Mach. Intell. **26**(1), 131–137 (2004)

J. Yang, D. Zhang, X. Yong, J.-Y. Yang, Two-dimensional discriminant transform for face recognition. Pattern Recogn. **38**(7), 1125–1129 (2005)

A.Y. Yang, S.S. Sastry, A. Ganesh, Y. Ma, in *Fast ℓ 1-minimization algorithms and an application in robust face recognition: a review*, Proceedings of IEEE International Conference on Image Processing (IEEE, 2010), pp. 1849–1852

W. Yang, C. Sun, L. Zhang, A multi-manifold discriminant analysis method for image feature extraction. Pattern Recogn. **44**(8), 1649–1657 (2011)

J. Yang, L. Zhang, Y. Xu, J.-Y. Yang, Beyond sparsity: The role of L 1-optimizer in pattern classification. Pattern Recogn. **45**(3), 1104–1118 (2012)

D. Zhang. *Advanced pattern recognition technologies with applications to biometrics* (IGI Global, 2009)

X. Zhang, Y. Gao, Face recognition across pose: a review. Pattern Recogn. **42**(11), 2876–2896 (2009)

L. Zhang, M. Yang, X. Feng. in *Sparse representation or collaborative representation: which helps face recognition?* Proceedings of IEEE International Conference on Computer Vision (IEEE, 2011), pp. 471–478

Chapter 8
Sparse Representation-Based Methods for Face Recognition

Abstract Sparse representation has attracted much attention from researchers in fields of signal processing, image processing, computer vision, and pattern recognition. Sparse representation also has a good performance in both theoretical research and practical applications. Many different algorithms have been proposed for sparse representation. In this chapter, we will mainly introduce the application of the sparse representation in fields of face recognition.

8.1 Introduction

Sparse representation, from the viewpoint of its origin, is directly related to Compressed Sensing (CS) (Candès et al. 2006; Donoho 2006), which is one of the most popular research topics in computer science in recent years.

For face classification, from the viewpoint of "atoms," available sparse representation methods can be categorized into two general groups: naive sample-based sparse representation and dictionary learning-based sparse representation. The Naive Sample-based Sparse Representation Classification (NSSRC) method takes the original training samples as a dictionary to represent the test samples for face recognition (Wright et al. 2009). The NSSRC algorithm always first assumes that the test image sample can be sufficiently represented by samples from the same subject. Specifically, SRC exploits the linear combination of training samples to represent the test sample and computes sparse representation coefficients of the linear representation system, and then calculates the reconstruction residuals of each class employing the sparse representation coefficients and training samples. The test sample will be classified as a member of the class, which leads to the minimum reconstruction residual. The NSSRC algorithm requires that the l_1 norm of the coefficient vector of the linear combination is as small as possible. The method depends on this "optimal" linear combination to classify the test sample. We refer to this kind of method as l_1 norm-based representation method. Later, some researchers proposed l_2 norm-based representation methods such as the Collaborative Representation Classification (CRC) method (Zhang et al. 2011) and the Two-Phase Test Sample Sparse Representation (TPTSSR) method (Xu et al. 2011a). These methods also first obtain the "optimal" linear combination of the training samples to represent the test sample and then exploit this linear combination to classify the test sample. However, they differ from the naive sparse representation method (NRBC) as follows (Xu et al. 2012c; Shi et al. 2011). First, they require that the l_2 norm rather than l_1 norm of the coefficient vector of the linear combination be minimized. Second, they have analytic solutions whereas NRBC have no such solutions. The l_2 norm-based representation methods show good performance in biometrics such as face recognition and palmprint recognition (Yang et al. 2012; Xu et al. 2012a). Linear Regression Classification (LRC) can be viewed as a l_2 norm-based representation method (Naseem et al. 2010, 2012). However, as LRC and conventional l_2 norm-based representation methods use a linear combination of the training samples from each class and all the training samples to represent the test sample, they should solve C and one linear system for classifying the test sample. C is the number of the classes. The recently proposed kernel Representation-Based Classification Method (RBCM) is a nonlinear extension of RBCM (Yang et al. 2011; Yin et al. 2012). The l_2 norm-based representation method has also been extended to the complex space (Xu et al. 2011b). The corresponding method performs very well in bimodal biometrics.

The above conventional representations, which exploit the training samples to obtain a representation of the test sample. For face recognition, the Representation-Based Classification (RBC) algorithm also has the following drawback: when it exploits a linear combination of the training samples to represent a test sample, it indeed just tries to make the test sample look like the training samples. For real-world pattern classification applications, the test sample might be very much different from the training samples from the same class. A typical example is that a face image varies with illuminations, poses, and facial expressions, so the probe face image is usually different from the gallery images from the same subject. As a consequence, in face recognition, RBC probably cannot well deal with the great difference between the training samples and test sample. In this chapter, we will mainly present two improved RBC algorithms which are able to obtain better performance than some state-of-art algorithms in case of various poses and illuminations, et al.

8.2 Inverse Sparse Representation for Face Recognition

In this section, we present a face recognition method by integrating conventional representation and the inverse representation. The method indeed uses two complementary ways to reflect and evaluate the similarity between the test sample and each class. A reasonable score level fusion strategy is used to combine the similarities generated from the two ways and classify the test sample. This enables us to obtain higher classification accuracy.

8.2.1 Main Steps of the Method

We assume that there are C classes and each class has n training samples. Let $x_1, \ldots, x_N$ be all the N training samples $(N = Cn)$. $x_{(i-1)n+k}$ still stands for the kth training sample of the ith subject. Let y still stand for the test sample.

The main steps of the improved RBC method are as follows. The first step uses the mirror image of the face image to obtain virtual training samples and test samples. The detailed introduction of the mirror image is in Sect. 7.4.1 of Chap. 7. The second step obtains the "optimal" linear combination of the original and virtual training samples from every subject to represent the test sample and calculates the score of each subject. The third step uses the following procedure to implement the inverse representation: for the jth subject, it first combines all the original training samples from the other subjects, the original test sample and virtual test sample to form a set. It then produces the "optimal" linear combination of all samples from this set to represent each training sample from the jth subject. Based on this linear combination, the third step calculates the "distance" between the test sample and the training sample of the jth subject. Since a subject has more than one training sample, this step takes the mean of all the "distances" corresponding to all the training samples from the jth subject as the "distance" between the test sample and the jth subject. The fourth step integrates the scores and "distances," produced from the second and third steps for the ultimate classification. These steps are presented in detail below.

Step 1. Produce the virtual test sample for the original test sample. For original test sample y, the virtual test sample is defined as $y^v(p,q) = y(p, Q - q + 1)$, $p = 1, \ldots, P, q = 1, \ldots, Q$. P and Q stand for the numbers of the rows and columns of the face image matrix, respectively. $y(p,q)$ and $y^v(p,q)$ denote the pixels located in the pth row and qth column of y and y^v, respectively. y^v is indeed the mirror image of y. The virtual training sample corresponding to each original training sample is also generated in the same way. Let $x_1^v, \ldots, x_N^v$ be the virtual training samples generated from $x_1, \ldots, x_N$, respectively. All the samples are converted into column vectors and still denoted by the previous notations.

Step 2. Let $X = [x_1 \ldots x_n x_1^v \ldots x_n^v \quad x_{n+1} \ldots x_{2n} x_{n+1}^v \ldots x_{2n}^v \ldots x_{(C-1)n+1} \ldots x_N x_{(C-1)n+1}^v \ldots x_N^v]$ $(N = Cn)$. For the ith subject, we establish linear system $y = X_i \alpha_i$, $X_i = \left[x_{(i-1)n+1} \ldots x_{in} x_{(i-1)n+1}^v \ldots x_{in}^v \right]$, $i = 1, \ldots, C$. In order to simultaneously minimize $||y - X_i \alpha_i||$ and $||\alpha_i||$, i.e., the norm of the solution vector, we define an objective function as $\min ||y - X_i \alpha_i|| + \lambda ||\alpha_i||$, where λ is a small positive constant. Thus, we solve α_i using $\hat{\alpha}_i = (X_i^T X_i + \lambda I)^{-1} X_i^T y$. Hereafter $|| \cdot ||$ always denotes the l_2 norm. λ and I stand for a small positive constant and the identity matrix, respectively. We calculate the score between the test sample and the ith subject using $s_i = ||y - X_i \hat{\alpha}_i||$.

Step 3. For the jth subject, we first combine all the original training samples from the other subjects, the original test sample and virtual test sample to form matrix $Z = \begin{bmatrix} X_1 \ldots X_{j-1} & X_{j+1} \ldots X_C & y & y^v \end{bmatrix}$, $X_i = \begin{bmatrix} x_{(i-1)n+1} \ldots x_{in} x^v_{(i-1)n+1} \ldots x^v_{in} \end{bmatrix}$.

We establish a linear system for each original training sample from the jth subject. For the kth $(k = 1, \ldots, n)$ original training sample from the jth subject, the linear system is defined as $\tilde{x}_k = Z\beta_k$, $\tilde{x}_k = x_{(j-1)*n+k}$. β_k is solved using $\hat{\beta}_k = (Z^T Z + \lambda I)Z^T \tilde{x}_k$. $d_k^0 = \left\| \tilde{x}_k - \hat{\beta}_k^{(C-1)n+1} y - \hat{\beta}_k^{(C-1)n+2} y^v \right\|$ is viewed as the "distance" between the test sample and the kth training sample of the jth subject. $\hat{\beta}_k^{(C-1)n+1}$, and $\hat{\beta}_k^{(C-1)n+2}$ are the $(C-1)n+1$-th and $(C-1)n+2$-th components of $\hat{\beta}_k$, respectively. For the jth subject, the mean of d_k^0 is used as the "distance" between the test sample and the jth subject and is denoted by d_j.

Step 4.   For test sample y, we first normalize its scores and "distances" with respect to all the subjects using $s'_j = (s_j - s^{min})/(s^{max} - s^{min})$ and $d'_j = (d_j - d^{min})/(d^{max} - d^{min})$, where $s^{min} = \min(s_1, \ldots, s_C)$, $s^{max} = \max(s_1, \ldots, s_C)$, $d^{min} = \min(d_1, \ldots, d_C)$, $d^{max} = \max(d_1, \ldots, d_C)$. We use $t_j = w_1 s'_j + w_2 d'_j$ to calculate the ultimate score with respect to the jth subject. w_1 and w_2 are the weights and $w_1 + w_2 = 1$. Because conventional representation seems to be more reliable in evaluating the similarity than the inverse representation, our method assigns a larger value to w_1 in comparison with w_2. If $k = \arg \min_j t_j$, then test sample y is assigned to the kth subject.

8.2.2   Analysis of the Method

8.2.2.1   Interpretation of the Main Steps

As introduced in the previous Chap. 7, the combination of the original and mirror training samples reflect more possible variation of the face image and enables the test sample to be easier and correctly classified. Secondly, in the second step of the method, the simultaneous use of the original and virtual training samples will enable the representation result to be more useful for classifying the face.

The advantage of integrating the inverse representation and conventional representation can be formally presented as follows. As we know, in real-world applications, the error exists in both the test sample and training sample. However, as conventional representation is based on the least-squares algorithm, it takes only the error in the test sample into account. Actually, for conventional LRC algorithm which was introduced in Sect. 7.1 of Chap. 7, the representation formula can be rewritten as

$$X_i A_i = y = y_0 + \Delta y, \tag{8.1}$$

where $y_0, \Delta y$ stand for the true test sample and error, respectively. According to the theoretical analysis, $\hat{A}_i$, i.e., the solution of A_i obtained using conventional representation is indeed generated with the following objective function (Fierro and Bunch 1994, 1996; Fierro et al. 1997):

$$\left\{\hat{A}_i, \Delta y\right\} = \arg\min\|\Delta y\| \text{ s.t. } X_i A_i = y_0 + \Delta y. \tag{8.2}$$

Moreover, the inverse representation in our method takes only the error in the raining sample into account. Specially, in the inverse representation in our method, $Z\beta_k = \tilde{x}_k$ can be rewritten as

$$Z\beta_k = \tilde{x}_{k_0} + \Delta\tilde{x}_k, \tag{8.3}$$

where $\tilde{x}_{k_0}, \Delta\tilde{x}_k$ stand for the true value of $\tilde{x}_k$ and error, respectively. It is easy to know that $\hat{\beta}_k$ is generated with the following objective function:

$$\left\{\hat{\beta}_k, \Delta\tilde{x}_k\right\} = \arg\min(\|\Delta\tilde{x}_k\| + \lambda\|\beta_k\|) \text{ s.t. } Z\beta_k = \tilde{x}_{k_0} + \Delta\tilde{x}_k. \tag{8.4}$$

From the above presentation, we observe that the integration of the inverse representation and conventional representation allows the error in the test sample and training sample to be simultaneously taken into account and processed. This will be beneficial for achieving good face recognition performance.

8.2.2.2   More Quantitative Analysis

In this subsection, we perform the correlation analysis to show the difference between the score and distance, respectively, obtained using step 2 and step 3 of the presented method. In score level fusion, if correlation coefficient between the two kinds of scores to fuse is low, the fusion result is usually good. In other words, a smaller correlation coefficient is able to lead to a greater improvement in accuracy. As we know, the correlation coefficient between two variables x and y are defined as $\rho(x, y) = \frac{\text{cov}(x,y)}{\sqrt{\text{cov}(x,x)}\sqrt{\text{cov}(y,y)}}$, where $\text{cov}(x, y) = E[(x - E(x))(y - E(y))]$. For a test sample, we use $s = [s_1 \ldots s_C]^T$ and $d = [d_1 \ldots d_C]^T$ to stand for all the scores and distances. We refer to s and d as score vector and distance vector, respectively. We calculate the correlation coefficient between the score and distance of the test sample using $\rho(s, d) = \frac{\text{cov}(s,d)}{\sqrt{\text{cov}(s,s)}\sqrt{\text{cov}(d,d)}}$, where $\text{cov}(s, d) = \frac{1}{C}\sum_{j=1}^{C}(s_j - \bar{s})$ $(d_j - \bar{d})$, $\bar{s} = \frac{1}{C}\sum_{j=1}^{C} s_j$, $\bar{d} = \frac{1}{C}\sum_{j=1}^{C} d_j$.

Table 8.1 shows the mean of all the correlation coefficients of the scores and distances of the test samples from the ORL database. We see that the maximum mean

Table 8.1 The mean of all
the correlation coefficients of
the scores and distances
obtained using Step 2 and
Step 3 of the presented
method

Training samples per class	3	4	5
Mean of all the correlation coefficients	0.545	0.520	0.496

The first three, four, and five face images of each subject in the
ORL database are used as training samples and the others are
taken as test samples. © 2014 IEEE. Reprinted, with permission,
from Xu et al. (2014)

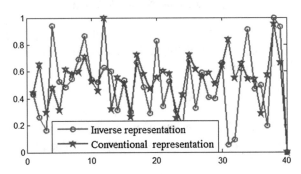

Fig. 8.1 The scores and distances, of the last test sample, obtained using Step 2 and Step 3 of the
presented method, respectively. The first five face images of each subject in the ORL database are
used as training samples and the others are taken as test samples. The *vertical axis* shows the
values of the score and distance. The *horizontal axis* shows No. of the component of the score
vector and distance vector. The scores and distances have been normalized. © 2014 IEEE.
Reprinted, with permission, from Xu et al. (2014)

is only 0.545. Figure 8.1 depicts the scores and distances, of the last test sample,
obtained using Step 2 and Step 3 in the case where the first five face images of each
subject in the ORL database are used as training samples and the others are taken as
test samples. Figure 8.2 depicts the scores and distances, of the last test sample from
the subset of the FERET database, obtained using Step 2 and Step 3 in the case where
the first four face images of each subject are used as training samples and the others
are taken as test samples. These two figures also visually tell us that the correlation
between the scores and distances is low. This means that the distances generated from
Step 3 are very complementary to the scores generated from Step 2 in recognizing the
faces. Figure 8.3 shows some test samples that were erroneous and correctly classified by LRC and our method, and the corresponding training sample from the
subject to which the test sample was erroneously assigned by LRC.

8.2.3 *Experimental Results*

We used the FERET, ORL, and Georgia Tech (GT) face databases to conduct
experiments. Each sample was converted into a unit vector in advance. Tables 8.2,
8.3, 8.4, and 8.5 show the experiment results of different algorithms which are

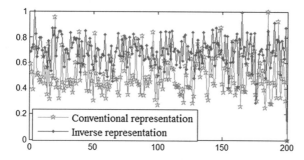

Fig. 8.2 The scores and distances, of the last test sample, obtained using Step 2 and Step 3 of the presented method, respectively. The first four face images of each subject in the subset of the FERET database are used as training samples and the others are taken as test samples. The *vertical axis* shows the values of the score and distance. The *horizontal axis* shows No. of the component of the score vector and distance vector. The scores and distances have been normalized. © 2014 IEEE. Reprinted, with permission, from Xu et al. (2014)

Fig. 8.3 Some test samples that were classified erroneously and correctly by LRC and the presented method, and the corresponding training sample from the subject to which the test sample was erroneously assigned by LRC. The *first row* shows the test samples. The *second row* shows one training sample from the subject to which the test sample was erroneously assigned by LRC. The *first face* image of each subject in the ORL database were used as training samples and the others were taken as test samples. w_1 and w_2 were set to 0.6 and 0.4, respectively. © 2014 IEEE. Reprinted, with permission, from Xu et al. (2014)

performed on above databases, respectively. For FERET database, each image was resized to a 40 × 40 image using the down-sampling algorithm. For ORL face database, each image was resized to an image with one half of the original size by using the downsampling algorithm. For GT database, we use the face image with the background removed, and each used image has the size of 30 by 40.

The above algorithms are also tested on corrupted face images. The sets of training samples and test samples are the same as those in Tables 8.1, 8.2, 8.3, and 8.4, respectively. For obtaining corrupted face images, we use Matlab function

Table 8.2 Classification accuracies (%) of different methods on the FERET face database

Training samples per class	1	2	3
LRC	44.92	64.20	59.62
CRC	44.33	58.40	44.37
RCR	41.67	55.10	46.12
SRC	50.25	64.80	60.00
The improved RBC method $(w_1 = 0.8)$	55.17	78.10	78.63
The improved RBC method $(w_1 = 0.7)$	53.83	75.40	75.00
The improved RBC method $(w_1 = 0.6)$	51.08	75.40	69.50

The first 1, 2, and 3 face images of each subject are treated as original training samples and the remaining face images are taken as test samples. © 2014 IEEE. Reprinted, with permission, from (Xu et al. 2014)

Table 8.3 Classification accuracies (%) of different methods on the ORL face database

Training samples per class	2	3	4
LRC	79.06	81.79	85.00
CRC	83.44	86.07	89.17
RCR	77.19	81.07	82.08
SRC	85.00	85.71	90.00
The improved RBC method $(w_1 = 0.8)$	85.62	89.64	89.17
The improved RBC method $(w_1 = 0.7)$	86.88	90.36	90.83
The improved RBC method $(w_1 = 0.6)$	86.88	89.64	91.67

The first 2, 3, and 4 face images of each subject are treated as original training samples and the remaining face images are taken as test samples. © 2014 IEEE. Reprinted, with permission, from Xu et al. (2014)

Table 8.4 Classification accuracies (%) of different methods on the GT face database

Training samples per class	3	4	5
LRC	51.00	55.27	59.40
CRC	45.33	47.09	48.80
RCR	36.67	38.36	40.80
SRC	52.00	56.73	59.80
The improved RBC method $(w_1 = 0.9)$	57.00	60.36	62.20
The improved RBC method $(w_1 = 0.8)$	55.33	57.82	62.20
The improved RBC method $(w_1 = 0.7)$	55.33	57.82	59.60

The first 3, 4, and 5 face images of each subject are used as training samples, respectively. The remaining images are taken as test samples. © 2014 IEEE. Reprinted, with permission, from Xu et al. (2014)

Fig. 8.4 Some of the corrupted face images. The *first two rows* show the corrupted face images of two subjects in the used FERET subset. The *third and fourth rows* show some of the corrupted face images of two subjects in the GT database. The *last two rows* show some of the corrupted face images of two subjects in the ORL database. © 2014 IEEE. Reprinted, with permission, from Xu et al. (2014)

Table 8.5 Classification accuracies (%) of different methods on the corrupted FERET face database

Training samples per class	1	2	3
LRC	19.75	39.00	38.00
CRC	25.67	27.90	18.63
RCR	18.58	16.80	12.50
SRC	34.50	46.90	43.00
The improved RBC method ($w_1 = 0.8$)	36.92	55.50	54.13
The improved RBC method ($w_1 = 0.7$)	36.50	50.80	49.12
The improved RBC method ($w_1 = 0.6$)	35.58	45.70	44.75

© 2014 IEEE. Reprinted, with permission, from Xu et al. (2014)

"imnoise" to add Gaussian white noise of zero mean and variance of 0.01 to the tested face images whereas the training samples are not dealt with so. Figure 8.4 shows some of the corrupted face images. Table 8.5, 8.6 and 8.7 show the classification accuracies of all the methods on the corrupted FERET, ORL and GT face images, respectively.

Table 8.6 Classification accuracies (%) of different methods on the corrupted ORL face database

Training samples per class	2	3	4
LRC	74.06	77.14	83.33
CRC	81.56	82.86	89.17
RCR	74.69	76.79	79.17
SRC	82.81	83.93	89.58
The improved RBC method $(w_1 = 0.8)$	85.00	87.86	89.58
The improved RBC method $(w_1 = 0.7)$	84.69	88.57	90.00
The improved RBC method $(w_1 = 0.6)$	84.06	89.29	89.58

© 2014 IEEE. Reprinted, with permission, from Xu et al. (2014)

Table 8.7 Classification accuracies (%) of different methods on the corrupted GT face database

Training samples per class	3	4	5
LRC	45.67	48.91	51.60
CRC	37.50	42.00	41.60
RCR	24.17	24.00	23.80
SRC	46.17	49.27	51.20
The improved RBC method $(w_1 = 0.9)$	52.33	57.09	57.60
The improved RBC method $(w_1 = 0.8)$	52.33	55.09	57.20
The improved RBC method $(w_1 = 0.7)$	51.33	53.09	55.80

© 2014 IEEE. Reprinted, with permission, from Xu et al. (2014)

8.3   Robust Sparse Representation by Incorporating the Original Training Sample and Its Reasonable Variant for Face Recognition

In this section, we present another improved RBC algorithm to overcome the problems of various poses and illuminations. The main ideas are as follows: besides the test sample is represented via a linear combination of the original training samples, which is implemented by the conventional RBC, and the deviation of the test sample from each class is calculated, we also exploit nearest neighbors of the test sample to produce an alternative set of the original training samples and use this set to obtain a representation of the test sample. The obtained alternative set can present possible variation of the original training samples and the representation of the test sample generated from this set is complementary to that obtained using the set of the original training samples. The integration of these two representations allow us to obtain higher accuracy. Finally, these two representations are fused for ultimate classification of the test sample.

We assume that there are L classes and each class has m training samples. Let $n = mL$. There are n training samples in total. We denote the m training samples of the cth $(c \leq L)$ class by $x_{m(c-1)+1} \ldots x_{cm}$. As a result, all of the n training samples are denoted by $x_1 \ldots x_n$, respectively. Let $X = [x_1 \ldots x_n]$ and $X_i = [x_{m(i-1)+1} \ldots x_{im}]$, $c \leq L$. y is the test sample to be classified. $x_1 \ldots x_n$, and y are supposed to be column vectors.

8.3.1   Main Steps of the Method

The main steps of the method are described below. These steps are repeatedly implemented for each test sample. In other words, we perform classification every test sample using the following same steps.

Step 1. RBC algorithm is implemented to solve $y = XA$ and the solution is denoted by $\hat{A}$. The deviation of test sample y from the j-class is calculated using $s_j^1 = \left\| y - X_j \hat{A}_j \right\|_2$. X_j is the matrix consisting of the training samples of the j-class. $\hat{A}_j$ is composed of m components of $\hat{A}$. Let $\hat{A} = [\hat{a}_1 \ldots \hat{a}_n]^T$, then $\hat{A}_j = [\hat{a}_{m(j-1)+1} \ldots \hat{a}_{mj}]^T$, $1 \leq j \leq L$. We also refer to $\hat{A}_j$ as the coefficient vector consisting of the training samples of the j-class.

Step 2. k-nearest neighbors of test sample y are selected from the set of the original training samples. Let these k-nearest neighbors be denoted by vectors $n_1 \ldots, n_k$, respectively, and let $N = [n_1 \ldots n_k]$. Equation $N = X\tilde{A}$ is constructed and the solution to unknown $\tilde{A}$ is obtained using $\tilde{A} = (X^T X + \gamma I)^{-1} X^T N$. γ is a small positive constant and I is the identity matrix.

Step 3. Equation $N = U\bar{\tilde{A}}$ is constructed and the solution to unknown, U is obtained using $\hat{U} = N(\bar{\tilde{A}})^T (\bar{\tilde{A}} \bar{\tilde{A}}^T + \gamma I)^{-1}$.

Step 4. The RBC algorithm is implemented again to solve equation $y = \hat{U}B$ and the solution is denoted by $\hat{B} = [\hat{b}_1 \ldots \hat{b}_n]^T$. The deviation of test sample y from the j-class is calculated using $s_j^2 = \left\| y - \hat{U}_j \hat{B}_j \right\|_2$, where $\hat{B}_j = [\hat{b}_{m(j-1)+1} \ldots \hat{b}_{mj}]^T$. Let $\hat{U} = [\hat{u}_1 \ldots \hat{u}_n]$, then $\hat{U}_j = [\hat{u}_{m(j-1)+1} \ldots \hat{u}_{mj}]^T$.

Step 5. s_j^1 and s_j^2 are fused using $S_j = \alpha s_j^1 + (1 - \alpha) s_j^2$, $0 \leq \alpha \leq 1$. Test sample y is classified into the k-class if $k = \arg \min_j S_j$.

It should be pointed out that Steps 1 and 4 can select an arbitrary same RBC algorithm from the l_2 RBC, l_1 RBC, and $l_{2,1}$ RBC algorithms. In the experimental section presented later, several typical RBC algorithms will be used and tested. The detailed introduction of RBC algorithms is in Sect. 7.2 of Chap. 7.

8.3.2   *Analysis of the Method*

The presented method is reasonable owing to the following factors. First, to generate more available training samples can obtain more accurate recognition of the test sample. Second, by using Steps 2 and 3, the presented method indeed constructs an alternative set of the original all training samples. In particular, these two steps exploit k-nearest neighbors of the test sample to modify the set of the original training samples. As a result, the produced alternative set of training samples contain complementary information on the original set and the simultaneous use of these two sets is very helpful for recognition of the test sample. The sample in the alternative set is also referred to as alternative training sample. Actually, alternative training samples are reasonable variants of the original training samples. It is clear that in Sect. 8.3.1 $\hat{U}$ consist of alternative training samples and the ith column of $\hat{U}$ is the column vector corresponding to the ith alternative training sample. Another rationale of the improved RBC method is that the weighted fusion scheme presented in Step 4 allows us to properly take advantage of the two kinds of deviations. Experiments presented in Sect. 8.3.3 show that when the two kinds of deviations are assigned with different weights from 0 to 1 (i.e., $0 < \alpha < 1$), the improved RBC method can always obtain a satisfactory accuracy which is better than that of the naïve RBC method.

A few previous works also made efforts in exploiting nearest neighbors of the test sample when constructing representation of the test sample (Ma et al. 2010; Zhang and Yang 2010). The improved RBC method is distinguished from them as follows: these works just directly use the nearest neighbors, but the improved RBC method indeed exploits the test sample, its nearest neighbors, and the set of original training samples to obtain alternative training samples. As a result, alternative training samples contain more information than the nearest neighbors used in (Ma et al. 2010; Zhang and Yang 2010), and seem to be more helpful. Moreover, in the methods in (Ma et al. 2010; Zhang and Yang 2010) the test sample is classified only on the basis of the nearest neighbors, whereas improved RBC method classifies the test sample by simultaneously using the original training samples and alternative training samples. The diagram of the improved RBC method can be depicted by Fig. 8.5.

The following insight is also helpful to understand the rationale of the presented method. Figure 8.6 shows some original training samples and alternative training samples of one subject in the ORL face database. From this figure, we see that alternative training samples are usually different from original training samples of the same subject. This visually shows that alternative training samples and original training samples are complementary in representing the test sample. Moreover, as shown in Fig. 8.7, the first and second kinds of deviations of the test sample have low correlation.

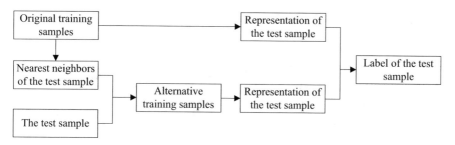

Fig. 8.5 The diagram of the improved RBC method

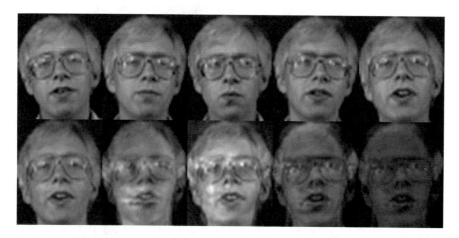

Fig. 8.6 Some original training samples and alternative training samples of one subject in the ORL face database. The *first row shows* five original training samples of one subject in the ORL face database. The *second row* shows alternative training samples of the same subject shown in the first row. In this case, the *first five face* images of each subject are used as training samples and the *other face* images are used as test samples

8.3.3 Experimental Results

In this section, we use the FERET[1] and ORL[2] face databases to test and verify the effectiveness of the presented method. In order to evaluate the performance of the improved RBC method, we apply it to CRC (Zhang et al. 2011) and the Sparse Representation-based Classification (SRC) algorithm proposed in (Kim et al. 2007). We also test an improvement to the nearest neighbor classifier (INNC) (Xu et al. 2012b), FISTA (Beck and Teboulle 2009), and a Fusion Classification Method

---

[1]http://www.itl.nist.gov/iad/humanid/feret/feret_master.html.

[2]http://www.cl.cam.ac.uk/research/dtg/attarchive/facedatabase.html.

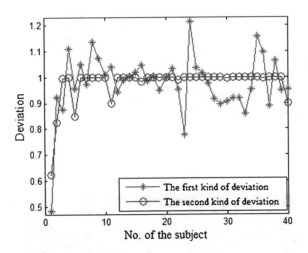

Fig. 8.7 The first and second kinds of deviations. The first five face images of each subject in the ORL database are used as training samples and the other face images are used as test samples. The first and second kinds of deviations of the first test sample are depicted. As each class (subject) has two deviation values (one first kind of deviation value, and one second kind of deviation value) and there are 40 subjects, the first test sample has 80 deviation values in total

Table 8.8 Classification error rates using different methods on the FERET face database

Number of the training samples per subject	1	2	3	4	5	6
Improvement of CRC ($\alpha = 0.15$)	0.5266	0.3780	0.4175	0.2783	0.1750	0.1850
Improvement of CRC ($\alpha = 0.2$)	0.5266	0.3760	0.4112	0.2766	0.1775	0.1850
Improvement of CRC ($\alpha = 0.25$)	0.5250	0.3740	0.4100	0.2716	0.1775	0.1800
Improvement of CRC ($\alpha = 0.3$)	0.5241	0.3720	0.4100	0.2800	0.1775	0.1650
CRC	0.5567	0.4160	0.5563	0.4467	0.3150	0.2550
Improvement of SRC ($\alpha = 0.15$)	0.5525	0.3720	0.4225	0.2566	0.1675	0.1800
Improvement of SRC ($\alpha = 0.2$)	0.5533	0.3700	0.4175	0.2566	0.1675	0.1650
Improvement of SRC ($\alpha = 0.25$)	0.5541	0.3690	0.4162	0.2566	0.1600	0.1550
Improvement of SRC ($\alpha = 0.3$)	0.5525	0.3700	0.4137	0.2566	0.1600	0.1600
SRC	0.5800	0.4160	0.4887	0.3633	0.2225	0.1800
INNC	0.5567	0.4170	0.4950	0.4600	0.3125	0.2050
FISTA	0.5283	0.4120	0.4625	0.2983	0.2150	0.1750
FCM (Liu et al. 2013)	0.5691	0.4280	0.5262	0.4350	0.3175	0.3000

The first 1, 2, 3, 4, 5, and 6 face images of each subject are selected as original training samples and the remaining face images are treated as testing samples

(FCM) proposed in (Liu et al. 2013) for comparison. In the experiments, parameter γ is set to 0.01, and k is set to two times of the number of original training samples of every subject. The experiment results are shown in Tables 8.8 and 8.9.

Table 8.9 Classification error rates using different methods on the ORL face database

Number of the training samples per subject	2	3	4	5
Improvement of CRC ($\alpha = 0.15$)	0.1562	0.1107	0.0833	0.0800
Improvement of CRC ($\alpha = 0.2$)	0.1531	0.1107	0.0833	0.0850
Improvement of CRC ($\alpha = 0.25$)	0.1468	0.1178	0.0833	0.0850
Improvement of CRC ($\alpha = 0.3$)	0.1437	0.1142	0.0916	0.0850
CRC	0.1656	0.1392	0.1083	0.1150
Improvement of SRC ($\alpha = 0.15$)	0.1843	0.1321	0.0917	0.0850
Improvement of SRC ($\alpha = 0.2$)	0.1781	0.1321	0.0916	0.0950
Improvement of SRC ($\alpha = 0.25$)	0.1750	0.1250	0.0916	0.0900
Improvement of SRC ($\alpha = 0.3$)	0.1750	0.1321	0.0875	0.0950
SRC	0.1844	0.1571	0.1125	0.1200
INNC	0.2125	0.2178	0.1750	0.1700
FISTA	0.1750	0.1535	0.1125	0.1150
FCM (Liu et al. 2013)	0.1656	0.1429	0.1042	0.1100

The first 2,3,4, and 5 face images of each subject are selected as original training samples and the remaining face images are treated as testing samples. Each image was also resized to a 56 by 46 image matrix by using the down-sampling algorithm

8.4 Summary

Sparse representation has been widely adopted for face recognition. In this chapter, two improved face recognition algorithms based on sparse representation are presented. The first improved algorithm used a novel inverse representation approach to improve the accuracy. The second improved algorithm improved the performance via the combination of the original and alternative training samples, which consolidates the representation of test image. The rationales of the presented methods are also analyzed in detail. The experiments also show that both two methods can greatly improve the accuracy of traditional sparse representation methods.

References

A. Beck, M. Teboulle, A fast iterative shrinkage-thresholding algorithm for linear inverse problems. SIAM J. Imaging Sci. **2**(1), 183–202 (2009)

E.J. Candès, J. Romberg, T. Tao, Robust uncertainty principles: exact signal reconstruction from highly incomplete frequency information. IEEE Trans. Inf. Theory **52**(2), 489–509 (2006)

D.L. Donoho, Compressed sensing. IEEE Trans. Inf. Theory **52**(4), 1289–1306 (2006)

R.D. Fierro, J.R. Bunch, Collinearity and total least squares. SIAM J. Matrix Anal. Appl. **15**(4), 1167–1181 (1994)

R.D. Fierro, J.R. Bunch, Perturbation theory for orthogonal projection methods with applications to least squares and total least squares. Linear Algebra Appl. **234**, 71–96 (1996)

R.D. Fierro, G.H. Golub, P.C. Hansen, D.P. O'Leary, Regularization by truncated total least squares. SIAM J. Sci. Comput. **18**(4), 1223–1241 (1997)

S.-J. Kim, K. Koh, M. Lustig, S. Boyd, D. Gorinevsky, An interior-point method for large-scale l 1-regularized least squares. IEEE J. Sel. Top. Sig. Process. **1**(4), 606–617 (2007)

Z. Liu, J. Pu, T. Huang, Y. Qiu, A novel classification method for palmprint recognition based on reconstruction error and normalized distance. Appl. Intell. **39**(2), 307–314 (2013)

L. Ma, B. Xiao, C. Wang, *Sparse representation based on K-nearest neighbor classifier for degraded Chinese character recognition*, in Advances in Multimedia Information Processing-PCM 2010 (Springer, 2010)

I. Naseem, R. Togneri, M. Bennamoun, Linear regression for face recognition. IEEE Trans. Pattern Anal. Mach. Intell. **32**(11), 2106–2112 (2010)

I. Naseem, R. Togneri, M. Bennamoun, Robust regression for face recognition. Pattern Recogn. **45**(1), 104–118 (2012)

Q. Shi, A. Eriksson, A. Van Den Hengel, C. Shen, *Is face recognition really a compressive sensing problem?* in Proceedings of IEEE Conference on Computer Vision and Pattern Recognition (IEEE, 2011), pp. 553–560

J. Wright, A.Y. Yang, A. Ganesh, S.S. Sastry, Y. Ma, Robust face recognition via sparse representation. IEEE Trans. Pattern Anal. Mach. Intell. **31**(2), 210–227 (2009)

Y. Xu, D. Zhang, J. Yang, J.-Y. Yang, A two-phase test sample sparse representation method for use with face recognition. IEEE Trans. Circuits Syst. Video Technol. **21**(9), 1255–1262 (2011a)

Y. Xu, A. Zhong, J. Yang, D. Zhang, Bimodal biometrics based on a representation and recognition approach. Opt. Eng. **50**(3), 037202–037202-7 (2011b)

Y. Xu, Z. Fan, Q. Zhu, Feature space-based human face image representation and recognition. Opt. Eng. **51**(1), 017205-1–017205-7 (2012a)

Y. Xu, Q. Zhu, Y. Chen, J.-S. Pan, An improvement to the nearest neighbor classifier and face recognition experiments. Int. J. Innov. Comput. Inf. Control **8**(12), 1349–4198 (2012b)

Y. Xu, W. Zuo, Z. Fan, Supervised sparse representation method with a heuristic strategy and face recognition experiments. Neurocomputing **79**, 125–131 (2012c)

Y. Xu, X. Li, J. Yang, Z. Lai, D. Zhang, Integrating conventional and inverse representation for face recognition. IEEE Trans. Cybern. **44**(10), 1738–1746 (2014)

H. Yang, Z. Xu, J. Ye, I. King, M.R. Lyu, Efficient sparse generalized multiple kernel learning. IEEE Trans. Neural Networks **22**(3), 433–446 (2011)

M. Yang, L. Zhang, D. Zhang, S. Wang, *Relaxed collaborative representation for pattern classification*, in Proceedings of IEEE Conference on Computer Vision and Pattern Recognition (IEEE, 2012), pp. 2224–2231

J. Yin, Z. Liu, Z. Jin, W. Yang, Kernel sparse representation based classification. Neurocomputing **77**(1), 120–128 (2012)

L. Zhang, M. Yang, X. Feng, *Sparse representation or collaborative representation: Which helps face recognition?* in Proceedings of IEEE International Conference on Computer Vision (IEEE, 2011), pp. 471–478

N. Zhang, J. Yang, *K nearest neighbor based local sparse representation classifier*, in Proceedings of Chinese Conference on Pattern Recognition (IEEE, 2010), pp. 1–5

Part V
Multi-biometrics

Chapter 9
Fusion Methodologies of Multiple Traits

Abstract Multi-biometrics can provide higher identification accuracy than single biometrics, so it is more suitable for some real-world personal identification applications that need high-standard security. Among various biometrics technologies, palmprint identification has received much attention because of its good performance. In this chapter, we will present two novel fusion methodologies of multi-traits for personal identification. We first present an effective palmprint identification method via the fusion of the left and right palmprints, which can be viewed as the fusion method of multiple traits with the same category. Then, we introduce another personal identification method via the fusion of the palmprint and palmvein, which uses multiple traits from the different category.

9.1 Introduction

No single biometric technique can meet all requirements in circumstances (Jain et al. 2004). To overcome the limitation of the unimodal biometric technique and to improve the performance of the biometric system, multimodal biometric methods are designed by using multiple biometrics or using multiple modals of the same biometric trait, which can be fused at four levels: image (sensor) level, feature level, matching score level, and decision level (Xu et al. 2011; Tulyakov and Govindaraju 2008; Zhang et al. 2010; Hao et al. 2007).

Conventional multimodal biometrics methods treat different traits independently. However, some special kinds of biometric traits have a similarity and these methods cannot exploit the similarity of different kinds of traits. For example, the left and right palmprint traits of the same subject can be viewed as this kind of special biometric traits owing to the similarity between them, which will be demonstrated later. However, there is almost no any attempt to explore the correlation between the left and right palmprint and there is no 'special' fusion method for this kind of biometric identification. In this chapter, we will present a novel framework of combining the left with right palmprint at the matching score level.

© Springer Science+Business Media Singapore 2016
D. Zhang et al., *Discriminative Learning in Biometrics*,
DOI 10.1007/978-981-10-2056-8_9

As a unique and reliable biometric characteristic, palmprint verification has achieved a great success. However, palmprint alone may not be able to meet the increasing demand of highly accurate and robust biometric systems. Recently, palmvein, which refers to the palm feature under near-infrared spectrum, has been attracting much research interest. Since palmprint and palmvein can be captured simultaneously by using specially designed devices, the joint use of palmprint and palmvein features can effectively increase the accuracy, robustness, and anti-spoof capability of palm-based biometric techniques. Thus, in this chapter, we will also present a verification method via the fusion of palmprint and palmvein.

9.2 Fusion of the Left and Right Palmprint

9.2.1 Correlation Between the Left and Right Palmprints

In this section, the illustration of the correlation between the left and right palmprints is presented. Figure 9.1 shows palmprint images of four subjects. Figure 9.1a–d show four left palmprint images of these four subjects. Figure 9.1e–h show four right palmprint images of the same four subjects. Images in Fig. 9.1i–l are the four reverse palmprint images of those shown in Fig. 9.1e–h. It can be seen that the left palmprint image and the reverse right palmprint image of the same subject are somewhat similar.

Figure 9.2a–d depict the principal lines images of the left palmprint shown in Fig. 9.1a–d. Figure 9.2e–h are the reverse right palmprint principal lines images corresponding to Fig. 9.1i–l. Figure 9.2i–l show the principle lines matching images of Fig. 9.2a–h, respectively. Figure 9.2m–p are matching images between the left and reverse right palmprint principal lines images from different subjects. The four matching images of Fig. 9.2m–p are: (a) and (f) principal lines matching image, (b) and (e) principal lines matching image, (c) and (h) principal lines matching image, and (d) and (g) principal lines matching image, respectively.

Figure 9.2i–l clearly show that principal lines of the left and reverse right palmprint from the same subject have very similar shape and position. However, principal lines of the left and right palmprint from different individuals have very different shape and position, as shown in Fig. 9.2m–p. This demonstrates that the principal lines of the left palmprint and reverse right palmprint can also be used for palmprint verification/identification.

9.2.2 Main Steps of the Method

This subsection presents a personal identification method via the fusion framework of the left and right palmprint. The framework first works for the left palmprint

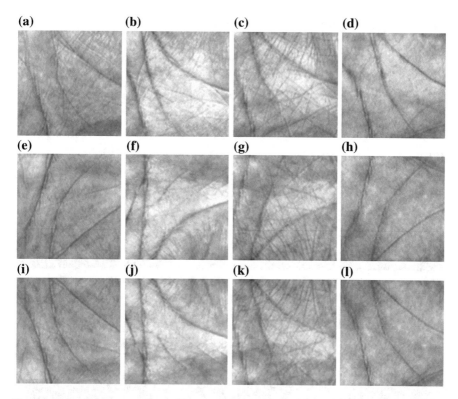

Fig. 9.1 Palmprint images of four subjects. **a–d** Are four left palmprint images; **e–h** are four right palmprint corresponding to **a–d**; **i–l** are the reverse right palmprint images of **e–h**. © 2015 IEEE. Reprinted with permission, from Xu et al. (2015)

images and uses a palmprint identification method to calculate the scores of the test sample with respect to each class. Then, it applies the palmprint identification method to the right palmprint images to calculate the score of the test sample with respect to each class. After the crossing matching score of the left palmprint image for testing with respect to the reverse right palmprint images of each class is obtained, the proposed framework performs matching score-level fusion to integrate these three scores to obtain the identification result. The method is presented in detail below.

We suppose that there are C subjects, each of which has m available left palmprint images and m available right palmprint images for training. Let X_i^k and Y_i^k denote the ith left palmprint image and ith right palmprint image of the kth subject, respectively, where $i = 1, \ldots, m$ and $k = 1, \ldots, C$. Let Z_1 and Z_2 stand for a left palmprint image and the corresponding right palmprint image of the subject to be identified. Z_1 and Z_2 are the so-called test samples.

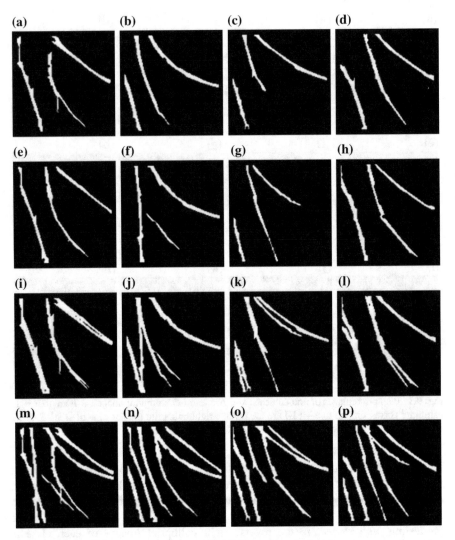

Fig. 9.2 Principal lines images. **a–d** Are four left palmprint principal lines images, **e–h** are four reverse right palmprint principal lines image, **i–l** are principal lines matching images of the same people, and **m–p** are principal lines matching images from different people. © 2015 IEEE. Reprinted with permission, from Xu et al. (2015)

Step 1. Generate the reverse images $\tilde{Y}_i^k$ of the right palmprint images Y_i^k. Both Y_i^k and $\tilde{Y}_i^k$ will be used as training samples. $\tilde{Y}_i^k$ is obtained by: $\tilde{Y}_i^k(l, c) = Y_i^k(L_Y - l + 1, c)$, $(l = 1 \ldots L_Y,\ c = 1 \ldots C_Y)$, where L_Y and C_Y are the row number and column number of Y_i^k, respectively.

Step 2. Use Z_1, X_i^ks and a palmprint identification method, such as the method introduced in previous chapter, to calculate the score of Z_1 with respect to each class. The score of Z_1 with respect to the ith class is denoted by s_i.

Step 3. Use Z_2, Y_i^ks and the palmprint identification method used in Step 2 to calculate the score of Z_2 with respect to each class. The score of Z_2 with respect to the ith class is denoted by t_i.

Step 4. $\tilde{Y}_j^k$ ($j = 1, \ldots, m'$, $m' \leq m$), which have the property of $\text{Sim\_score}(\tilde{Y}_j^k, X^k)$ $\geq \text{match\_threshold}$, are selected from $\tilde{Y}^k$ as additional training samples, where match_threshold is a threshold. $\text{Sim\_score}(\tilde{Y}_j^k, X^k)$ is defined as:

$$\text{Sim\_score}(Y, X^k) = \sum_{t=1}^{T}(S(\hat{Y}, X^k))/T, \tag{9.1}$$

and

$$S(\hat{Y}, X^k) = \max_t(\text{Score}(\hat{Y}, \hat{X}_i^k)), \quad i = \{1 \ldots m\}, \tag{9.2}$$

where Y is a palmprint image. X^k are a set of palmprint images from the kth subject and X_i^k is one image from X^k. $\hat{X}_i^k$ and $\hat{Y}$ are the principal line images of X_i^k and Y, respectively. T is the number of principal lines of the palmprint and t represent the tth principal line. $\text{Score}(Y, X)$ is calculated as formula (9.3) and the $\text{Score}(Y, X)$ is set to 0 when it is smaller than sim_threshold, which is empirically set to 0.15.

$$S(A, B) = \left(\sum_{i=1}^{m}\sum_{j=1}^{n}A(i,j)\&\bar{B}(i,j)\right)/N_A, \tag{9.3}$$

where A and B are two palmprint principal lines images, "&" represents the logical "AND" operation, N_A is the number of pixel points of A, and $\bar{B}(i,j)$ represents a neighbor area of $B(i,j)$.

Step 5. Treat $\tilde{Y}_j^k$s obtained in Step 4 as the training samples of Z_1. Use the palmprint identification method used in Step 2 to calculate the score of Z_1 with respect to each class. The score of the test sample with respect to $\tilde{Y}_j^k$s of the ith class is denoted as g_i.

Step 6. The weighted fusion scheme $f_i = w_1 s_i + w_2 t_i + w_3 g_i$, where $0 \leq w_1, w_2 \leq 1$ and $w_3 = 1 - w_1 - w_2$, is used to calculate the score of Z_1 with respect to the ith class. If $q = \arg\min_i f_i$, then the test sample is recognized as the qth subject.

9.2.3 *Analysis of the Proposed Method*

In the framework, the final decision-making is based on three kinds of information: the left palmprint, the right palmprint, and the correlation between the left and right palmprint. As we know, fusion in multimodal biometric systems can be performed at four levels. In the image (sensor) level fusion, different sensors are usually required to capture the image of the same biometric. Fusion at decision level is too rigid since only abstract identity labels decided by different matchers are available, which contain very limited information about the data to be fused. Fusion at feature level involves the use of the feature set by concatenating several feature vectors to form a large one-dimensional vector. The integration of features at the earlier stage can convey much richer information than other fusion strategies. So feature level fusion is supposed to provide a better identification accuracy than fusion at other levels. However, fusion at the feature level is quite difficult to implement because of the incompatibility between multiple kinds of data. Moreover, concatenating different feature vectors also lead to a high-computational cost. The advantages of the score-level fusion have been concluded in Jain et al. (2004), Jain and Feng (2009), Tulyakov and Govindaraju (2008) and the weight-sum score-level fusion strategy is effective for component classifier combination to improve the performance of biometric identification. The strength of individual matchers can be highlighted by assigning a weight to each matching score. Consequently, the weight-sum matching score-level fusion is preferable due to the ease in combining three kinds of matching scores of the proposed method.

Figure 9.3 shows the basic fusion procedure of the proposed method at the matching score level. The final matching score is generated from three kinds of matching scores. The first and second matching scores are obtained from the left and right palmprint, respectively. The third kind of score is calculated based on the crossing matching between the left and right palmprint. $w_i (i = 1, 2, 3)$, which

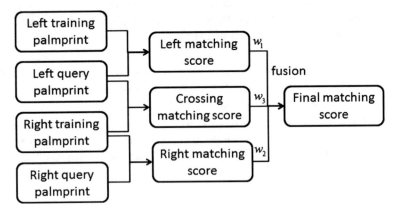

Fig. 9.3 Fusion at the matching score level of the proposed framework. © 2015 IEEE. Reprinted with permission, from Xu et al. (2015)

denotes the weight assigned to the ith matcher, can be adjusted and viewed as the importance of the corresponding matchers.

Differing from the conventional matching score-level fusion, the proposed method introduces the crossing matching score to the fusion strategy. When $w_3 = 0$, the proposed method is equivalent to the conventional score-level fusion. Therefore, the performance of the proposed method will at least be as good as or even better than conventional methods by suitably tuning the weight coefficients.

9.2.4 Experimental Results

More than 7000 different images from both the contact-based and the contactless palmprint databases are employed to evaluate the effectiveness of the proposed method. Typical state-of-the-art palmprint identification methods, such as the RLOC method, the competitive code method, the ordinal code method, the BOCV method, and the SMCC method (Zuo et al. 2010), are adopted to evaluate the performance of the proposed framework. Moreover, several recent developed contactless-based methods, such as the SIFT methods (Lowe 2004) and the OLOF +SIFT method (Morales et al. 2011), are also used to test the proposed framework. For the sake of completeness, we compare the performance of our method with that of the conventional fusion-based methods.

9.2.4.1 Palmprint Databases

The PolyU palmprint database (version 2)[1] contains 7752 palmprint images captured from a total of 386 palms of 193 individuals. The samples of each individual were collected in two sessions, where the average interval between the first and second sessions was around 2 months. In each session, each individual was asked to provide about 10 images of each palm. We notice that some individual provide few images. For example, only one image of the 150th individual was captured in the second session. To facilitate the evaluation of the performance of our framework, we set up a subset from the whole database by choosing 3740 images of 187 individual, where each individual provide 10 right palmprint images and 10 left palmprint images, to carry out the following experiments. Figure 9.4 shows some palmprint samples on the PolyU database.

The public IITD palmprint database[2] is a contactless palmprint database. Images in IITD database were captured in the indoor environment, which acquired contactless hand images with severe variations in pose, projection, rotation, and translation. The main problem of contactless databases lies in the significant

[1]http://www.comp.polyu.edu.hk/~biometrics/.

[2]http://www4.comp.polyu.edu.hk/~csajaykr/IITD/Database_Palm.htm.

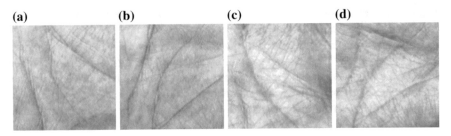

Fig. 9.4 a–d Are two pairs of the left and right palmprint images of two subjects from PolyU database. © 2015 IEEE. Reprinted with permission, from Xu et al. (2015)

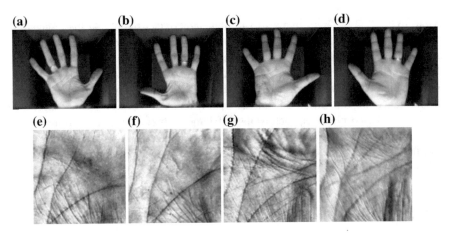

Fig. 9.5 a–d Are two pairs of the left and right hand images of two subjects from IITD database. **e–h** are the corresponding ROI images extracted from **a** and **d**. © 2015 IEEE. Reprinted with permission, from Xu et al. (2015)

intra-class variations resulting from the absence of any contact or guiding surface to restrict such variations (Morales et al. 2011). The IITD database consists of 3290 hand images from 235 subjects. Seven hand images were captured from each of the left and right hand for each individual in every session. In addition to the original hand images, the region of interest (ROI) of palmprint images are also available in the database. Figure 9.5 shows some typical hand images and the corresponding ROI palmprint images in the IITD palmprint database. Compared to the palmprint images in the PolyU database, the images in the IITD database are more close to the real-applications.

9.2.4.2   Matching Results Between the Left and Right Palmprint

To obtain the correlation between the left and right palmprint in both the PolyU and the IITD databases, each left palmprint is matched with every right palmprint of each subject and the principal line matching score is calculated for the left palmprint and this subject. A match is counted as a genuine matching if the left palmprint is from the class; if otherwise, the match is counted as an imposter matching.

The PolyU palmprint subset has 1870 left palmprint images and 1870 right palmprints from 187 individuals. Therefore, there are 1870 (1870 * 1) genuine matches and 347,820 (1870 * 186) impostor matches in total. In the IITD palmprint database, there are 1645 left palmprint images and 1645 right palmprints from 235 different subjects. So in the IITD database the total number of genuine matching and imposter matching are 1645 (1645 * 1) and 384,930 (1645 * 234), respectively. The training sample number of each class in both experiments are set as 3 and 2, respectively. Figure 9.6a, b shows the matching results of both databases. The false accept rate (FAR), false reject rate (FRR), and equal error rate (EER) (the point where FAR is equal to FRR) (Kong et al. 2009) are adopted to evaluate the similarity between the left and right palmprints. The receiver operating characteristic (ROC) curve, which is a graph of FRR against FAR for all possible thresholds, is introduced to describe the performance of the proposed method. The ROC curves of both the PolyU and IITD databases are plotted in Fig. 9.6c.

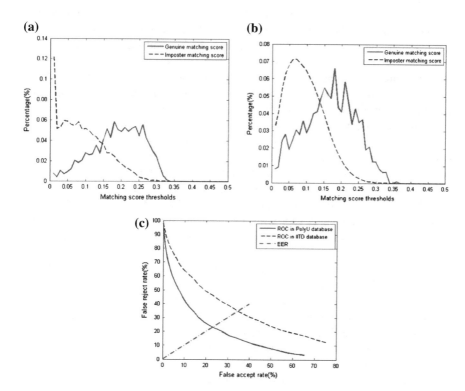

Fig. 9.6 **a** and **b** Are matching score distributions of the PolyU and IITD databases, respectively. **c** is ROC curves of the PolyU and IITD databases. © 2015 IEEE. Reprinted with permission, from Xu et al. (2015)

Figure 9.6a, b show that the genuine matching generally have larger principal lines matching scores than those of the imposter matching. The distribution of the genuine matching and imposter matching are separable and the genuine class and the imposter class can be roughly discriminated by using a linear classifier. The EERs of two databases are 24.22 and 35.82 %, respectively. One can observe that the EER obtained using the IITD database is much larger than that obtained using the PolyU database. The main reason is that palmprint images in IITD database have serious variations in rotation and translation. The experimental results still illustrate that the left palmprint and right palmprint of the same people generally have higher similarity than those from different subjects.

9.2.4.3 Experimental Results on PolyU Palmprint Database

In identification experiments, different kinds of palmprint recognition methods are applied in the framework, including the line-based method (Huang et al. 2008), coding-based methods, subspace-based methods, and representation-based methods.

In the experiments, match_threshold is empirically set to 0.2. The conventional fusion scheme only fuses the left palmprint and right palmprint features, but does not integrate the crossing similarity between the left and right palmprint. So the conventional fusion scheme is a special case of the proposed framework with $w_3 = 0$. Three weight coefficients are assigned to three scores. The weight coefficients w_1, w_2 and w_3 are tuned in step of 0.05. The left palmprint matching scores and right palmprint matching scores should have larger weights than the crossing matching score between the left palmprint and reverse right palmprint.

It is impossible to exhaustively verify all possible weight coefficients to find the optimal coefficients. Due to the limit of space, only a set of representative weight coefficients that minimize the final identification error rate of our framework and conventional fusion methods are reported. Empirically, the score that has the lower identification error rate usually has a larger weight coefficient. In addition, the optimal weight coefficients vary with the methods, since each method adopted in the proposed framework utilizes different palmprint feature extraction algorithm.

The first m left and m right palmprint are selected as the training samples to calculate the left matching score s_i and the right matching score t_i, respectively. The rest of the left and right palmprints are used as test samples. m reverse right palmprints are also selected as the training samples to calculate the crossing matching score g_i based on the rule of the proposed framework. Tables 9.1, 9.2, 9.3, 9.4, 9.5 and 9.6 list the identification error rate of the proposed framework using different palmprint identification methods.

The experimental results of the PolyU database show that the identification error rate of the proposed method is about 0.06 to 0.2 % lower than that of conventional fusion methods. The comparison between the best identification results of the

Table 9.1 Results of the rloc with m as 2 and the competitive code method with m as 1. © 2015 IEEE

RLOC				Competitive code method			
w_1	w_2	w_3	Error rate (%)	w_1	w_2	w_3	Error rate (%)
0.5	0.5	0	5.21	0.4	0.6	0	0.48
0.6	0.4	0	5.95	0.5	0.5	0	0.48
0.55	0.45	0	5.82	0.6	0.4	0	0.83
0.45	0.5	0.05	5.15	0.45	0.5	0.05	0.42
0.45	0.45	0.1	5.01	0.3	0.6	0.1	0.30

Reprinted with permission, from Xu et al. (2015)

Table 9.2 Results of the ordinal code method with m as 1 and the fusion code method with m as 1. © 2015 IEEE

Ordinal code method				Fusion code method			
w_1	w_2	w_3	Error rate (%)	w_1	w_2	w_3	Error rate (%)
0.4	0.6	0	0.83	0.5	0.5	0	0.59
0.35	0.65	0	0.89	0.3	0.7	0	0.59
0.55	0.45	0	0.89	0.45	0.55	0	0.59
0.35	0.6	0.05	0.77	0.4	0.55	0.05	0.53
0.4	0.55	0.05	0.83	0.3	0.65	0.05	0.53

Reprinted with permission, from Xu et al. (2015)

Table 9.3 Results of the palmcode method with m as 1 and the bocv method with m as 1. © 2015 IEEE

Palmcode				BOCV			
w_1	w_2	w_3	Error rate (%)	w_1	w_2	w_3	Error rate (%)
0.4	0.6	0	0.77	0.5	0.5	0	0.71
0.6	0.4	0	0.65	0.4	0.6	0	0.59
0.55	0.45	0	0.42	0.35	0.65	0	0.53
0.45	0.45	0.1	0.36	0.3	0.65	0.05	0.48
0.5	0.45	0.05	0.36	0.35	0.6	0.05	0.48

Reprinted with permission, from Xu et al. (2015)

Table 9.4 Results of the 2DPCA based method with m as 2 and the 2DLDA based method with m as 3. © 2015 IEEE

2DPCA				2DLDA			
w_1	w_2	w_3	Error rate (%)	w_1	w_2	w_3	Error rate (%)
0.5	0.5	0	4.81	0.55	0.45	0	0.46
0.6	0.4	0	4.75	0.4	0.6	0	0.38
0.35	0.65	0	4.88	0.6	0.4	0	0.53
0.5	0.4	0.05	4.55	0.4	0.5	0.1	0.31
0.45	0.45	0.1	4.61	0.5	0.45	0.05	0.31

Reprinted with permission, from Xu et al. (2015)

Table 9.5 Results of the pca based method with m as 4 and the lda based method with m as 2. © 2015 IEEE

PCA				LDA			
w_1	w_2	w_3	Error rate (%)	w_1	w_2	w_3	Error rate (%)
0.45	0.55	0	0.27	0.5	0.5	0	0.13
0.6	0.4	0	0.27	0.4	0.6	0	0.13
0.35	0.65	0	0.36	0.6	0.4	0	0.13
0.55	0.4	0.05	0.18	0.4	0.4	0.2	0.07
0.45	0.45	0.1	0.18	0.5	0.4	0.1	0.07

Reprinted with permission, from Xu et al. (2015)

Table 9.6 Results of the TPTSSR method with m as 1 and the CRC based method with m as 1. © 2015 IEEE

TPTSSR				CRC			
w_1	w_2	w_3	Error rate (%)	w_1	w_2	w_3	Error rate (%)
0.5	0.5	0	0.83	0.5	0.5	0	0.83
0.6	0.4	0	1.43	0.55	0.45	0	0.77
0.3	0.7	0	1.13	0.45	0.55	0	1.07
0.4	0.5	0.1	0.65	0.5	0.45	0.05	0.65
0.4	0.55	0.05	0.71	0.4	0.5	0.1	0.65

Reprinted with permission, from Xu et al. (2015)

proposed method and conventional fusion scheme are depicted as Fig. 9.7, which shows that the framework using different methods outperform the conventional fusion schemes.

9.2.4.4 Experimental Results on IITD Palmprint Database

Experiments are also conducted on the IITD contactless palmprint database. For the space limited, not all methods employed in the PolyU database but several promising contactless palmprint identification methods, including coding-based methods, the SIFT-based method, the OLOF+SIFT method and the SMCC method, are adopted to carry out the experiments. In addition, LDA-and CRC-based methods are also tested by the database. Large-scale translation will cause serious false position problem in the IITD database. To reduce the effect of the image translation between the test image and the training image, the test image will be vertically and horizontally translated with one to three pixels, and the best matching result obtained from the translated matching is recorded as the final matching result. The experimental results are listed in Tables 9.7, 9.8, 9.9 and 9.10. The corresponding comparison between the best identification accuracies of the proposed method and conventional fusion schemes are plotted as Fig. 9.8.

Fig. 9.7 The comparative
results between the proposed
method and the conventional
fusion method on the PolyU
database. © 2015 IEEE.
Reprinted with permission,
from Xu et al. (2015)

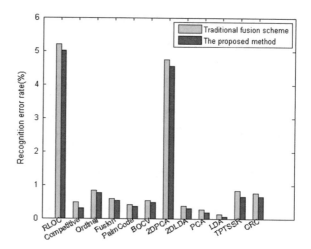

Table 9.7 Results of oridinal code method with m as 2 and the sift based method with m as 2. © 2015 IEEE

Ordinal code method				SIFT			
w_1	w_2	w_3	Error rate (%)	w_1	w_2	w_3	Error rate (%)
0.5	0.5	0	1.16	0.5	0.5	0	5.94
0.4	0.6	0	1.74	0.4	0.6	0	5.94
0.6	0.4	0	1.30	0.6	0.4	0	6.09
0.4	0.	0.2	1.01	0.4	0.5	0.1	5.36
0.5	0.4	0.1	1.16	0.45	0.5	0.05	5.51

Reprinted with permission, from Xu et al. (2015)

Table 9.8 Results of olof + sift with m as 2 and the bocv method m as 2. © 2015 IEEE

OLOF+SIFT				BOCV			
w_1	w_2	w_3	Error rate (%)	w_1	w_2	w_3	Error rate (%)
0.5	0.5	0	0.72	0.5	0.5	0	2.03
0.4	0.6	0	0.58	0.45	0.55	0	2.17
0.35	0.65	0	0.58	0.6	0.4	0	2.46
0.4	0.5	0.1	0.43	0.45	0.45	0.1	2.03
0.3	0.6	0.1	0.58	0.5	0.45	0.05	1.74

Reprinted with permission, from Xu et al. (2015)

Both Figs. 9.7 and 9.8 clearly show that the palmprint identification accuracy of the proposed framework is higher than that of the direct fusion of the left and right palmprint for both the PolyU database and the IITD contactless database. As a result, we infer that the use of the similarity between the left and right palmprint is effective for improving the performance of palmprint identification.

Table 9.9 Results of palmcode method with m as 2 and the smcc method with m as 1.© 2015 IEEE

Palmcode				SMCC			
w_1	w_2	w_3	Error rate (%)	w_1	w_2	w_3	Error rate (%)
0.5	0.5	0	3.04	0.4	0.6	0	0.54
0.4	0.6	0	3.77	0.5	0.4	0	0.54
0.6	0.4	0	3.48	0.45	0.55	0	0.54
0.45	0.45	0.1	2.90	0.4	0.	0.2	0.43
0.5	0.4	0.1	2.90	0.45	0.45	0.1	0.43

Reprinted with permission, from Xu et al. (2015)

Table 9.10 Results of lda method with m as 2 and the crc method with m as 1. © 2015 IEEE

LDA				CRC			
w_1	w_2	w_3	Error rate (%)	w_1	w_2	w_3	Error rate (%)
0.5	0.5	0	10.29	0.5	0.5	0	12.90
0.4	0.6	0	10.29	0.4	0.6	0	14.06
0.35	0.65	0	10.43	0.6	0.4	0	13.33
0.45	0.5	0.05	10.14	0.4	0.5	0.1	12.75
0.4	0.55	0.05	10.29	0.4	0.4	0.2	12.75

Reprinted with permission, from Xu et al. (2015)

Fig. 9.8 The comparative results between the proposed method and the conventional fusion method in the IITD database. © 2015 IEEE. Reprinted with permission, from Xu et al. (2015)

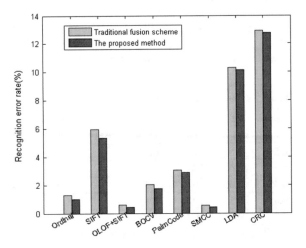

It seems that the crossing matching score can also be calculated based on the similarity between the right query and left training palmprint. We also conduct experiments to fuse both crossing matching scores to perform palmprint identification. However, as the use of the two crossing matching scores does not lead to more accuracy improvement, we exploit only one of them in the fusion method.

9.3 Joint Palmprint and Palmvein Verification

Although palmprint recognition has achieved a great success, it has some intrinsic weaknesses. For example, some people may have similar palm lines, especially principal lines (Zhang et al. 2003); also it is not so difficult to forge a fake palmprint (Kong et al. 2009). These problems can be addressed by using multi-biometric systems, such as fusing facial trait and palmprint trait (Yao et al. 2007), fusing iris and palmprint traits (Wu et al. 2007) or fusing the palmvein trait and palmprint trait (Zhang et al. 2011). The veins of the palm mainly refer to the inner vessel structures beneath the skin and the palmvein images can be collected using both far infrared (FIR) and near-infrared (NIR) light (Zharov et al. 2004). Obviously, palmvein is much harder to fake than palmprint. Intuitively, since both palmprint and palmvein are from the palm, it is possible to establish a convenient multi-biometric system to acquire and use the two traits jointly, and the complementary information provided by the two traits will make the system more accurate in personal identification and more robust to spoof-attack. In this section, we will present an effective personal verification method via the fusion of the palmprint and palmvein information.

9.3.1 Main Steps of the Method

The flowchart of the joint palmprint and palmvein verification system is illustrated in Fig. 9.9. It has four main stages. First, the region of interest (ROI) is extracted; then a liveness detection algorithm based on image brightness and texture is applied; if the input images pass the liveness detection, palmprint features will be extracted by texture coding and palmvein by matched filters; finally, the score-level fusion is applied through dynamic weighted sum for decisionmaking. The details of ROI extraction can be found in Zhang et al. (2003). Figure 9.10 shows some samples of ROI. In the following, we discuss the processing of other stages.

9.3.1.1 Liveness Detection

There are various liveness detection methods in biometric systems. For example, perspiration detection in a sequence of fingerprint images (Parthasaradhi et al. 2005); using additional hardware to acquire life signs; utilizing inherent liveness features, such as facial thermograms (Schuckers 2002). However, these methods can be time-consuming, require addition hardware and costly. In the system, the low-cost NIR LED is used for illumination. It has been proved that 700–1000 nm NIR light could penetrate human skin 1–3 mm inside, and blood will absorb more NIR energy than the surrounding tissues (e.g., fat or melanin), so the vein structure is darker than other areas in the palmvein image (Zharov et al. 2004). However, since the skin of some people, especially female, is relatively thicker (Lee and

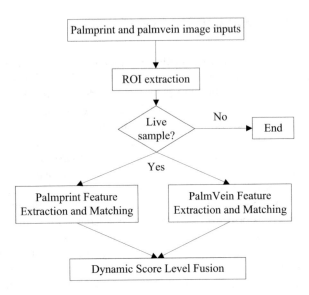

Fig. 9.9 Flowchart of online joint palmprint and palmvein verification. Reprinted from Zhang et al. (2011), with permission from Elsevier

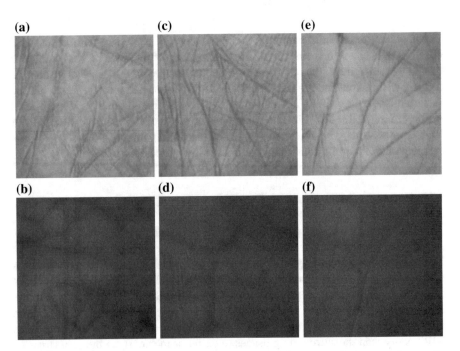

Fig. 9.10 ROI sample images. Each column comes from the same palm. **a**, **c** and **e** are the palmprint ROIs, **b**, **d** and **f** are the associated palmvein ROIs. Reprinted from Zhang et al. (2011), with permission from Elsevier

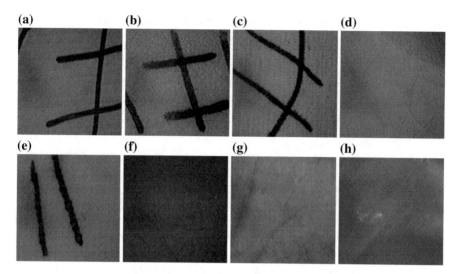

Fig. 9.11 NIR palmvein images of fake palms made from **a** cardboard; **b** foam; **c** glove; **d** plaster; **e** plastic; **f** plasticine; **g** print paper; **f** wax. Reprinted from Zhang et al. (2011), with permission from Elsevier

Hwang 2002), their palmvein structures cannot be clearly captured (e.g., Fig. 9.10f). On the other hand, the fake palm made by some materials can also lead to dark lines under NIR illumination, e.g., Fig. 9.11a. Therefore, it will be difficult to apply liveness detection by detecting only the existence of dark lines in the palmvein image.

As human skin has special reflectance and absorbance properties under the NIR spectral, the features associated with these properties can be extracted from the image brightness and texture for telling true palm from fake palms. Figure 9.13 shows the palmvein images of several fake palms we made from different materials. After observing these images and palmvein images from true palms, we found that the image brightness and Gray Level Co-occurrence Matrix (GLCM) (Haralick et al. 1973) entropy could provide enough discriminant information to distinguish them. Thus, we propose a liveness detection algorithm by analyzing palmvein image brightness and texture features.

The brightness feature is defined as the average of the intensity over the image:

$$B = \frac{1}{M * N} \sum_{x=1}^{M} \sum_{y=1}^{N} f(x, y), \tag{9.4}$$

where $f(x, y)$ represents the gray value at pixel (x, y), and M and N represent the numbers of rows and columns in the image. On the other hand, the GLCM is a widely used texture operator in image processing and pattern recognition. For a given angle θ and distance d, a GLCM is defined as:

Table 9.11 The brightness and GLCM entropy of true and fake palm samples

	Fig. a	Fig. b	Fig. c	Fig. d	Fig. e	Fig. f	Fig. g	Fig. h
B	110.2	108.0	115.5	126.7	113.9	71.1	127.6	114.4
E	6.6	7.5	7.2	6.3	6.5	6.8	6.6	6.5

$$p_{\theta,d}(i,j) = \frac{\#\{[(x_1,y_1),(x_1+\Delta x, y_1+\Delta y)] \in S | f(x_1,y_1) = i \& f(x_1+\Delta x, y_1+\Delta y) = j\}}{\#S},$$

$$(9.5)$$

where $\Delta x = d * \cos \theta$ and $\Delta y = d * \sin \theta$. S is the set of pixels in the image and "#" means the number of the elements in a set. (i, j) is the coordinate in the GLCM.

With GLCM, several statistics could be computed, such as entropy, contrast, correlation, energy, homogeneity, etc. Among them, entropy is a popular feature to represent the uniformity of image texture. The more uniform the texture distributes, the bigger the entropy is. The GLMC entropy is computed as

$$E = \sum_{i=1}^{L} \sum_{j=1}^{L} p(i,j) * (- \ln p(i,j)),$$

$$(9.6)$$

where L is the level of quantization.

Table 9.11 shows the brightness and GLCM entropy of the palmvein images in Fig. 9.11. We can see the brightness and GLCM entropy values of fake palms and true palms are very different. Therefore, with some training samples, a classifier can be learned to tell the true palm from fake palms. In Sect. 9.3.2, we will establish a training dataset and learn the classifier. A testing dataset is also built to test the liveness detection method.

9.3.1.2 Palmprint Feature Extraction and Matching

In general there are three kinds of palmprint feature extraction algorithms, subspace learning (Wu et al. 2003; Connie et al. 2005; Ribaric and Fratric 2005; Hu et al. 2007), line detection (Han et al. 2003) and texture-based coding (Zhang et al. 2003; Kong and Zhang 2004b). Among them, orientation texture-based coding (Kong and Zhang 2004b) is preferred for online system as it could achieve high accuracy. It is also fast for matching and can be easily implemented in real-time.

The orientation of palm lines is stable and can serve as distinctive features for personal identification. To extract the orientation features, six Gabor filters along different orientations ($\theta_i = j\pi/6$, where $j = \{0, 1, 2, 3, 4, 5\}$) are applied to the palmprint image. Here, the real part of the Gabor filter is used and it is defined as:

$$\psi(x, y, \omega, \theta) = \frac{\omega}{\sqrt{2\pi\kappa}} e^{-\frac{\omega^2}{8\kappa^2}(4x'^2 + y'^2)} \left(e^{i\omega x'} - e^{-\frac{\kappa^2}{2}} \right), \tag{9.7}$$

where $x' = (x - x_0)\cos\theta + (y - y_0)\sin\theta$, $y' = -(x - x_0)\sin\theta + (y - y_0)\cos\theta$, (x_0, y_0) is the center of the function; ω is the radial frequency in radians per unit length and θ is the orientation of the Gabor functions in radians. κ is defined by $\kappa = \sqrt{2\ln 2}\left(\frac{2^\delta + 1}{2^\delta - 1}\right)$, where δ is the half-amplitude bandwidth of the frequency response. To reduce the influence of illumination, the direct current is removed from the filter.

By regarding palm lines as the negative lines, the orientation corresponding to the minimal Gabor filtering response (i.e., the negative response but with the highest magnitude) is taken as the feature for this pixel (Kong and Zhang 2004). Because the contour of Gabor filters is similar to the cross-section profile of palm lines, the higher the magnitude of the response, the more likely there is a line. Since six filters are used to detect the orientation of each pixel, the detected orientation {0, $\pi/6$, $\pi/3$, $\pi/2$, $2\pi/3$, $5\pi/6$} can then be coded by using 3 bits {000, 001, 011, 111, 110, 100} (Kong and Zhang 2004). Figure 9.12 shows an example of the extracted orientation feature map, where different gray levels represent different orientation.

Based on the extracted 3-bit orientation feature maps, the Hamming distance between two maps can be calculated as follows:

$$D(P, Q) = \frac{\sum_{y=0}^{M} \sum_{x=0}^{N} \sum_{i=1}^{3} (P_i^b(x, y) \otimes Q_i^b(x, y))}{3M * N}, \tag{9.8}$$

where P and Q are two feature maps, $P_i^b(Q_i^b)$ is the ith bit plane of $P(Q)$ and $\otimes$ is bitwise exclusive OR. To further reduce the influence of imperfect ROI extraction, we translate one of the two feature maps vertically and horizontally from -4 to 4

(a)   **(b)**

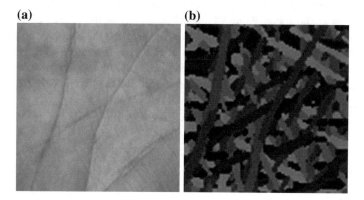

Fig. 9.12 Orientation feature map of palmprint. **a** Original palmprint image; and **b** extracted feature map (different gray levels represent different orientation). Reprinted from Zhang et al. (2011), with permission from Elsevier

(a)   **(b)**   **(c)**

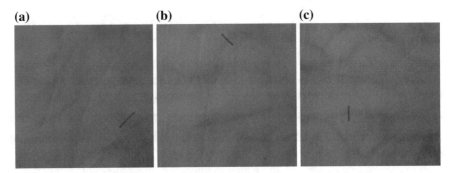

Fig. 9.13 a–c Some palmvein images and **d** the cross-section of vein structures. Reprinted from Zhang et al. (2011), with permission from Elsevier

when matching with another feature map. The minimal distance obtained by translated matching is regarded as the final distance.

9.3.1.3 Palmvein Feature Extraction and Matching

It is observed that the cross-sections of palmveins are similar to Gaussian functions. Figure 9.13 shows some examples. Based on this observation, the matched filters (Hoover et al. 2000; Zhang et al. 2007), which are widely used in retinal vessel extraction, can be a good technique to extract these palmveins. The matched filters are Gaussian-shaped filters along angle θ:

$$g_{\theta}^{\sigma}(x,y) = -\exp\left(-\frac{x'^2}{\sigma^2}\right) - m, \quad \text{for } |x'| \leq 3\sigma, \quad |y'| \leq L/2, \qquad (9.9)$$

where $x' = x\cos\theta + y\sin\theta, y' = -x\sin\theta + y\cos\theta$, σ is the standard deviation of Gaussian, m is the mean value of the filter, and L is the length of the filter in y direction which is set empirically. In order to suppress the background pixels, the filter is designed as a zero-sum. For one σ, four different angle filters ($\theta_j = j\pi/4$, where $j = \{0, 1, 2, 3\}$) are applied for each pixel, and the maximal response among these four directions is kept as the final response for the given scale[3]:

$$\begin{aligned}
R_F^{\sigma} &= \max(R_{\theta_j}^{\sigma}(x,y)), \quad j = \{0,1,2,3\}, \\
R_{\theta_j}^{\sigma}(x,y) &= g_{\theta_j}^{\sigma}(x,y) * f(x,y),
\end{aligned} \qquad (9.10)$$

where $f(x, y)$ is the original image and $*$ denotes the convolution operation.

---

[3]Different from the CompCode in Sect. 9.3.1.2 where the minimal response is used, here, the shape of used matched filters is identical to the cross-section of vein, thus the maximal response is kept.

As shown in Bao et al. (2005), Zhang et al. (2007), the multiscale product of filtering responses is a good way to enhance the edge structures and suppress noise. The product of matched filter responses at two scales σ_1 and σ_2 is defined as:

$$P(x,y) = R_F^{\sigma_1}(x,y) \cdot R_F^{\sigma_2}(x,y). \tag{9.11}$$

The scale parameters σ_1 and σ_2 are set empirically. After computing the multiscale production, we binarize it by using a threshold which is empirically set based on a training dataset. The vein pixel, whose scale production response is greater than the threshold, is represented by "1," while the background pixel is represented by "0." At last, some postprocessing operations are performed to remove some small regions. Figure 9.14 illustrates the whole procedure of palmvein extraction.

The extracted palmvein maps are binary images, and the distance between two palmvein maps is computed as:

$$D(P,Q) = 1 - \frac{\sum_{y=0}^{M}\sum_{x=0}^{N}\left(P^b(x,y) \,\&\, Q^b(x,y)\right)}{\sum_{y=0}^{M}\sum_{x=0}^{N}\left(P^b(x,y) | Q^b(x,y)\right)}, \tag{9.12}$$

where P and Q are two palmvein feature maps, "&" is bitwise AND operator and "|" is bitwise OR operator. The dissimilarity measurement in (9) is different from the Hamming distance used in Zhang et al. (2007). This is because most of pixels in the palmvein map are non-palmvein pixels. For example, in our database the average ratio of non-palmvein pixels is about 86 %. Such an uneven distribution of palm-vein and non-palmvein pixels makes the Hamming distance less the discriminative (Daugman 2003).

Similar to that in palmprint feature map matching, we translate one of the palmvein feature maps vertically and horizontally from −4 to 4 and match it with another palmvein feature map. The minimal distance obtained by translated matching is regarded as the final distance.

9.3.1.4 Palmprint and Palmvein Fusion

The information presented by multiple traits can be fused at various levels: image level, feature level, matching score level, or decision level (Ross et al. 2006). Although image and feature level fusion can integrate the information provided by different biometric, the required registration procedure is too time-consuming (Wang et al. 2008). As to matching score fusion and decision level fusion, it has been found (Ross et al. 2006) that the former usually works better than the later because match scores contain more information about the input pattern and it is easy to access and fuse the scores generated by different matchers. For these reasons, matching score-level fusion is the most commonly used approach in multimodal biometric systems. In this work, we test sum and weighted sum on palmprint and palmvein matching score fusion:

Fig. 9.14 Palmvein feature
extraction. **a** Original
palmvein images; **b** matched
filter response with scale σ_1;
c matched filter response with
scale σ_2; **d** response product
of the two scales; **e** binary
image after thresholding;
f final vein map after
post-processing. Reprinted
from Zhang et al. (2011), with
permission from Elsevier

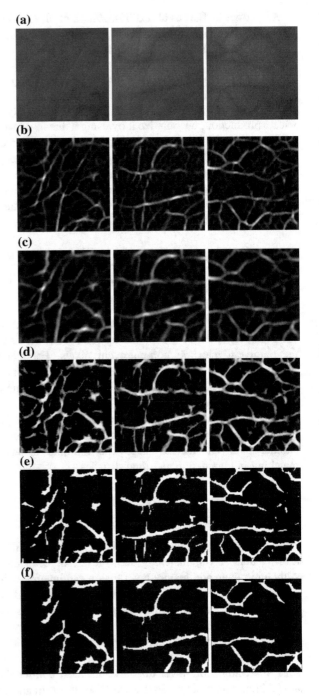

$$FD_{Sum} = D_{Palmprint} + D_{Palmvein}, \tag{9.13}$$

$$FD_{WeightSum} = W_{Palmprint}D_{Palmprint} + W_{Palmvein}D_{Palmvein}, \tag{9.14}$$

where $D_{Palmprint}$ and $D_{Palmvein}$ are the palmprint and palmvein matching scores obtained by Eq. (9.8) and (9.12), respectively. $W_{Palmprint}$ and $W_{Palmvein}$ are the weights for palmprint and palmvein feature in the fusion.

Considering that not all palmvein images have clear vein structures (referring to Fig. 9.10), it is intuitive that good quality palmvein images should have higher weight in the fusion than those poor quality images. Here, a dynamic weighted sum fusion scheme by incorporating the palmvein image quality is proposed. We define an objective criterion (Daugman 2003) to evaluate the palmvein image quality:

$$d' = \frac{|\mu_{vein} - \mu_{non-vein}|}{\sqrt{(\sigma_{vein}^2 + \sigma_{non-vein}^2)/2}}, \tag{9.15}$$

where μ_{vein} and $\mu_{non-vein}$ are the average intensity values of vein pixels and non-vein pixels extracted by in Sect. 9.3.1.4, and σ_{vein} and $\sigma_{non-vein}$ are the standard deviation of vein and non-vein pixels, respectively. For a clear palmvein image, the boundary between vein and non-vein structures is clear, so a higher d' will be obtained. While for an unclear palmvein image, the boundary is not clear and the d' will be smaller. For example, the d' values of Fig. 9.10b, d, f are 1.63, 1.11, and 0.16, respectively. It shows that these images could be well classified by the proposed criterion.

By incorporating the palmvein image quality into consideration, a dynamic weighted sum scheme is proposed as:

$$\begin{aligned} FD_{WeightSum} &= W_{Palmprint}D_{Palmprint} + W_{Palmvein}D_{Palmvein}, \\ &= \left(1 - \frac{\bar{d}'}{2}\right)D_{Palmprint} + \frac{\bar{d}'}{2}D_{Palmvein}, \end{aligned} \tag{9.16}$$

$$\bar{d}' = \frac{d' - d'_{min}}{d'_{max} - d'_{min}}, \tag{9.17}$$

where d'_{min} and d'_{max} are the minimal and maximal value of d' computed by a training dataset. As shown in Eq. (9.16), if quality of palmvein image is very good, the weights of both palmprint and palmvein will be close to 0.5; if quality of palmvein image is very poor, the system will depend on palmprint solely. The experiments in Sect. 9.3.2.4 will validate the effectiveness of our dynamic fusion scheme.

9.3.2 Experimental Results

9.3.2.1 Database Establishment

By using the developed joint palmprint and palmvein device, we established a database which includes palmprint and palmvein images from 500 different palms. The subjects were mainly volunteers from the Shenzhen Graduate School of Harbin Institute of Technology and The Hong Kong Polytechnic University. In this database, 396 palms are from male and age ranges from 20 to 60. The images were captured by two separate sessions. The average time interval between two sessions was 9 days. On each session, the subject was asked to provide 6 samples from his/her palms. For each shot, the device collected one palmprint and one palmvein image simultaneously (less than 1 s). Finally, the database contains 6000 palmprint and palmvein images of resolution 352 * 288.

9.3.2.2 Experimental Results of Liveness Detection

We established a fake palm database, which includes 489 images from the fake palms made by eight different materials: cardboard, foam, glove, plaster, plastic, plasticine, print paper, and wax. This data set is randomly partitioned into two equal parts, a training set and a test set. The same division strategy is applied to the true palm database. The distribution of brightness (B, refer to Eq. 9.4) and entropy (E, refer to Eq. 9.7) of the training and test sets are plotted in Fig. 9.15. Because the skin reflectance and absorbance are different from those eight materials, we can see there is a clear boundary between them. In most of cases, different materials are clustered into specific regions as they have specific properties under NIR illumination. Four thresholds (i.e., the boundaries of the rectangle in Fig. 9.15) are computed based on the training samples:

$$B_{\min} = \min(B(TS)) - \sigma_{B(TS)}, B_{\max} = \max(B(TS)) + \sigma_{B(TS)},$$
$$E_{\min} = \min(E(TS)) - \sigma_{E(TS)}, E_{\max} = \max(E(TS)) + \sigma_{E(TS)}, \tag{9.18}$$

where TS represents the whole training set, $\sigma_{B(TS)}$ and $\sigma_{E(TS)}$ are the standard deviation values of B and E in the training set, respectively.

With these four thresholds, all of the training samples could be correctly classified as shown in Fig. 9.15a. For the test set, only one genuine palmvein is wrongly rejected as shown in Fig. 9.15b. In practice, we can use more strict thresholds to reject the imposter palms. In case, the user is wrongly rejected, he/she may put his/her palm one more time on the system for verification. Currently, the fake palm database is a relatively small, and setting up a large fake palm database and investigate more advance feature extraction methods will be our future focus.

Fig. 9.15 Brightness and GLCM entropy distribution of fake and true palm under NIR illumination. The *rectangle* is the boundary learned from the training set. **a** Distribution of the training set. **b** Distribution of the test set. Reprinted from Zhang et al. (2011), with permission from Elsevier

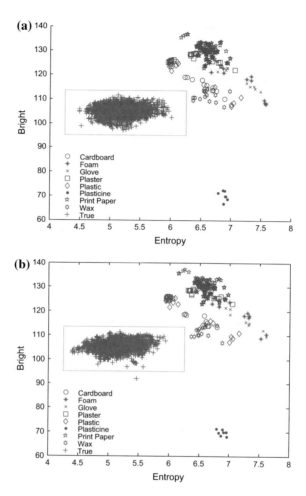

9.3.2.3 Experimental Results on Palmprint Verification

To obtain the verification accuracy for palmprint, each palmprint image is matched with all the other palmprint images. A match is counted as genuine matching if the two palmprint images are from the same palm; otherwise, the match is counted as impostor matching. The total number of palmprint matches is $6000 \times 5999/2 = 17,997,000$, and among them there are 33,000 (12 * 11/2 * 500) genuine matching, others are impostor matching. Equal Error Rate (EER), a point when false accept rate (FAR) is equal to false reject rate (FRR), is used to evaluate the performance.

The distance distribution of genuine and impostor is shown in Fig. 9.16 and the receiver operating characteristic (ROC) curve is showed in Fig. 9.17. Using palmprint, we can get FRR = 2.10 % when FAR = 5.6e−6 %. The EER is about 0.0352 %. The accuracy on palmprint is comparable to those of state-of-the-art

Fig. 9.16 Matching distance
distribution of palmprint.
Reprinted from Zhang et al.
(2011), with permission from
Elsevier

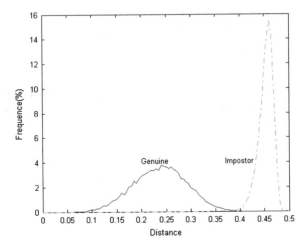

Fig. 9.17 ROC curve of
palmprint. Reprinted from
Zhang et al. (2011), with
permission from Elsevier

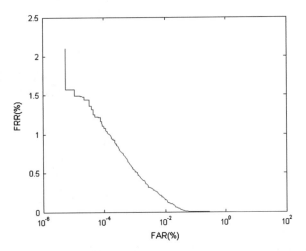

(EER: 0.024 %, multiscale feature extraction) (Zuo et al. 2008) on the public
palmprint database[4] collected under white illumination.

9.3.2.4 Experimental Results on Palmvein Verification

Using the same matching scheme as in Sect. 9.3.2.4, the distance distribution of
genuine and impostor of palmvein images is illustrated in Fig. 9.18. The ROC
curve is displayed in Fig. 9.19. For comparison, the curve by using Hamming
Distance as in Zhang et al. (2007) is also plotted.

---

[4]PolyU Palmprint Database (2006). <http://www.comp.polyu.edu.hk/_biometrics>.

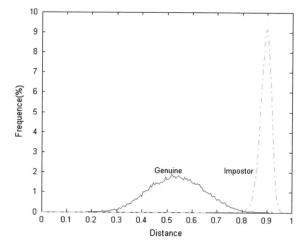

Fig. 9.18 Matching distance distribution of palmvein. Reprinted from Zhang et al. (2011), with permission from Elsevier

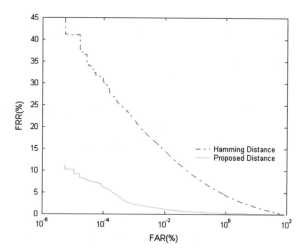

Fig. 9.19 ROC curve of palmvein. Reprinted from Zhang et al. (2011), with permission from Elsevier

From Fig. 9.19, we can see the proposed dissimilarity measurement could improve the verification accuracy significantly over the widely used Hamming distance. The EER of palmvein verification is about 0.3091 %, which is not as accurate as palmprint verification but better than the result reported in Ref. Zhang et al. (2007) (98.8 % GAR when FAR = 5.5 %). This is largely due to the relatively low quality of palmvein images.

To better evaluate the effect of image quality on the verification accuracy, we partition the palmvein images into three equal sets by the proposed criterion d': good quality images, average quality images, and poor quality images. The ROC curves for three sets are plotted in Fig. 9.20. Good quality palmvein image set has much better results than poor quality image set. The EER values for good, average, and poor quality image sets are is 0.0898, 0.1214 and 0.3199 %, respectively.

Fig. 9.20 ROC curves of palmvein on different image quality. Reprinted from Zhang et al. (2011), with permission from Elsevier

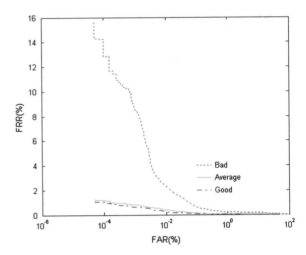

9.3.2.5 Experimental Results by Palmprint and Palmvein Fusion

The distance distributions of palmprint and palmvein are different, which can be seen in Figs. 9.16 and 9.18. For example, the impostor scores of palmprint concentrate on 0.45 with standard deviation being 0.015, and that of palmvein concentrates on 0.89 with standard deviation being 0.023. Thus normalizing the matching scores before fusion is necessary. As the impostor distribution looks like a Gaussian shape, the z-normalization (Ross et al. 2006) is used here:

$$D_N = \frac{D - \mu_{\text{impostor}}}{\sigma_{\text{impostor}}}. \tag{9.19}$$

The ROC curves of palmprint and palmvein fusion are shown in Fig. 9.21. The EER values of sum (Eq. 9.14) and weighted sum (Eq. 9.15) are 0.0212 and 0.0158 % respectively. Because palmvein contains complementary information to palmprint, the fusion of them could improve the system accuracy significantly. Figure 9.22 shows an example, the two palms have similar palmprint patterns and they will be falsely accepted by using only palmprint images as inputs. However, their palmvein patterns are very different. Thus, by combining palmprint with palmvein, they could be separated easily. Since the proposed weighted sum fusion incorporates palmvein image quality, better accuracy could be achieved as shown in Fig. 9.21. Compared with the sum rule, the weighted sum could reduce the EER up to 25 %.

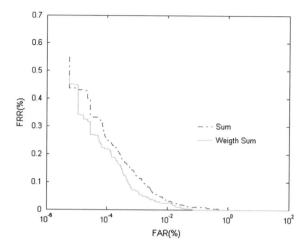

Fig. 9.21 ROC curves for different fusion schemes. Reprinted from Zhang et al. (2011), with permission from Elsevier

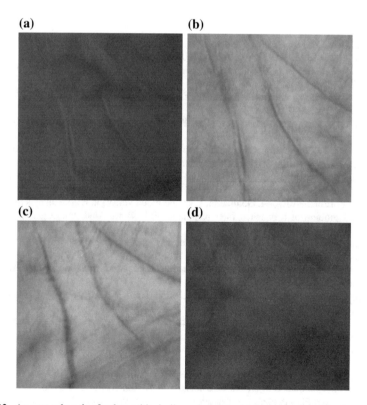

Fig. 9.22 An example pair of palms with similar palmprint which may be recognized wrongly by palmprint, but different palmvein features could separate them well. **a–b** from one palm; **c–d** from another palm. Reprinted from Zhang et al. (2011), with permission from Elsevier

9.4 Summary

In this chapter, we first present a fusion approach of the left and right palmprint for palmprint identification. Three kinds of scores generated from the left and right palmprint images are fused. Extensive experiments demonstrate that the fusion of the left and right palmprint obtains very high accuracy and the use of the similarity score between the left and right palmprint leads to important improvement in the accuracy.

Then in Sect. 9.3 we present another palmprint and palmvein fusion scheme for personal verification. The experiment shows that palmprint and palmvein contain complementary information, and the fusion of both two features is able to achieve much higher accuracy than using either of them, respectively.

The work in this chapter also seems to be helpful in motivating people to explore potential relation between the traits of other bimodal biometrics issues.

References

P. Bao, L. Zhang, X. Wu, Canny edge detection enhancement by scale multiplication. IEEE Trans. Pattern Anal. Mach. Intell. **27**(9), 1485–1490 (2005)

T. Connie, A.T.B. Jin, M.G.K. Ong, D.N.C. Ling, An automated palmprint recognition system. Image Vis. Comput. **23**(5), 501–515 (2005)

J. Daugman, The importance of being random: statistical principles of iris recognition. Pattern Recogn. **36**(2), 279–291 (2003)

C.-C. Han, H.-L. Cheng, C.-L. Lin, K.-C. Fan, Personal authentication using palm-print features. Pattern Recogn. **36**(2), 371–381 (2003)

Y. Hao, Z. Sun, T. Tan., Comparative studies on multispectral palm image fusion for biometrics, in *Computer Vision–ACCV 2007* (Springer, Berlin, 2007)

R.M. Haralick, K. Shanmugam, I.H. Dinstein, Textural features for image classification. IEEE Trans. Syst. Man Cybern. **6**, 610–621 (1973)

A. Hoover, V. Kouznetsova, M. Goldbaum, Locating blood vessels in retinal images by piecewise threshold probing of a matched filter response. IEEE Trans. Med. Imaging **19**(3), 203–210 (2000)

D. Hu, G. Feng, Z. Zhou, Two-dimensional locality preserving projections (2DLPP) with its application to palmprint recognition. Pattern recogn. **40**(1), 339–342 (2007)

D.-S. Huang, W. Jia, D. Zhang, Palmprint verification based on principal lines. Pattern Recogn. **41**(4), 1316–1328 (2008)

A.K. Jain, J. Feng, Latent palmprint matching. IEEE Trans. Pattern Anal. Mach. Intell. **31**(6), 1032–1047 (2009)

A.K. Jain, A. Ross, S. Prabhakar, An introduction to biometric recognition. IEEE Trans. Circuits Syst. Video Technol. **14**(1), 4–20 (2004)

A. Kong, D. Zhang, M. Kamel, A survey of palmprint recognition. Pattern Recogn. **42**(7), 1408–1418 (2009)

A.K. Kong, D. Zhang, Competitive coding scheme for palmprint verification, in *Proceedings of the 17th International Conference on Pattern Recognition* (IEEE, 2004), pp. 520–523)

Y. Lee, K. Hwang, Skin thickness of Korean adults. Surg. Radiol. Anat. **24**(3–4), 183–189 (2002)

D.G. Lowe, Distinctive image features from scale-invariant keypoints. Int. J. Comput. Vision **60**(2), 91–110 (2004)

A. Morales, M. Ferrer, A. Kumar, Towards contactless palmprint authentication. IET Comput. Vision **5**(6), 407–416 (2011)

S.T. Parthasaradhi, R. Derakhshani, L. Hornak, S.A. Schuckers, Time-series detection of perspiration as a liveness test in fingerprint devices. IEEE Trans. Syst. Man Cybern. Part C Appl. Rev. **35**(3), 335–343 (2005)

S. Ribaric, I. Fratric, A biometric identification system based on eigenpalm and eigenfinger features. IEEE Trans. Pattern Anal. Mach. Intell. **27**(11), 1698–1709 (2005)

A.A. Ross, K. Nandakumar, A.K. Jain, *Handbook of multibiometrics* (Springer Science & Business Media, Berlin, 2006)

S.A. Schuckers, Spoofing and anti-spoofing measures. Inform. Secur. Tech. Rep. **7**(4), 56–62 (2002)

S. Tulyakov, V. Govindaraju, Use of identification trial statistics for the combination of biometric matchers. IEEE Trans. Inform. Forensics Secur. **3**(4), 719–733 (2008)

J.-G. Wang, W.-Y. Yau, A. Suwandy, E. Sung, Person recognition by fusing palmprint and palm vein images based on "Laplacianpalm" representation. Pattern Recogn. **41**(5), 1514–1527 (2008)

X. Wu, D. Zhang, K. Wang, Fisherpalms based palmprint recognition. Pattern Recogn. Lett. **24** (15), 2829–2838 (2003)

X. Wu, D. Zhang, K. Wang, N. Qi, Fusion of palmprint and iris for personal authentication, in *Advanced Data Mining and Applications* (Springer, Berlin, 2007)

Y. Xu, L. Fei, D. Zhang, Combining left and right palmprint images for more accurate personal identification. IEEE Trans. Image Process. **24**(2), 549–559 (2015)

Y. Xu, Q. Zhu, D. Zhang, Combine crossing matching scores with conventional matching scores for bimodal biometrics and face and palmprint recognition experiments. Neurocomputing **74** (18), 3946–3952 (2011)

Y.-F. Yao, X.-Y. Jing, H.-S. Wong, Face and palmprint feature level fusion for single sample biometrics recognition. Neurocomputing **70**(7), 1582–1586 (2007)

D. Zhang, Z. Guo, G. Lu, L. Zhang, Y. Liu, W. Zuo, Online joint palmprint and palmvein verification. Expert Syst. Appl. **38**(3), 2621–2631 (2011)

D. Zhang, Z. Guo, G. Lu, L. Zhang, W. Zuo, An online system of multispectral palmprint verification. IEEE Trans. Instrum. Meas. **59**(2), 480–490 (2010)

D. Zhang, W.-K. Kong, J. You, M. Wong, Online palmprint identification. IEEE Trans. Pattern Anal. Mach. Intell. **25**(9), 1041–1050 (2003)

Y-B. Zhang, Q. Li, J. You, P. Bhattacharya, Palm vein extraction and matching for personal authentication, in *Advances in Visual Information Systems* (Springer, Berlin, 2007)

V.P. Zharov, S. Ferguson, J.F. Eidt, P.C. Howard, L.M. Fink, M. Waner, Infrared imaging of subcutaneous veins. Lasers Surg. Med. **34**(1), 56–61 (2004)

W. Zuo, Z. Lin, Z. Guo, D. Zhang, The multiscale competitive code via sparse representation for palmprint verification, in *Proceedings of IEEE Conference on Computer Vision and Pattern Recognition* (IEEE, 2010), pp. 2265–2272

W. Zuo, F. Yue, K. Wang, D. Zhang, Multiscale competitive code for efficient palmprint recognition, in *Proceedings of International Conference on Pattern Recognition* (IEEE, 2008), pp. 1–4

Part VI
Discussion

Chapter 10
Discussions and Future Work

Abstract Recently, the reliable authentication of human identity based on biometrics in the complex environments has attracted much attention. This book provides with several representative methods of discriminative learning for biometric recognition. The ideas, algorithms, experimental evaluation, and underlying rationales are also provided for the better understanding of these methods. In this chapter, we will give a further discussion about the book and present some remarks on the future development of discriminative learning for biometric recognition.

10.1 Metric Learning and Sparse Representation-Based Classification

In Chaps. 2 and 3, we have introduced two types of representative discriminative learning methods, i.e., metric learning (ML) and sparse representation (SR).

10.1.1 Metric Learning

Metric learning aims to find an effective distance metric that enables samples of different classes to have larger distances and samples of the same class to have smaller distances (Bellet et al. 2013). Versatile supervised distance metric learning algorithms have been proposed, such as large margin nearest neighbor (LMNN) (Weinberger et al. 2009), information theoretic metric learning (ITML) (Davis et al. 2007) and logistic discriminant metric learning (LDML) (Guillaumin et al. 2009). In Chap. 2, we present a generalized kernel classification framework to unify the existing metric learning approaches, e.g., LMNN, LDML, and ITML. Based on this framework, we introduce two novel metric learning methods, i.e., doublet-SVM and triplet-SVM, which can achieve competitive classification accuracy and can be solved efficiently by the off-the-shelf SVM solvers. Taking the positive semi-definite (PSD) constraint into account, we further introduce two other metric

© Springer Science+Business Media Singapore 2016
D. Zhang et al., *Discriminative Learning in Biometrics*,
DOI 10.1007/978-981-10-2056-8_10

learning methods, i.e., the positive-semi-definite constrained metric learning (PCML) and the nonnegative-coefficient constrained metric learning (NCML). Both PCML and NCML are convex and their global optimum can be obtained efficiently with the associated optimization algorithms.

Despite the great success of metric learning in biometric recognition, there remain several issues which deserve further investigation. In the following, we discuss them from three aspects: metric learning models, feature representation, and applications.

- In terms of metric learning models, (i) most existing models learn the distance metric based on either pairwise constraints or triplet comparison, and proper integration of both pairwise and triplet comparison can be used to further improve the recognition performance (Wang et al. 2015); (ii) rather than only learning distance metric, we can consider to boost performance by joint learning of distance and similarity metrics (Li et al. 2013; Chen et al. 2012); (iii) to alleviate the labor of sample labeling and annotation, semi-supervised and weakly supervised metric learning has attracted considerable research interests (Chang and Yeung 2004).
- In terms of feature representation, most existing methods learn metrics in image space or based on handcrafted feature representation (e.g., SIFT). Therefore, it is interesting to develop appropriate feature descriptor for specific biometric recognition task, such as Local Maximal Occurrence (LOMO) for person reidentification (Liao et al. 2015). Recently, deep learning, especially convolutional neural network (CNN), has exhibited promising performance in many learning tasks. And the integration of metric and feature learning is also a promising direction in metric learning (Yi et al. 2014).
- In terms of applications, metric learning methods now are mainly used in image-based face recognition. Therefore, it is interesting to apply them to other biometric recognition tasks, e.g., video-based face recognition, person reidentification, palmprint recognition, and multi-biometrics. Moreover, metric learning can also be adopted in the applications on biometric data analysis, e.g., face attribute analysis, kinship recognition, gender recognition.

10.1.2 Sparse Representation-Based Classification

Sparse representation-based classification (SRC) has achieved great success in face recognition. In Chapter 3, we introduce the frameworks of sparse representation with l_0-norm minimization, l_1-norm minimization, l_p-norm ($0 \le p \le 1$) minimization, l_2-norm, and $l_{2,1}$-norm minimization, respectively. Then, supervised dictionary learning, semi-supervised dictionary learning, and unsupervised dictionary learning are further summarized for the improvement of sparse representation. Finally, we present a novel multiple representations of original images for image classification, which are served as virtual images. Both the original and virtual images are used separately to produce different results which are integrated by a flexible score fusion scheme. The multiple representation algorithm is very simple and computationally quite efficient, also lead to satisfactory performance in image classification and face recognition.

Even though sparse representation-based classification has achieved great success, there still lacks in-depth analyses on its intrinsic classification mechanism. The work of probabilistic subspace methods (Moghaddam 2002) may provide some new insights on the interpretation of SRC/CRC from a probabilistic viewpoint. In sparse representation, the dictionary can be simply predefined, but it has been demonstrated that learning the dictionary from data instead of using off-the-shelf bases significantly improves signal reconstruction performance. Many discriminative dictionary learning (DL) methods have been proposed and achieved state-of-the-art performance in various tasks. We will give a discussion from the following two aspects: task-driven and discriminative dictionary learning, and analysis/synthesis dictionary learning.

- The conventional data-driven approach of DL has been well adapted to reconstruction tasks. Recent studies have shown that the better performance can be achieved when the dictionary is tuned to the specific task, such as compressed sensing (Duarte and Sapiro 2009), signal classification (Bagnell and Bradley 2009). For biometric recognition task, it is interesting to design dictionary from task-driven and discriminative learning perspective (Zhang and Li 2010; Mairal et al. 2009). In the existing discriminative DL methods, the discrimination of dictionaries can be enforced by three major strategies, i.e., structural regularization (Yang et al. 2011), explicit discrimination term (Zhang and Li 2010), and pairwise constraint (Cai et al. 2014). The relationships among these three strategies, however, are not investigated yet, moreover, for most discriminative DL methods, the coding schemes are inconsistent in the training and the testing stages, which cannot guarantee that the dictionaries learned in the training stage work well in the test stage. In the future studies, it is encouraging to analyze the relationships and employ the complementarity among different discriminative DL models. As to the inconsistent coding issue, the development of two-level optimization models provides an elaborate solution.
- Most existing DL models are based on the synthesis model, where a sample is represented by the multiplication of the dictionary and the coding coefficient vector. Analysis DL has also achieved great success in image modeling and restoration (Rubinstein et al. 2013; Roth and Black 2009). Unfortunately, even numerous algorithms have been proposed (Lee et al. 2006; Hale et al. 2008), for synthesis DL computation efficiency remains a critical issue to be addressed. Compared with synthesis DL, analysis DL is usually computationally efficient. Therefore, it is encouraged to investigate discriminative analysis DL methods to borrow the efficiency of analysis models without loss of discriminative capability. Moreover, analysis and synthesis DL models characterize the complement subspaces of signals (Elad 2012). It is natural to integrate them into a joint dictionary learning framework for simultaneous improvement on both efficiency and effectiveness (Gu et al. 2014).

10.2 Discriminative Learning for Palmprint Authentication

In the last two decades, versatile methods have been developed for representation and matching of palmprint images (Zhang et al. 2003; Lowe 2004; Huang et al. 2008; Yue et al. 2008, 2009; Xu et al. 2013). Among these methods, a class of coding-based methods (Zhang et al. 2003; Kong et al. 2006; Wu et al. 2006; Kong and Zhang 2004; Sun et al. 2005) has attracted considerable attention due to its promising performance and computational efficiency. In Chap. 4, we presented two improved coding-based palmprint authentication methods. For the first method, fuzzy C-Means (Bezdek et al. 1987) is extended to angular domain for orientation selection in the competitive coding framework. For the second method, binary orientation cooccurrence vector (BOCV) (Guo et al. 2009) is provided for the compact encoding of the filtering responses along all enumerated directions.

In Chap. 5, we further introduce several issues related with orientation coding-based palmprint authentication, including multiscale fusion, accurate orientation representation, and improved angular matching (Zhang et al. 2003; Kong et al. 2006; Han et al. 2008; Zuo et al. 2008). First, we present two multiscale orientation coding methods to fusing multiscale information either in feature-level (e.g., SMCC) (Zuo et al. 2010) or in decision level (e.g., MCC) (Zuo et al. 2008). Second, we describe the steerable filter-based (Jacob and Unser 2004) method (Zuo et al. 2011) for accurate orientation extraction, and generalize the angular distance by considering the tolerance for small angular differences and the equivalence of sufficient large angular differences. Based on this framework, we discuss the effect of discrete representation and generalized angular distance for palmprint recognition.

In Chap. 6, we describe a multifeature palmprint authentication system by fusing both 2D and 3D features. Specifically, competitive coding is adopted to extract 2D feature (Li et al. 2002; Kumar et al. 2003; Connie et al. 2005; Hennings et al. 2007), and surface curvature maps are used for 3D feature representation (Ross and Jain 1999; Sanchez et al. 2000; Kumar et al. 2003; Woodard and Flynn 2005). Finally, a decision level fusion module is introduced for palmprint authentication. And the experimental results show the effectiveness of multifeature palmprint authentication and its robustness against spoof attacks.

Despite the great advances in palmprint authentication, there remain several critical issues deserved further investigations on palmprint feature extraction, representation, and matching:

- Most promising palmprint authentication methods are based on orientation encoding. On the one hand, a number of approaches utilized multiscale (e.g., SMCC) (Zuo et al. 2010), multi-orientation (e.g., BOCV) (Guo et al. 2009), and multi-region information to improve verification accuracy by including more discriminative features. On the other hand, feature selection has also been introduced in palmprint authentication to reduce redundancy. By putting them together, one may develop more promising palmprint recognition method with optimal tradeoff between accuracy and efficiency. Moreover, this study also provides a complete framework to investigate the proper combination of multiscale, multi-orientation, multiregion, and feature selection toward better performance.

- Recently, deep learning methods, such as convolutional networks (CNNs), have achieved great success in many computer vision tasks, e.g., image classification (Hinton et al. 2012), face recognition (Back et al. 1997), visual tracking (Lu et al. 2015), and object detection (Donahue et al. 2014; Girshick et al. 2015). For palmprint authentication, the competitive code can also be treated as a specialized pooling and nonlinearity scheme on filtering output. Thus, it is interesting to develop specific CNN architecture and learning models for palmprint recognition.

- Robustness against spoof attacks is also an important issue in palmprint authentication. To tackle this issue, like Chap. 7, one can involve more features, e.g., 3D and multispectral information (Woodard and Flynn 2005; Xu et al. 2014), into the system. Besides, some dynamic features may also benefit the distinction between real and faked palms.

- Most palmprint authentication methods only consider the rigid deformation in their matching algorithms. Nonrigid deformation, however, is pervasive in real scenarios. Several histogram-based methods (e.g., LBP) (He et al. 2011) and correlation filter-based methods (e.g., BLPOC) (Ito et al. 2004; Zhang et al. 2009) are more robust to non-rigid deformation but generally cannot achieve state-of-the-art performance. Therefore, one can consider to exploit the complementarity between histogram-based approaches and orientation coding methods to develop better algorithms.

10.3 Sparse Representation for Face Recognition Problem

The sparse representation-based classification (SRC) has achieved great achievements in face recognition, but there are still some challenging issues, such as the limitation of available training samples, the changes of face images due to illumination, expressions and poses. In Chap. 7, we propose some effective schemes to generate virtual face images, such as the 'symmetrical face,' the mirror images of face, and the 'mean faces,' which are effective in improving the face recognition accuracy.

In Chap. 8, we introduce two sparse representation-based methods for face recognition, i.e., inverse sparse representation and an improved robust sparse representation. The inverse sparse representation takes the training error into consideration, while conventional SRC takes only the test error into account. The improved robust sparse representation is presented for improving the robustness against pose and illumination variations. Both methods obtain better recognition results than conventional SRC.

Sparse representation-based classification (SRC), collaborative representation classification (CRC), and linear regression classification (LRC) have been widely used in biometrics, such as face recognition and palmprint recognition (Wright et al. 2010; Zhang et al. 2011; Naseem et al. 2012). However, the working mechanism of SRC is still not clear. Researchers have tried to figure out why it can improve the face recognition accuracy and most of them attribute the good performance to sparsity, which is measured by the l_0-norm. Since the l_0-minimization is NP-hard, then its closest convex function l_1-minimization is employed. The l_1-minimization problem can be solved by using the iterative methods, such as gradient projection, iterative shrinkage-thresholding, proximal gradient, and augmented Lagrange multiplier (ALM). To alleviate the computational burdern, the l_2-norm-based collaborative representation has also been developed with closed-form solution and competitive performance. In summary, it is valuable to further study SRC for addressing the limited training set issue and better understanding of its working mechanism.

- To solve the problem of lacking training samples, one may consider other possible ways to extend the training data or the dictionaries. For example, Deng et al. assumed that the intraclass variations can be approximated by a sparse linear combination of other intraclass variations, and proposed an extended SRC method to apply the intraclass variant dictionary to represent the possible variation between the training and testing images (Deng et al. 2012). In the future studies, it is interesting to investigate more on the principled solutions for generating virtual images and dictionaries to improve the performance and robustness of SRC.
- By far, the debate is continuing on which form of regularizer is more effective for SRC/CRC. Shi et al. showed that l_2-norm method is significantly more accurate than SRC and l_1-norm regularizer does not lead to the robustness or desired performance (Shi et al. 2011). Zhang et al. further claimed that the collaborative representation plays a more critical role than the sparse regularizer in face recognition (Zhang et al. 2011). Deng et al. proposed a simple variant of SRC by representing the test sample as a sparse linear combination of the class centroid and the differences to the class centroid with an enormous improvement under the uncontrolled training conditions (Deng et al. 2013). Wright et al., conducted a comparative study to analyze the effect of norms of the representation term and the regularizer, and suggested to check the assumptions and choose the proper norms which favor the correct solution (Wright et al. 2010). However, it remains a challenging issue to adaptively select the correct assumption and proper norms for a specific task or dataset.
- Recent progress in process-centric sparse modeling provides some new insight on developing SRC methods. Gregor and LeCun designed a framework to train a neural network to predict the optimal approximation of sparse coding (Gregor and LeCun 2010). Bronstein et al. further extended this idea by developing a process-centric perspective for sparse modeling (Bronstein et al. 2012). Rather than design of the dictionaries and the norms for representation and

regularization terms, they suggested to directly learn a deterministic pursuit process for implicit sparse modeling. These methods provide a more flexible way for learning dictionary and selection norms from training data for a specific task, and the complexity is controllable in the inference stage. Therefore, one can consider to follow this line to develop SRC/CRC models for adaptive selection of norms and optimal tradeoff between performance and complexity.

10.4 Multi-biometrics Methodologies

Biometrics are described as the science of recognizing an individual based on his physiological or behavioral traits, such as the fingerprints, hand geometry, iris, retina, face, hand vein, facial thermogram, signature, voice, etc., which are used for determining an individual's identity. Most existing biometric systems deployed in real world are unimodal with single biometric. While no single biometric technique can satisfy all requirements in circumstances (Jain et al. 2004). Unimodal biometric system may suffer from noisy data, intraclass variations, interclass similarities, insufficient-universality, spoof attacks etc., which promotes the emergence of multi-biometrics methodologies.

Due to that a certain module contains the specific type of information, different levels of fusion are defined, such as, sensor level fusion, feature-level fusion, score-level fusion, decision level fusion, rank level fusion in multi-biometrics. In Chap. 9, we present two fusion methods to combine multi-modality of biometric features for personal identification at the matching score level: the fusion of the left and right palmprints from the perspective of multiple traits in the same category, the fusion of the palmprint and palmvein from the perspective of multiple traits in different categories. Experiments show that both fusion methods improve the performance.

A variety of issues should be considered for a multimodal biometric system, such as choice of biometric traits, feature extraction of the chosen biometric traits, and fusion method, etc. In the following, we discuss these issues in the context of palmprint identification.

- Ceases, including principal lines and wrinkles, are the main discriminative features for low resolution palmprint recognition. Among the three types of palmprint recognition methods, the studies in (Zhang et al. 2012) indicate that holistic-based methods are less correlated with the feature-based ones. Therefore, it is interesting to develop powerful fusion methods for combining different types of algorithms, especially holistic and feature-based ones, for palmprint recognition.
- Many state-of-the-art palmprint recognition methods, such as FusionCode (Kong et al. 2006), CompCode (Kong and Zhang 2004), and sparse multi-scale competitive code (SMCC) (Zuo et al. 2010) can also be explained from the viewpoint of feature-level fusion. This motivates us to further investigate the

proper feature-level fusion approaches to integrate multi-filter, multidirectional and multiscale discriminative information into compact code to facilitate efficient and effective palmprint matching.

- Palmprints identification has its own intrinsic weaknesses. From example, it is difficult to distinguish the fake palmprints from the real ones. Different from palmprint, palmvein as the palm feature under infrared spectrum can be captured simultaneously with palmprint by using specially designed devices, and is difficult to fake. Joint use of palmprint and palmvein features can thus effectively increase the accuracy, robustness, and anti-spoof capability of palm-based biometric techniques.
- Recently, 3D palmprint has been developed (Zhang et al. 2015). In Chap. 6, we also discussed the fusion of competitive code-based-2D and surface curvature-based-3D palmprint features. We believe proper fusion of 2D and 3D features from single biometric or multiple biometrics can further improve personal identification performances.

References

A.D. Back, C.L. Giles, S. Lawrence, A.C. Tsoi, Face recognition: a convolutional neural-network approach. IEEE Trans. Neural Networks **8**, 98–113 (1997)

J.A. Bagnell, D.M. Bradley, *Differentiable Sparse Coding*, in Advances in Neural Information Processing Systems (2009), pp. 113–120

A. Bellet, A. Habrard, M. Sebban, A survey on metric learning for feature vectors and structured data. arXiv preprint (2013) arXiv:1306.6709

J.C. Bezdek, R.J. Hathaway, M.J. Sabin, W.T. Tucker, Convergence theory for fuzzy c-means: counterexamples and repairs. IEEE Trans. Syst. Man Cybern. **17**(5), 873–877 (1987)

A. Bronstein, P. Sprechmann, G. Sapiro, *Learning efficient structured sparse models*. arXiv preprint (2012), arXiv:1206.4649

S. Cai, W. Zuo, L. Zhang, X. Feng, P. Wang, *Support vector guided dictionary learning*, in Computer Vision–ECCV 2014 (Springer, 2014), pp. 624–639

H. Chang, D. Yeung, *Locally linear metric adaptation for semi-supervised clustering*. in Proceedings of the Twenty-first International Conference on Machine Learning (ACM, 2004)

D. Chen, X. Cao, L. Wang, F. Wen, J. Sun, *Bayesian face revisited: a joint formulation*. in Computer Vision–ECCV 2012 (Springer Berlin Heidelberg, 2012), pp. 566–579

T. Connie, A.T.B. Jin, M.G.K. Ong, D.N.C. Ling, An automated palmprint recognition system. Image Vis. Comput. **23**(5), 501–515 (2005)

J.V. Davis, B. Kulis, P. Jain, S. Sra, I.S. Dhillon, *Information-theoretic metric learning*. in Proceedings of Proceedings of the 24th international conference on Machine learning (ACM, 2007), pp. 209–216

W. Deng, J. Hu, J. Guo, Extended SRC: undersampled face recognition via intraclass variant dictionary. IEEE Trans. Pattern Anal. Mach. Intell. **34**(9), 1864–1870 (2012)

W. Deng, J. Hu, J. Guo, *In defense of sparsity based face recognition*, in Proceedings of the IEEE Conference on Computer Vision and Pattern Recognition (2013), pp. 399–406

J. Donahue, T. Darrell, R.B. Girshick, J. Malik, Rich feature hierarchies for accurate object detection and semantic segmentation (CoRR, 2014) abs/1311.2524

J.M. Duarte-Carvajalino, G. Sapiro, Learning to sense sparse signals: simultaneous sensing matrix and sparsifying dictionary optimization. IEEE Trans. Image Process: Publ. IEEE Sig. Process. Soc. **18**(7), 1395–1408 (2009)

M. Elad, Sparse and redundant representation modeling—what next? IEEE Signal Process. Lett. **19**(12), 922–928 (2012)

R.B. Girshick, K. He, S. Ren, J. Sun, Faster R-CNN: towards real-time object detection with region proposal networks (NIPS, 2015)

K. Gregor, Y. Lecun, *Learning fast approximations of sparse coding*, in Proceedings of the 27th International Conference on Machine Learning (ICML-10) (2010), pp. 399–406

S. Gu, L. Zhang, W. Zuo, X. Feng, *Projective dictionary pair learning for pattern classification*. in Advances in Neural Information Processing Systems (2014), pp. 793–801

M. Guillaumin, J. Verbeek, C. Schmid, *Is that you? Metric learning approaches for face identification*. in Proceedings of IEEE International Conference on Computer Vision (IEEE, 2009), pp. 498–505

Z. Guo, D. Zhang, L. Zhang, W. Zuo, Palmprint verification using binary orientation co-occurrence vector. Pattern Recogn. Lett. **30**(13), 1219–1227 (2009)

E.T. Hale, W. Yin, Y. Zhang, Fixed-point continuation for L_1-minimization: methodology and convergence. SIAM J. Optim. **19**(3), 1107–1130 (2008)

Y. Han, Z. Sun, T. Tan, *Combine hierarchical appearance statistics for accurate palmprint recognition*, in Proceedings of International Conference on Pattern Recognition (IEEE, 2008), pp. 1–4

Y. He, R. Huang, N. Sang, Local binary pattern histogram based texton learning for texture classification (ICIP 2011)

P.H. Hennings-Yeomans, B. Kumar, M. Savvides, Palmprint classification using multiple advanced correlation filters and palm-specific segmentation. IEEE Trans. Inf. Forensics Secur. **2**(3), 613–622 (2007)

G.E. Hinton, A. Krizhevsky, I. Sutskever, ImageNet classification with deep convolutional neural networks (NIPS 2012)

D.-S. Huang, W. Jia, D. Zhang, Palmprint verification based on principal lines. Pattern Recogn. **41**(4), 1316–1328 (2008)

K. Ito, H. Nakajima, K. Kobayashi, T. Aoki, T. Higuchi, *A fingerprint matching algorithm using phase-only correlation*. in Ieice Transactions (2004), pp. 682–691

M. Jacob, M. Unser, Design of steerable filters for feature detection using canny-like criteria. IEEE Trans. Pattern Anal. Mach. Intell. **26**(8), 1007–1019 (2004)

A.K. Jain, A. Ross, S. Prabhakar, An introduction to biometric recognition. IEEE Trans. Circ. Syst. Video Technol. **14**(1), 4–20 (2004)

A.W.K. Kong, D. Zhang, *Competitive coding scheme for palmprint verification*, in Proceedings of the 17th International Conference on Pattern Recognition, 2004. ICPR 2004, vol. 1 (IEEE, 2004), pp. 520–523

A. Kong, D. Zhang, M. Kamel, Palmprint identification using feature-level fusion. Pattern Recogn. **39**(3), 478–487 (2006)

A. Kumar, D.C. Wong, H.C. Shen, A.K. Jain, *Personal verification using palmprint and hand geometry biometric*, in Proceedings of Audio-and Video-Based Biometric Person Authentication (Springer, 2003), pp. 668–678

H. Lee, A. Battle, R. Raina, A.Y. Ng, *Efficient sparse coding algorithms*, in Advances in Neural Information Processing Systems (2006), pp. 801–808

W. Li, D. Zhang, Z. Xu, Palmprint identification by Fourier transform. Int. J. Pattern Recognit. Artif. Intell. **16**(04), 417–432 (2002)

Z. Li, S. Chang, F. Liang, T. Huang, L. Cao, J. Smith, *Learning locally-adaptive decision functions for person verification*. in Proceedings of the IEEE Conference on Computer Vision and Pattern Recognition (2013), pp. 3610–3617

S. Liao, Y. Hu, X. Zhu, S.Z. Li, *Person re-identification by local maximal occurrence representation and metric learning*. in Proceedings of the IEEE Conference on Computer Vision and Pattern Recognition (2015), pp. 2197–2206

D.G. Lowe, Distinctive image features from scale-invariant keypoints. Int. J. Comput. Vision **60** (2), 91–110 (2004)

H. Lu, W. Ouyang, L. Wang, X. Wang, Visual tracking with fully convolutional networks (ICCV, 2015)

J. Mairal, J. Ponce, G. Sapiro, A. Zisserman, F.R. Bach, *Supervised dictionary learning*. in Advances in neural information processing systems (2009), pp. 1033–1040

B. Moghaddam, Principal manifolds and probabilistic subspaces for visual recognition. IEEE Trans. Pattern Anal. Mach. Intell. **24**(6), 780–788 (2002)

I. Naseem, R. Togneri, M. Bennamoun, Robust regression for face recognition. Pattern Recogn. **45** (1), 104–118 (2012)

A. Ross, A. Jain, *A prototype hand geometry-based verification system*, in Proceedings of 2nd Conference on Audio and Video Based Biometric Person Authentication (1999), pp. 166–171

S. Roth, M.J. Black, Fields of experts. Int. J. Comput. Vision **82**(2), 205–229 (2009)

R. Rubinstein, T. Peleg, M. Elad, Analysis K-SVD: a dictionary-learning algorithm for the analysis sparse model. IEEE Trans. Signal Process. **61**(3), 661–677 (2013)

R. Sanchez-Reillo, C. Sanchez-Avila, A. Gonzalez-Marcos, Biometric identification through hand geometry measurements. IEEE Trans. Pattern Anal. Mach. Intell. **22**(10), 1168–1171 (2000)

Q. Shi, A. Eriksson, A. Van Den Hengel, C. Shen, *Is face recognition really a compressive sensing problem?* in 2011 IEEE Conference on Computer Vision and Pattern Recognition (CVPR) (IEEE, 2011), pp. 553–560

Z. Sun, T. Tan, Y. Wang, S.Z. Li, *Ordinal palmprint representation for personal identification*, in Proceedings of IEEE Conference on Computer Vision and Pattern Recognition (IEEE, 2005), pp. 279–284

F. Wang, W. Zuo, L. Zhang, D. Meng, D. Zhang, A kernel classification framework for metric learning. IEEE Trans. Neural Networks Learn. Syst. **26**(9), 1950–1962 (2015)

K.Q. Weinberger, J. Blitzer, L.K. Saul, Distance metric learning for large margin nearest neighbor classification. J. Mach. Learn. Res. **10**, 207–244 (2009)

D.L. Woodard, P.J. Flynn, Finger surface as a biometric identifier. Comput. Vis. Image Underst. **100**(3), 357–384 (2005)

J. Wright, Y. Ma, J. Mairal, G. Sapiro, T.S. Huang, S. Yan, Sparse representation for computer vision and pattern recognition, Proc. IEEE **98**(6), 1031–1044 (2010)

X. Wu, K. Wang, D. Zhang, *Palmprint texture analysis using derivative of Gaussian filters*, in Proceedings of International Conference on Computational Intelligence and Security (IEEE, 2006), pp. 751–754

Y. Xu, Z. Fan, M. Qiu, D. Zhang, J.-Y. Yang, A sparse representation method of bimodal biometrics and palmprint recognition experiments. Neurocomputing **103**, 164–171 (2013)

Y. Xu, X. Li, J. Yang, D. Zhang, Integrate the original face image and its mirror image for face recognition. Neurocomputing **131**, 191–199 (2014)

M. Yang, L. Zhang, X. Feng, D. Zhang, *Fisher discrimination dictionary learning for sparse representation*, in 2011 IEEE International Conference on Computer Vision (ICCV) (IEEE, 2011), pp. 543–550

D. Yi, Z. Lei, S. Liao, S.Z. Li, *Deep metric learning for person re-identification*. in 2014 22nd International Conference on Pattern Recognition (ICPR) (IEEE, 2014), pp. 34–39

F. Yue, W. Zuo, K. Wang, D. Zhang, *A performance evaluation of filter design and coding schemes for palmprint recognition*, in Proceedings of International Conference on Pattern Recognition (IEEE, 2008), pp. 1–4

F. Yue, W. Zuo, D. Zhang, K. Wang, Orientation selection using modified FCM for competitive code-based palmprint recognition. Pattern Recogn. **42**(11), 2841–2849 (2009)

D. Zhang, W.-K. Kong, J. You, M. Wong, Online palmprint identification. IEEE Trans. Pattern Anal. Mach. Intell. **25**(9), 1041–1050 (2003)

Q. Zhang, B. Li, *Discriminative K-SVD for dictionary learning in face recognition*, in 2010 IEEE Conference on Computer Vision and Pattern Recognition (CVPR) (IEEE, 2010), pp. 2691–2698

L. Zhang, L. Zhang, D. Zhang, Finger-knuckle-print verification based on band-limited phase-only correlation (CAIP 2009)

L. Zhang, M. Yang, X. Feng, *Sparse representation or collaborative representation: which helps face recognition?* in 2011 IEEE International Conference on Computer Vision (ICCV) (IEEE, 2011), pp. 471–478

D. Zhang, W. Zuo, F. Yue, A comparative study of palmprint recognition algorithms. ACM Comput. Surv. (CSUR) **44**(1), 2 (2012)

L. Zhang, Y. Shen, H. Li, J. Lu, 3D palmprint identification using block-wise features and collaborative representation. IEEE Trans. Pattern Anal. Mach. Intell. **37**(8), 1730–1736 (2015)

W. Zuo, F. Yue, K. Wang, D. Zhang, *Multiscale competitive code for efficient palmprint recognition*, in Proceedings of International Conference on Pattern Recognition (IEEE, 2008), pp. 1–4

W. Zuo, Z. Lin, Z. Guo, D. Zhang, The multiscale competitive code via sparse representation for palmprint verification (2010)

W. Zuo, F. Yue, D. Zhang, On accurate orientation extraction and appropriate distance measure for low-resolution palmprint recognition. Pattern Recogn. **44**(4), 964–972 (2011)

Index

© Springer Science+Business Media Singapore 2016
D. Zhang et al., *Discriminative Learning in Biometrics*,
DOI 10.1007/978-981-10-2056-8

Printed in the United States
By Bookmasters